RAF

AN ILLUSTRATED HISTORY FROM 1918

ROY CONYERS NESBIT

SUTTON PUBLISHING

First published in 1998 by
Sutton Publishing Limited · Phoenix Mill
Thrupp · Stroud · Gloucestershire · GL5 2BU

This new revised paperback edition first published in 2007

British Library Cataloguing in Publication Data
A catalogue record for this book is available from the British Library

ISBN 978-0-7509-4289-8

For Margaret

Front endpaper: the Royal Aircraft Factory SE5a is often classed as the best single-seat fighter to serve in the RAF in the First World War. Armed with a Vickers gun on the port side of the fuselage and a Lewis gun on the upper wing, it entered squadron service with the RFC on the Western Front in June 1917 and gained a high reputation for its flying qualities and ruggedness. Together with the Sopwith Camel, it established the RAF's superiority over the German Air Force in 1918. Most went out of service after the war, but some continued until 1919. The SE5a serial C5303 in this photograph was flown by Lt L.N. Franklin while on the strength of 56 Squadron.

J.M. Bruce/G.S. Leslie collection

Back endpaper: the Panavia Tornado GR1 is a two-seat supersonic aircraft with variable geometry wings, employed on tactical strike work and reconnaissance. It first entered RAF squadron service in January 1982, armed with two 27 mm Mauser cannon and capable of carrying a warload of 18,000 lb. These two Tornado GR1As of 13 Squadron, equipped with infrared linescans, were photographed near RAF Honington in Suffolk on 19 May 1990.

British Crown Copyright/MOD/Sgt Rick Brewell

Typeset in 10/14pt Sabon and 9/11pt Gill Sans.
Typesetting and origination by
Sutton Publishing Limited.
Printed and bound in Great Britain by
J.H. Haynes & Co. Ltd, Sparkford.

CONTENTS

CHAPTER ONE

HARD-WON VICTORY

The Royal Air Force that came into being on 1 April 1918, as Britain's third armed service, was a huge organization compared to the air arms which had been formed only a few years earlier. These were the Royal Flying Corps, which began life with the granting of a Royal Warrant on 13 April 1912, and the Royal Naval Air Service, which became officially recognized on 1 July 1914. It had been intended in 1912 that the RFC would have a Military Wing and a Naval Wing, with a Central Flying School serving both, but the Admiralty refused to enter into this arrangement and went its own way with a Naval Wing and a Central Flying School, before becoming the RNAS.

In turn, these air arms stemmed from the balloons and kites which had been part of the British Army for many years, although some military commanders had regarded them as providing little more than an amusing sport. It was not until the Boer War that the value of balloons as observation posts became fully recognized, even though a balloon establishment had been set up in Woolwich in 1878 as a branch of the Royal Engineers. Similarly, the military establishment took little note of the aeroplane after the first powered flight made on 17 December 1903 by the biplane *Flyer* designed by Wilbur and Orville Wright. It was Louis Blériot's flight across the Channel on 25 July 1909 which caused them to think afresh. The prospect of French invaders landing behind British coastal fortifications sent ripples of alarm around military circles.

The attitude of the War Office towards the aeroplane was different from that of the Admiralty. The War Office saw the aeroplane primarily as an instrument serving similar purposes to the balloons and non-rigid airships with which the Air Battalion of the Royal Engineers was equipped, although their airships were transferred to the Admiralty in October 1913. The aeroplane would be useful for artillery spotting and reconnaissance of enemy positions in the field. Experiments with airborne wireless took place and were moderately successful. Types of airborne cameras were devised by enthusiasts within the Service. The main criterion for the aeroplane was stability, since so many accidents and deaths were being caused during training with monoplanes. Thus designers within the Royal Aircraft Factory, a name which was authorized at the same time as the RFC, met the initial needs of the War Office with slow and stable two-seater biplanes which look rudimentary but delightful to modern eyes. These were far easier to handle than monoplanes, but the period allotted to training remained short. Pilot errors still occurred while engine and structural failures were not uncommon.

On the other hand the Admiralty, which controlled the most powerful navy in the world and usually insisted on attacking the enemy on sight, saw the aeroplane as an instrument of aggression in addition to that of air reconnaissance. Thus it issued specifications to private firms to meet its particular needs. Gun platforms were fitted to aircraft in order to bring down Zeppelins, which had been considered potential menaces since the first flight had been made in Germany on 2 July 1900. As early as December 1911, the first aircraft was flown off the deck of a ship and a form of arrester gear was proposed. The purpose of this was primarily to give the Royal Navy advance warning of the presence of enemy warships and enable it to sail into battle. In addition, seaplanes could be carried on warships and lowered over the side to bomb enemy ports and vessels. Patterns of anti-submarine patrols were devised for shore-based aircraft and seaplanes. Bombsights were designed and bomb-aiming trials were carried out. The art of air navigation over long stretches of sea was pioneered, including methods of calculating wind velocity. A lightweight wireless set was produced for mounting in an aircraft. On 28 July 1914, a seaplane made by Short Brothers was successful in taking off with a torpedo. The Admiralty also became interested in the possibility of long-range bombing operations and shortly after the declaration of war specified 'a bloody paralyser of an aeroplane' to bomb targets in Germany, particularly Zeppelin bases. In many ways, the Admiralty foresaw more accurately the roles which the future Royal Air Force would perform, although it must be said that some of the more traditional admirals were extremely sceptical of the value of the aeroplane.

The First World War began on 28 July 1914 when Austria-Hungary declared war on Serbia and Russia began to mobilize. Germany declared war on Russia on 1 August and began to enter Luxembourg the following day as a prelude to invading Belgium. The Fatherland then declared war on France on 3 August. When Britain declared war on Germany on 4 August, the RFC consisted of seven squadrons on paper, of which five were sufficiently operational to be sent to France, together with their 'aircraft park'. The RNAS possessed eight Naval Air Stations equipped with 71 aircraft and 7 'dirigibles', as airships were known. It sent two squadrons to Antwerp, from where they began air raids on Germany, primarily against Zeppelin sheds, but these had to pull out as the Germans advanced. Other RNAS units were sent to Ostend and Dunkirk, but the Ostend base was also lost.

The air war which developed over the Western Front swung to and fro, sometimes in favour of the Allies and sometimes the Germans, over the next terrible years. The war on the ground, originally one of movement, became almost static with a line of trenches and fortifications which stretched from Nieuport on the Belgian coast to the Swiss border. The RFC aircraft shed their Union flag symbols on wing undersurfaces, replacing them with the roundel which has become so familiar on British aircraft, although modified over the years. The folly of sending up RFC biplanes with no armament except rifles and side arms was exposed when German aircraft armed with machine-guns began to wreak havoc over the battlefields. This became almost a rout in the summer of

The two-seat Royal Aircraft Factory BE2c was built to satisfy a requirement of the War Office for an extremely stable reconnaissance aircraft. The first examples, which were unarmed, arrived in France in late 1914 and soon proved unable to outmanoeuvre enemy monoplane fighters and too slow to escape them. Later versions were armed with a Lewis gun, operated by the observer in the front cockpit. They could carry a bomb load of up to 224 lb. BE2cs were more successful in areas where the opposition was less severe, such as against the Turks. This photograph of serial 4135 of 30 Squadron, showing a C-type camera in the rear cockpit, was taken in Mesopotamia. BE2cs continued in service until the end of the First World War.

M.H. Goodhall

'THE FLAT IRON' by Charles J. Thompson
The first flush deck carrier was HMS *Argus*, formerly the Italian liner *Conte Rosso*, which was converted before being commissioned in September 1918. This painting shows a Sopwith Pup and a Sopwith 1½-Strutter on deck landing trials in 1918. HMS *Argus* was placed in reserve in 1930 but reconditioned as a 'Queen Bee' parent ship in 1937 and then used for training deck landing during the Second World War. She was scrapped in 1947.

The two-seat Avro 504 was designed in 1913 and saw service with both the RFC and the RNAS in the early months of the First World War. Early aircraft were unarmed but later variants were fitted with a Lewis gun in the front cockpit for the observer and carried about 80 lb of bombs. However, Avro 504s are best remembered for the trainer versions, for the 504N continued in service until 1933. This 504J, serial B930, was photographed in 1917 at the Gosport Instructors' Course.

J.M. Bruce/G.S. Leslie collection

1915 when the agile Fokker E-type monoplane appeared, armed with a machine-gun synchronized to fire through the propeller arc. Of course, the RFC responded with machine-guns mounted on rings in observers' cockpits as well as others in forward-firing positions for the pilots, and the balance of superiority swung back again. Single-seat fighters also appeared in the RFC.

The air battles which followed caught the imagination of the public. The pilots became 'knights of the air' and the more successful were revered as national heroes. The rapid advance of technology also contributed to the high standing of the RFC and the RNAS in the eyes of the public. A pilot who brought down one of the hated Zeppelins which began to bomb England in January 1915 was awarded a Victoria Cross almost automatically. The Zeppelins were either set on fire with incendiary bullets or blown up by bombs dropped from above.

However, the reality of air combat did not correspond exactly with the public conception. Much of the flying took place in cramped and bitterly cold conditions. There was undoubtedly some chivalry as well as heroism. The British and German aviators respected each other and dropped messages over their opponents' lines giving information about aircraft shot down and the fate of their occupants, while enquiring about their own losses. But most fighter pilots sought to manoeuvre so as to shoot an opponent in the back or in the vulnerable underbelly. They also pounced in packs on less well-armed enemy aircraft, especially those seen to be in difficulties. Most victories were scored against inferior aircraft rather than those which matched the aggressor. The crews often died agonizing deaths if their aircraft were set on fire, for parachutes were not carried during most of the war. Many aircraft were shot down by ground fire when attacking enemy positions. A high proportion of deaths or injuries occurred accidentally, either in training or on operational squadrons. Life in the air, on both sides, was usually unpleasant and short, even for the most proficient pilots.

The Western Front was not the only area in which air action took place. The RNAS supported the landings on Gallipoli, which began on 24 April 1915, against the forces of Turkey, which had entered the war in October 1914 in support of the Central Powers. This campaign resulted in much tragic loss of life before a withdrawal was completed on 8 January 1916. The conquest of Serbia by Austria and Hungary in November 1915 resulted in British troops landing in Salonika, where they were joined by a reconstituted Serbian Army the following year. Their main opponents were the Bulgarians, whose country had declared war on 12 October 1915. The RFC sent reconnaissance aircraft from Egypt to help the Allied forces, although at first these were outclassed by German fighters.

RNAS and RFC reconnaissance aircraft were also sent to support South African, British and Belgian troops fighting the enemy in German East Africa. A much larger campaign took place in Palestine, countering the advance of Turkish forces in the Sinai Desert which began in early 1915, threatening the Suez Canal. The RFC arrived in November 1915 and there were many combats with German fighters, although the British began to push back the Turks. In Mesopotamia, a small Indian force landed at Basra in November 1914, to protect the oil wells in the Persian Gulf, and advances were made up the Tigris, with the support of RFC and RNAS reconnaissance aircraft. Italy had entered the war in May 1915 on the side of the Allies, but when its forces were driven back by combined German and Austrian armies in October 1917, British and French forces, accompanied by several RFC squadrons, were sent to bolster the Italians.

The Short 184 seaplane could carry either a 14 inch torpedo or 520 lb of bombs and was armed with a single Lewis gun in the observer's cockpit. It entered service with the RNAS in the summer of 1915 and on 12 August one of these machines sank a Turkish merchant vessel in the Dardanelles, achieving the first success of an air-launched torpedo. The machine was tricky to fly and it was difficult to take off with the weight of a torpedo, but many were taken over by the RAF in April 1918 and continued well into 1919. This Short 184 serial 8033 was photographed while being hoisted on board the seaplane carrier *Vindex* of 2,950 tons.

J.M. Bruce/G.S. Leslie collection

All these theatres of war necessitated an enormous expansion of the British air arms, and there was no reluctance on the part of the government in authorizing this. In April 1915 there were only seven RFC squadrons and one flight in France, consisting of some 85 aircraft in the front line plus 20 in an aircraft park. It was originally proposed to increase the number of squadrons to 50 but the Secretary of State for War, Lord Kitchener, doubled this figure. The RNAS also underwent an expansion, although at a less rapid rate.

In the late spring of 1917, the German Air Force began to send long-range bombers to attack targets in England, supplementing the raids made by Zeppelins. One of these attacks, against London on 13 June 1917, resulted in heavy civilian casualties and led to the strengthening of anti-aircraft defences as well as a demand for more home-based fighters. Another outcome was the creation in October 1917 of the 41st Wing in northern France, consisting mainly of RNAS bombers which made retaliatory attacks against targets in Germany, usually in the area of the Ruhr. This Wing was expanded into the VIIIth Brigade in February 1918. Before this time, however, there was confusion as to the spheres of operations of the two air arms as well as their conflicting demands on the surface manufacturing resources available to all branches of the armed forces. Air Boards were set up to resolve these matters.

It is perhaps ironic that the man who was finally responsible for the formation of the Royal Air Force had fought against Britain. Lieutenant-General Jan Christian Smuts, a South African who had taken a degree at Cambridge

University, had become an effective guerrilla leader in the Boer War. He had also helped to negotiate his country's status as a self-governing Dominion in 1909 and was highly respected in Britain for his statesmanship and keen intellect. Moreover, in 1914 he suppressed a rebellion by Boers who were sympathetic to the German cause. In 1915 he commanded the South African forces that defeated the Germans in their colony of South West Africa. The following year, he moved against the Germans in East Africa. On the successful conclusion of this campaign, at heavy cost, he was invited in 1917 to join the British War Cabinet by the Prime Minister, David Lloyd George. It was hoped that, as an impartial observer, Smuts could devise a new structure for the burgeoning air arms of the War Office and the Admiralty and reconcile their differences.

In August 1917 Smuts advocated the creation of a Royal Air Force with an Air Ministry and an Air Staff. This was not dissimilar to the original concept of 1912 but the new service was on a much larger scale and of equal status to the War Office and the Admiralty, although considered junior to both. The War Cabinet approved his recommendation and an Act of Parliament was passed on 29 November 1917, but the measures did not become effective until 1 April 1918. By this time the RFC possessed 118 squadrons, of which 62 were serving in France and 19 in other theatres of war. The RNAS consisted of 50 squadrons, 14 of which were based in France and 5 in other theatres.

Major-General Sir Hugh Trenchard was appointed as Chief of Air Staff. A soldier who had been seriously wounded in the Boer War and later served in Nigeria, he had volunteered to join the RFC in 1912 and at the age of forty qualified as a pilot. He distinguished himself first as the Station Staff Officer to the Central Flying School and later in command of a Wing on the Western Front, and then the whole of the RFC in that theatre of war. However, Trenchard disagreed on matters of policy with the Secretary of State for Air, Lord Rothermere, and resigned his post almost immediately, together with some of his senior staff. Rothermere also resigned and was replaced by Sir William D. Weir. A new Chief of Air Staff was appointed on 12 April 1918. This was Major-General Sir Frederick Sykes, another officer who had been wounded in the Boer War. He had entered the RFC via the Balloon School and a pilot's course. Thereafter he had occupied a series of administrative posts, and his appointment was a compromise solution to a difficult political wrangle.

The newly created RAF faced a critical situation on the Western Front. Following the Bolshevik Revolution, Russia had signed an armistice with Germany on 15 December 1917. German troops on the Eastern Front were moved to the west and a massive offensive began on 21 March 1918. The Allies began a fighting retreat, helped by accurate air reconnaissance of enemy positions and concentrated air attacks against the advancing Germans.

The services of Trenchard were not lost to the war. In June 1918 the VIIIth Brigade was expanded into the Independent Air Force and he assumed command, after having been assured that it would operate under his sole control. Raids against Germany were intensified, causing some damage and casualties but not on the scale that the future would witness.

But on 6 April 1917 the USA had declared war on Germany and her fresh and well-equipped troops began to arrive. Following enormous losses, the German advance was stemmed and turned into retreat. Meanwhile British and Indian forces advanced in Mesopotamia and the Turks were also in retreat. Turkey surrendered on 30 October 1918 and Germany signed an armistice on 11 November 1918. The most destructive and bloodiest war in recorded history was over.

The Martinsyde G102 'Elephant' was a single-seater designed for long-range escort duties but it proved too heavy and unresponsive in this role when it appeared in early 1916 and was transferred to bombing, ground attack and air reconnaissance. It could carry up to 260 lb of bombs and was fitted with either one or two machine-guns. None survived in Britain after the end of the war, but a handful continued in the Middle East for a very short time.

J.M. Bruce/G.S. Leslie collection

The Royal Aircraft Factory BE12a was based on the two-seat BE2c but modified to a single-seat fighter with a more powerful engine. It first appeared in December 1916 and was fitted with a single Lewis gun. However, it was not successful in this role and was transferred to light bombing and air reconnaissance. Many continued until the Armistice, both at home and in Macedonia.

J.M. Bruce/G.S. Leslie collection

The Short 310-A4, sometimes known as the Short 320, was built in 1916 as a long-range seaplane capable of carrying a new torpedo of 1,000 lb. It was fitted with a more powerful engine than the Short 184 which preceded it. The armament consisted of a single Lewis gun in the front cockpit, but the observer had to clamber out of his seat and stand on decking to fire it. Short 310-A4s continued in service after the end of the First World War but the last were replaced in October 1919 by land-based torpedo-bombers.

J.M. Bruce/G.S. Leslie collection

The two-seat Sopwith 1½-Strutter first entered service with the RNAS in April 1916 and was soon in demand by the RFC. It became popular as it was the first British aircraft with a Vickers gun efficiently synchronized to fire through the propeller arc and also possessed good flying qualities. In addition, it had a single Lewis gun in the observer's position. On the Western Front, Strutters were replaced with Sopwith Camels in the summer of 1917 but some continued on home defence and training duties. A few RNAS machines were converted into single-seaters, carrying up to 260 lb of bombs. This Strutter, serial 7777 of 45 Squadron, was lost in action on 22 October 1916.

J.M. Bruce/G.S. Leslie collection

The Vickers ES2 was an experimental single-seater, fitted with a tractor engine instead of the pusher type fitted to the biplanes hitherto produced by this company. With some modifications and unofficially known as the 'Bullet', it appeared in August 1916 as the Vickers FB19, armed with a single Vickers gun synchronized to fire through the propeller arc. After trials in France, it was not accepted for operations over the Western Front, mainly owing to the pilot's restricted view, but some were sent to Macedonia and others were employed on home defence. This Vickers ES2 serial 7760 was photographed on 23 June 1917 while on the strength of 50 Squadron at Dover. This type of machine did not remain in RAF service after the Armistice.

47 Squadron Archives

The single-seat Spad VII Scout arrived on the Western Front in September 1916. This was a difficult time for the RFC, for its ageing aircraft with pusher engines were being outclassed by German fighters. Although not very manoeuvrable and armed with a single machine-gun firing through the propeller arc, the new Spad was one of the machines which helped to redress the balance. Most were retired by the end of the war but some were supplied to squadrons in Mesopotamia and continued until January 1919. This Spad VII Scout serial A253 was on the strength of 60 Squadron.

J.M. Bruce/G.S. Leslie collection

The single-seat Sopwith Pup was acclaimed for its excellent flying qualities when it appeared on the Western Front in the autumn of 1916. Armed with a single Vickers gun firing through the propeller arc, it gave a good account of itself in combat. With an upward-firing Lewis gun, it was also employed by the RNAS against Zeppelins, continuing to the end of the First World War.

J.M. Bruce/G.S. Leslie collection

The Royal Aircraft Factory RE8 entered service in November 1916. It was designed to provide the RFC with a well-defended reconnaissance aircraft and carried a Vickers gun firing through the propeller arc with either one or two Lewis guns in the observer's position. Although the RE8 could be out-manoeuvred by agile enemy fighters, it continued in service until the end of the First World War.

J.M. Bruce/G.S. Leslie collection

'FE2bs of 25 SQN RFC RETURN AFTER NIGHT BOMBING' by Mark Postlethwaite
The Royal Aircraft Establishment FE2b, a two-seater with a pusher engine and armed with two Lewis guns, was first delivered in May 1915 to squadrons in France. Its original role was that of a fighter but by November 1916 some were converted to bombers and employed on night operations until the end of the war.

The Handley Page O/100 was built soon after the outbreak of war in response to a requirement from the Air Department of the Admiralty for 'a bloody paralyser of an aeroplane' to bomb Germany. It was a twin-engined heavy bomber with a crew of four, with fittings for up to five Lewis guns in three positions, and a bomb-carrying capacity of 2,000 lb. It first appeared in November 1916 and was followed by the O/400, with higher powered engines. This O/100 of 216 Squadron, named *Le Tigre*, was photographed at Ochey in France in the spring of 1918.

J.M. Bruce/G.S. Leslie collection

The Armstrong Whitworth FK8 was a two-seat reconnaissance aircraft which arrived on the Western Front during January 1917. It was armed with a Vickers gun firing through the propeller arc and a Lewis gun in the observer's position. It was also capable of carrying 160 lb of bombs, and the crews preferred it to the contemporary RE8. This FK8 has a camera mounted vertically beside the pilot while another is being handed to the observer. FK8s continued in service until the summer of 1919.

J.M. Bruce/G.S. Leslie collection

'SOPWITH CAMEL' by Charles J. Thompson
The Sopwith Camel shared honours with the SE5a for the successes achieved over the Western Front, after its introduction in July 1917. A single-seat fighter armed with twin Vickers guns firing through the propeller arc, it was not easy to fly but was highly manoeuvrable in the hands of an experienced pilot. It was credited with destroying more enemy aircraft than any other type. This Camel, serial F6314, was built for the RAF in 1918.

The two-seat Airco DH4 was designed for high-speed day bombing, being capable of climbing above enemy fighters when it first reached France in March 1917. Most aircraft were fitted with a single Vickers gun firing through the propeller arc, but a few carried two. There was also a Lewis gun in the observer's position, while the bomb-carrying capacity was 460 lb. The DH4 in this photograph was on the strength of A Flight, 202 Squadron, at Bergues in France in 1918. Some continued with the RAF until January 1920.

J.M. Bruce/G.S. Leslie collection

The Bristol Fighter, known as the 'Brisfit', was a long-lived aircraft which first entered service with the RFC over the Western Front in April 1917. A two-seater armed with a Vickers gun firing through the propeller arc and a Lewis gun in the rear cockpit, it gave a good account of itself in combat and could also carry two 112 lb bombs. Bristol Fighters continued in RAF service for many years, some with overseas squadrons as late as 1932. Others continued as trainers after this time. This Bristol F2B Fighter was photographed at Farnborough in 1936, with Sgt D.J. Munro at the controls.

Author's collection

The Felixstowe F2A was a heavily armed flying boat which gave excellent service with the RNAS from November 1917 and then with the RAF until 1923. It was capable of long patrols and secured many successes against U-boats and Zeppelins. This machine, serial N4545, was photographed on 10 October 1918 when painted with the dazzle effect introduced to help rescuers locate aircraft forced down in the sea.

J.M. Bruce/G.S. Leslie collection

The single-seat Nieuport 27 Scout, usually fitted with a single machine-gun on the upper wing, proved a successful fighter when it appeared on the Western Front towards the end of 1917. The aircraft in this photograph, serial B3650, served with 1 Squadron and then 29 Squadron. The machines were retired by the end of the war.

J.M. Bruce/G.S. Leslie collection

The de Havilland 9A, known as the Ninak, was a two-seat day-bomber which entered squadron service in June 1918 and continued as a front-line aircraft and then as a trainer up to 1931. It was armed with a Vickers gun firing forward and a Lewis gun in the rear cockpit, and could carry 460 lb of bombs. Over two thousand of this reliable and long-serving aircraft were built. This example, serial J6963, was on the strength of 47 Squadron while stationed at Helwan in Egypt and then Khartoum in the Sudan.

47 Squadron Archives

The Handley Page V/1500 was the first four-engined bomber to enter service with the RAF, and was specifically designed to bring Berlin within reach of airfields in East Anglia. It was a long-range bomber with a crew of up to seven, armed with up to eight Lewis guns in four positions and carrying a bomb load of 7,500 lb. The first examples were supplied in October 1918 to 166 Squadron at Bircham Newton in Norfolk for this purpose, but the Armistice was signed before an operation could take place. V/1500s were withdrawn from squadron service by May 1919. This photograph was taken at Bircham Newton.

J.M. Bruce/G.S. Leslie collection

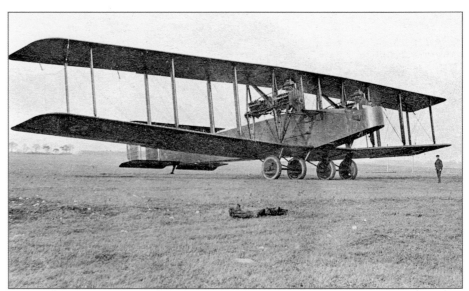

'SE5as AND FOKKER D.VIIs IN COMBAT' by Mark Postlethwaite
A painting depicting the aircraft considered to be the best British and German fighters of the First World War, meeting in combat. The Royal Aircraft Factory SE5a
arrived on the Western Front in June 1917 and the Fokker D.VII followed in April 1918.

The Bristol M1C Monoplane was condemned without trial before its introduction into squadron service, owing to a strong prejudice against aircraft of this type within the War Office, which preferred biplanes on the grounds of safety. A single-seat fighter, fast, manoeuvrable and fitted with a single Vickers gun firing through the propeller arc, it was eagerly awaited by RFC pilots on the Western Front who nicknamed it the 'Bullet'. In the event, small quantities were supplied only to squadrons in Mesopotamia towards the end of the war, where they soon proved their mettle. This example, serial C4990, was photographed in late 1918 at Detling in Kent.

J.M. Bruce/G.S. Leslie collection

The single-seat Sopwith Snipe, armed with two Vickers guns and with an improved performance, appeared on the Western Front in September 1918 as a replacement for the Camel. It proved a superior fighter in the last months of the war and was also employed on bomber escort work. Partly owing to financial economies applied to the postwar RAF, Snipes continued in squadrons at home and abroad up to November 1926, and some were employed as trainers for several years later. The Snipe in this photograph, serial E7337, was on the strength of 112 Squadron at Throwley in Kent for a short while.

J.M. Bruce/G.S. Leslie collection

CHAPTER TWO

POLITICAL FOOTBALL

The Royal Air Force of November 1918 possessed more aircraft than ever before or in its subsequent history. There were 22,544 machines, although only about 3,300 were on the strength of front-line squadrons, plus 103 airships. The personnel numbered 27,333 officers and 263,837 other ranks. In addition, there were about 25,000 in the Women's Royal Air Force (WRAF), which had been formed on 1 April 1918 from those serving in the air units of the Women's Royal Naval Service, the Women's Auxiliary Army Corps, the Voluntary Aid Detachment and the Women's Legion. The main fighting unit was the squadron, although some squadrons could be employed on non-operational duties such as training. There were usually about twelve aircraft in a front-line squadron, which was normally divided into three flights of four aircraft apiece. These squadrons required about twenty pilots plus a similar number of other aircrew if equipped with two-seat or multi-seat aircraft.

It was obvious that this enormous force could not be sustained in peacetime. Nevertheless the RAF in France remained at almost full strength until Germany signed the Peace Treaty on 28 June 1919, reluctantly accepting its harsh conditions. Thousands of aircraft were then collected in dumps and 'reduced to produce', to use the RAF's term for scrapping. Others were sold and converted to civil use. Most squadrons were disbanded, the process of demobilization being accelerated when women of the WRAF were sent to France to take the place of men, before this branch of the service was disbanded in 1920.

Some squadrons continued to fight. RAF units had accompanied ground forces sent to Murmansk in the summer of 1918, mainly to deny the base to German U-boats, and these remained after the Armistice to support the White Russians who were attempting to wrest control of the country from the Bolsheviks. Three squadrons were sent to South Russia from the end of 1918 as part of an RAF mission to give additional support. However, it became evident that this campaign was fruitless and the units were withdrawn by the end of 1919.

Trenchard was temporarily out of a job after the Armistice and was thinking about applying for a post in the Colonial Service. However, Churchill, who had taken over both the War Office and the Air Ministry in January 1919, invited him to resume his position as Chief of Air Staff. Trenchard took over this post on 31 March 1919, Sykes having moved to a new position of Controller-General of Civil Aviation.

By this time, the aeroplane was accepted as essential for the defence of the United Kingdom and as a potent method of retaliating against any aggressor. The Admiralty was pressing for the return of its air arm and it seemed possible that the RAF would be split into two parts once more. There was also the major question of finance, for the country had neared bankruptcy after a long and debilitating war. Most people had been sickened by the enormous casualties and wished to build up a peaceful country rather than sustain the armed forces. The need for a third service was questionable. In November 1918 Sykes wrote a memorandum recommending that the Empire be held together by civil aviation, with pilots and technicians drawn from the RAF, leaving a few squadrons for such tasks as home defence and to support the Royal Navy. However, a year later Trenchard submitted a memorandum which recommended the strength of the RAF for 1920 as 23 squadrons and 7 flights, at home and abroad, coupled with intensive training and research. His views prevailed.

Perhaps incongruously, it was financial stringency which ensured that the RAF survived as a separate service. In January 1920 an insurrection in Somaliland was crushed with the help of a single squadron of Airco DH9s which bombed the tribesmen's positions and put them to flight. The Camel Corps was then successful in establishing peace throughout a country which had been in turmoil. It became evident that a handful of RAF squadrons could partly replace the British Army overseas by garrisoning vast areas of the Empire, such as Iraq and

The Vickers Vimy was built as a twin-engined bomber capable of reaching Berlin from England, but it arrived too late for service in the First World War and instead equipped nine RAF squadrons or flights at home and abroad. On 14–15 June 1919 a modified Vimy, owned by Vickers and flown by Capt. John Alcock and Lt Arthur Whitten Brown, made the first flight across the Atlantic, from Newfoundland to Ireland. The Vimy was withdrawn from front-line service in 1924 but some continued as trainers until the early 1930s. This Vimy was photographed over Egypt.

Author's collection

the north-west frontier of India, far more effectively and at a much lower cost than hitherto. The usual method of controlling dissident tribes was to bomb their villages after giving due warning of an impending attack. These lessons were not lost either on the villagers or on a government seeking ways to reduce public expenditure.

Trenchard set about his tasks with astonishing foresight and unquenchable energy. The RAF Benevolent Fund was set up in October 1919 under his auspices. The RAF Nursing Service was formally established in 1921, later to become the Princess Mary's Royal Air Force Nursing Service. In February 1920 the RAF College at Cranwell was opened, where cadets underwent a rigorous two-year training course before qualifying as officers in the permanent RAF. In 1921 an apprentice scheme for boy entrants was opened at RAF Halton, where the trades of fitters and riggers were taught. Another trade taught to boy apprentices, that of wireless operator, was based temporarily at Cranwell. Those who performed well in these long courses could enter the RAF with ranks up to that of corporal. Adults who were recruited into the RAF were sent to Uxbridge and underwent training as aircraft hands, clerks, medical orderlies, ground gunners, service police, cooks and numerous other duties. Discipline was strict to the point of harshness, but life usually improved once the men were posted to squadrons. A few of the most successful were allowed to train as sergeant pilots and some of these later achieved very high commissioned rank in the RAF. In 1922 the RAF Staff College was opened in Andover for experienced officers who were expected to reach senior ranks.

Trenchard also knew the value of publicity. He formed the RAF Central Band in April 1920, and this gained a high professional standard. In July of that year the RAF staged its first pageant at Hendon. The North Atlantic had already been flown from west to east in a converted Vimy bomber, and an RAF airship had made the flight in both directions. Public interest in flying had been reawakened and crowds flocked to see the displays of aerobatics, formation flying and mock bombing attacks at Hendon. By this time RAF personnel were kitted out in their own light blue uniform. The names of their ranks were different, although equivalent, to those of the Royal Navy and Army. The majority of the officers were pilots and wore their distinctive wings, but some wore the air observer's brevet while others were ground personnel who carried out specialized duties. The RAF was considered an upstart service by some, but the combination of adventure and high technology was highly appealing to a forward-looking younger generation.

One matter which disturbed the development of the RAF as an independent service was the launching of aircraft carriers with decks designed for take-offs and landings. The first to appear had been HMS *Argus*, followed by the converted battleship HMS *Eagle* in 1923. The naval element of the RAF had been run down to two squadrons and three flights, but new aircraft suitable for carriers were coming into service. The squadrons were disbanded on 1 April 1923 to become flights of six aircraft apiece, and exactly a year later these were named the Fleet Air Arm of the Royal Air Force. It was inevitable that operational control would be exercised largely by the Admiralty.

During this period, an expansion of the RAF began, prompted by the knowledge that the home defences were far smaller than the French Air Force, which could muster as many as 600 aircraft. Although a friendly state, France was Britain's ancient enemy and conditions could change. In the following year, the Cabinet authorized a gradual increase to fifty-two squadrons for the Air Defence of Great Britain.

The F5 was the last of the Felixstowe flying boats, its wartime predecessors being the F2A, the F2C and the F3. It entered service in November 1918, too late for wartime operations, and became a standard flying boat with the RAF for the next seven years. The armament consisted of one machine-gun in the bows and three amidships, and it could carry 920 lb of bombs. The machine in this photograph, serial N4198, was on the strength of 480 Flight at Calshot in Hampshire.

J.M. Bruce/G.S. Leslie collection

Trenchard put several new measures into force to cater for this expansion. He divided the home forces into the Bombing Area, the Fighting Area, the Special Reserve and the Auxiliary Air Force. The last two were the RAF's equivalent of Britain's Territorial Army. The Special Reserve squadrons were manned by local volunteers, many of whom had served in wartime, with about one-third regular RAF personnel. The Auxiliary Air Force squadrons had a smaller core of regulars while the majority were volunteers who served only at weekends on airfields adjacent to the towns where they lived. The first to open was 602 (City of Glasgow) Squadron, in September 1925, but eventually sixteen of these squadrons were formed. Then there were the University Air Squadrons, which enabled undergraduates to begin flying training and learn generally about the RAF, encouraging them to join the service when they had taken their degrees. These began at Oxford and Cambridge but within a few years almost every university had its Air Squadron. Another measure was the introduction in early 1924 of the short service commission, which enabled young men to join the RAF as junior officers for a limited number of years, with the possibility of a permanent commission at the end of the period.

Backing these developments were several establishments committed to research and development of new aircraft and equipment. The Royal Aircraft Factory had been renamed the Royal Aircraft Establishment (RAE) in April 1918, to avoid confusion with the initials of the Royal Air Force. Based at Farnborough, the RAE was mainly concerned with research into aerodynamics and engines, together with the multitude of instruments which could be fitted in aircraft. The Aeroplane and Armament Experimental Establishment (AAEE), concerned with the practical testing of aircraft and equipment, was formed in 1924 at

Martlesham Heath in Suffolk, moving to Boscombe Down in Wiltshire on the outbreak of the Second World War. The Marine Aircraft Experimental Establishment (MAEE) had been set up by the Admiralty at Felixstowe in Suffolk and continued research and development into seaplanes, flying boats and land-based maritime aircraft, as well as practical testing. Experiments with the dropping of torpedoes were carried out by the Torpedo Development Unit (TDU), which had been formed in 1921 at Gosport in Hampshire.

Financial stringency coupled with a continued preference for safety and stability prevented any rapid development in the production of new designs. By and large the aircraft were improved versions of those which had existed at the time of the Armistice. Almost all were biplanes, with airframes of wood or metal, covered with fabric and braced with wire. Some of the single-seat fighters and two-seat general-purpose aircraft looked very elegant in their silver livery set off with squadron markings. Servicing was of a high quality and most of the machines handled well, while their airspeeds had been increased. However, there was little improvement in the armament or bomb-carrying capacity. The pace of design was far slower than in the desperate days of the First World War, when the German Air Force had acted as a spur. The major exceptions were the specialist aircraft, such as the monoplane seaplanes designed by Reginald J. Mitchell, in which RAF pilots began to win the coveted Schneider Trophy from 1927. In this period, the RAF lost interest in airships, following the destruction of *R.101*,

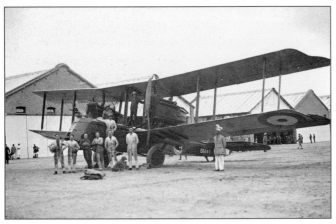

The de Havilland 10 Amiens day bomber appeared at the end of the First World War, too late for operational sorties. It accommodated a crew of four, was armed with up to four Lewis guns in nose and waist positions, and could carry a bomb load of 900 lb. Most of these bombers served overseas after the war, such as serial E6040 of 60 Squadron in this photograph dated 12 January 1922. The squadron was based at Risalpur in India and the aircraft was bombed-up preparatory to a raid against rebellious tribesmen at Dhatta Khel. Some of these bombers continued in service until April 1923.

J.M. Bruce/G.S. Leslie collection

which carried such high hopes when it left Cardington for Karachi on 4 October 1930 but tragically crashed a day later, killing all save six of the fifty-four on board.

Trenchard became the first Marshal of the Royal Air Force in 1927. He continued in this position until 1 January 1930, the longest-serving Chief of Air Staff, and was recognized thereafter as the 'Father of the Royal Air Force'. He handed over to one of his lieutenants, Air Chief Marshal Sir John Salmond, who served for a more normal period before his place was taken by Air Chief Marshal Sir Edward Ellington on 22 May 1933. Although the tenures of Trenchard and Salmond were periods when most of the world was at peace, Ellington was to experience the prelude to a shattering disaster. This was the rise of the most malignant dictator in living memory, Adolf Hitler, who became Chancellor of Germany in 1933. He was not the first nor the last in Europe, for Benito Mussolini had assumed power in Italy in 1922 and Francisco Franco became *Caudillo* of Spain in 1939.

In 1934 the home-based RAF consisted of only 42 of the 52 squadrons that had been authorized in 1924, with a front-line strength of 488 aircraft. Progress had been retarded by successive governments during a period when the public preferred disarmament. Meanwhile, Germany was busy assembling a secret air force, circumventing the provisions of the Versailles Peace Treaty of June 1919 which prohibited the establishment of such a force and the manufacture of military aircraft. German designers were able to improve their skills by working in Sweden, Switzerland, Italy and Turkey. Pilots were receiving elementary training on gliders and light aircraft in Germany, under the guise of sport. More advanced training for pilots, air observers and air gunners was taking place at Lipetsk in Russia. Civil airliners in service for Lufthansa were easily convertible to bombers. Although the Allied Control Commission in Germany had been

Only a few Nieuport Nighthawks were supplied to the RAF, the first appearing in January 1920. They were attached to 1 and 8 Squadrons and sent to Mesopotamia in 1923 for experimental purposes under tropical conditions. The distinctive feature was the new radial engine instead of the rotary engine of 1914–18 vintage. This machine set a pattern for the RAF single-seat fighters which entered service in the inter-war period. The Nighthawk was armed with twin Vickers guns firing through the propeller arc.

P. Ballie

disbanded in 1926, it was possible to estimate that the country would possess as many as a thousand front-line aircraft by 1935. Alarm bells began to ring in Britain.

Ellington proposed that the home-based RAF squadrons should be increased as rapidly as possible to 84, with the entire programme completed by March 1939. In spite of dissent from some quarters, this was authorized by Parliament in July 1934, after the Member for Epping, Winston Churchill, had stressed the vulnerability of cities such as London to air attack. The pace of expansion was accelerated in May 1935 when Parliament decreed that the number be increased to 125 squadrons by March 1937, to achieve parity with a further estimate of the growing Luftwaffe. Ten more squadrons were added the following year, supplementing the Fleet Air Arm and the RAF overseas.

With the purse-strings opened, the rate of progress became remarkable. There was much leeway to make up, for the designs of the RAF's operational aircraft had fallen behind those of Germany. Fortunately, Britain's aircraft industry responded immediately. This was the age when improvements such as all-metal construction, retractable undercarriages, variable pitch propellers, power-operated turrets and far more powerful engines were introduced. The American Browning machine-gun, with its improved rate of fire and reduced propensity to stoppages, replaced the Lewis gun and the forward-firing Vickers gun. New types of monoplanes, such as the Avro Anson, the Fairey Battle, the Vickers Wellington, the Armstrong Whitworth Whitley, the Handley Page Hampden, the Hawker Hurricane and the Supermarine Spitfire came off the production lines, although it has to be said that the pace of development was so fast that some of the earlier aircraft soon became obsolescent.

New airfields needed to be built to cater for the increase in squadrons, and Britain's construction industry rallied with alacrity, the number being increased from 52 to 138 by the outbreak of war, most of them in the east and south of England. Science came to the aid of the country's defences with the invention of radar, the detection of aircraft by cathode ray apparatus. Equipment known as IFF (Identification Friend or Foe) was fitted in RAF aircraft, producing recognizable blips on radar screens and enabling operators to distinguish them as friendly. A chain of twenty-two radar stations was built around the coasts of Britain, facing the potential enemy.

In 1936 the RAF was reorganized yet again. Bomber, Fighter and Coastal Commands were formed, supported by Training Command and a Maintenance Group which soon became a Command. Two years later a Balloon Command was formed. Overseas there were the Middle East, Palestine and Transjordan, Iraq, India, Mediterranean, Aden and Far East Commands. The chain of authority in the RAF stretched from the Cabinet to the Air Ministry, then to the Commands, Groups, Stations and Squadrons. The exception was the Fleet Air Arm, however, for this was returned to the formal control of the Admiralty in May 1939, although close collaboration continued with the RAF, particularly Coastal Command.

All this would not have been possible without a huge increase in manpower. It took about two years to train a pilot to operational readiness, and three years for the most skilled tradesmen. Recruitment into the regular RAF was expanded and the Royal Air Force Volunteer Reserve (RAFVR) was planned in 1936. From April of the following year, young men were able to train in their spare time as pilots, observers or gunner/wireless operators. This scheme was so popular that there were 10,000 recruits by the outbreak of war, although most were only partially trained. Many of those who flew in the Battle of Britain of 1940 had entered pre-war as RAFVRs. Those who volunteered as aircrew after the outbreak of war were also RAFVRs, and they coveted this distinction. In May 1939 the Women's Auxiliary Air Force (WAAF) was formed, absorbing the volunteers who had trained in an Auxiliary Territorial Service, and opening the door to wartime entrants.

The man who presided over much of this transformation, Sir Richard Ellington, handed over his duties to Air Marshal Sir Cyril Newall on 1 September 1937. Meanwhile the dictators continued their policy of aggression with little hindrance from the free world. The Saar, which had come under French administration in 1919, was returned to Germany in January 1935, following a plebiscite. Italy invaded Abyssinia in October of the same year, ruthlessly bombing villages and using poison gas, while international sanctions had little effect on her actions. German and Italian fliers were able to hone their skills as 'volunteers' in the Spanish Civil War which broke out in July 1936. Germany annexed Austria in February 1938, apparently with the acquiescence of most of the population of that country. Hitler's next move was to invade Bohemia and Moravia in March 1939, and Italy occupied Albania a month later. Germany and Russia signed their hypocritical 'non-aggression' pact in August 1939, and it became obvious to all but the most obtuse that war with the West was inevitable. Britain and France guaranteed the borders of Poland but Hitler ignored this and invaded that country on 1 September.

At 11.00 hours on 3 September, the sonorous voice of the Prime Minister, Neville Chamberlain, announced over the wireless that Germany had failed to respond to an ultimatum from France and Britain and that in consequence the two countries had declared war. A few minutes later, the air raid sirens wailed over London and people hurried to take shelter.

The Vickers Vernon was the first of the RAF's aircraft designed solely for troop-carrying duties. Before its arrival in March 1922, this function had been performed by converted bombers such as the Vimy. The Vernon carried a crew of two plus twelve passengers and equipped two squadrons in Iraq, flying over vast stretches of desert. The aircraft was also employed on air mail duties between Cairo and Baghdad, a charge of a shilling an ounce being levied for civil mail. Vernons continued in service until January 1927. This photograph shows serial J6977 of 45 Squadron, which was based at Hinaidi near Baghdad.

G. Quick

The Gloster Grebe was a single-seat fighter, armed with two Vickers machine-guns, which entered squadron service in October 1923. Four squadrons and one flight were equipped with Grebes, which were notable for their aerobatic qualities. They continued until the last was withdrawn in July 1929. The Grebe in this photograph, serial J7390, was on the strength of 19 Squadron.

Philip Jarrett collection

The Fairey Fawn was a two-seat day-bomber which first came into service in March 1924. It was fitted with a single Vickers gun firing forward and a Lewis gun in the rear cockpit, and could carry up to 460 lb of bombs. Although a cumbersome machine, it continued in service until 1929. The Fawn IIs in this photograph, serials J7219 and J7220, were on the strength of 11 Squadron in 1925, when it was based at Netheravon in Wiltshire.

Philip Jarrett collection

The Armstrong Whitworth Siskin III was a single-seat fighter, fitted with a radial engine and armed with twin Vickers guns, which entered squadron service in May 1924. Although its performance was impressive, this was a time of financial stringency and only two squadrons were equipped with the machine. Some continued in service until November 1931. The Siskin IIIA serial J8391 in this photograph was on the strength of 41 Squadron.

J.M. Bruce/G.S. Leslie collection

The Vickers Virginia was a heavy night-bomber, first introduced into squadron service in December 1924. There were ten Marks of this long-serving machine, I to X, the last continuing until 1937. It had a crew of four and was armed with three Lewis guns in nose and tail positions. The Mark X could carry about 3,200 lb of bombs. The example in this photograph, Virginia V serial J7430, was on the strength of 58 Squadron.

Philip Jarrett collection

The Fairey Fox was a two-seat day-bomber which surprised the authorities by its turn of speed when it first appeared in 1925. The armament consisted of a Vickers gun firing forward and a Lewis gun in the rear cockpit, and the machine could carry 460 lb of bombs. It equipped only 12 Squadron, from August 1925, but continued until January 1931 when the Hawker Hart arrived. The example here is serial J7945.

Philip Jarrett collection

The Hawker Woodcock was a single-seat fighter, armed with twin Vickers guns, which first entered squadron service in July 1925. Its main role was that of a night-fighter. Only two squadrons were equipped with Woodcocks, which continued until September 1928.

Philip Jarrett collection

The Supermarine Southampton, a reconnaissance flying boat with a crew of five, armed with three machine-guns and carrying a bomb load of 1,100 lb, entered service with 480 Flight in August 1925, replacing the ageing Felixstowe F5s. This flight became 201 Squadron in January 1929 and four other squadrons were equipped with Southamptons, which remained in service for over ten years. They became famous for their long-distance flights, particularly a trip to the Far East in 1927. This photograph is of Southampton II serial S1123.

J.M. Bruce/G.S. Leslie collection

The Handley Page Hyderabad was a heavy night-bomber with a crew of four, carrying up to 1,100 lb of bombs and armed with three Lewis guns in nose, dorsal and ventral positions. It began to enter squadron service in December 1925 and eventually equipped three squadrons, the last being withdrawn in December 1930.

Philip Jarrett collection

The Vickers Victoria began to replace the Vernon as a troop-carrier in January 1926; it was capable of carrying a crew of two and up to 22 troops. It served mainly in the Middle East, continuing for over ten years. This Victoria V serial JR8231 of 216 Squadron, based at Heliopolis in Egypt, was photographed at Amman in Jordan on 4 September 1936, at a time when the squadron was converting on to the newer Vickers Valentia.

A.R.J. Billinger via A.S. Thomas

The Gloster Gamecock, a single-seat fighter armed with two Vickers machine-guns, began to replace the Grebe in March 1926 for home defence. It was renowned for its aerobatic performances at the annual RAF displays at Hendon. Gamecocks were supplied to five squadrons and continued in service until March 1933. Those in this photograph were on the strength of 23 Squadron at Kenley in Surrey during 1927.

Philip Jarrett collection

The Hawker Horsley was introduced into squadron service in September 1926 as a day-bomber capable of carrying a load of up to 1,500 lb. It was followed by a torpedo-bomber version in June 1928. Armed with a Vickers gun firing forward and a Lewis gun firing aft, it gave good service up to July 1935. This Horsley II serial J8019 of 504 Squadron was photographed at Digby in Lincolnshire in 1929.

A.R.J. Billinger via A.S. Thomas

The Armstrong Whitworth Atlas was the first aircraft designed specifically for army co-operation, entering service in October 1927 to replace the Bristol Fighter. A two-seater armed with one machine-gun firing forward and another for the observer, its duties included artillery spotting, reporting by W/T, photo-reconnaissance, picking up messages with a hook on the undercarriage, and attacking with machine-guns or bombs. This Atlas I serial J9974 of 208 Squadron was photographed over the Jordan Valley in 1933.

J.M. Bruce/G.S. Leslie collection

The Westland Wapiti first appeared in 1927 as a replacement for the DH9A. It was a general-purpose aircraft, armed with a forward-firing Vickers gun and a Lewis gun in the rear cockpit, and could carry up to 580 lb of bombs. This Wapiti IIA serial J9854 served at Hinaidi in Iraq in 1935, where it was concerned with experiments relating to dropping containers by parachute. (Note the parachute emblem on the fin.)

J.M. Bruce/G.S. Leslie collection

The Fairey IIIF was a two-seat general-purpose aircraft, fitted with a Vickers gun firing forward and a Lewis gun in the rear cockpit. It came into service in December 1927 and was employed at home as a land-based day bomber, carrying up to 500 lb of bombs. Some overseas squadrons employed the machines as float planes, as can be seen in this 1929 photograph of serials J9796, J9809 and J9802 on the Nile. They were on the strength of 47 Squadron, which was based at Khartoum in the Sudan. Fairey IIIFs pioneered air routes in Africa and gave reliable service until the last were retired in August 1935.

47 Squadron Archives

The Hawker Tomtit was a two-seat *ab initio* trainer which was introduced from early 1929 as one of the RAF's replacements for the ageing Avro 504N. Tomtits were supplied to two flying schools, where they were popular for their flying qualities, and a few were also used for communication duties. They remained in service until 1935. Serial J9775 in this photograph is fitted with a blind-flying hood in the rear cockpit.

Philip Jarrett collection

The Boulton and Paul Sidestrand was a medium day bomber, with a crew of up to four, which first entered RAF service in March 1929. Armed with three Lewis guns in nose, dorsal and ventral positions, it could carry a bomb load of about 1,000 lb. Only eighteen were built and all were supplied to 101 Squadron, which was equipped with these machines up to January 1935. The Sidestrand IIIs in this photograph are serials J9769, J9176 and J9178.

Philip Jarrett collection

The Bristol Bulldog, a single-seat fighter fitted with two Vickers guns firing through the propeller arc, entered service in May 1929 and eventually equipped nine squadrons. It was a successful and long-serving machine which continued until September 1937. This Bulldog II serial K1088 was on the strength of 3 Squadron.

Philip Jarrett collection

'WAPITIS OVER KURDISTAN' by Mark Postlethwaite
A flight of Wapiti IIAs of 30 Squadron, based at Mosul in Iraq, on a reconnaissance mission over Kurdistan in the early 1930s, with serial K1989 in the foreground. The range of mountains in the background is the Iraqi border with Turkey.

The Handley Page Hinaidi which followed the Hyderabad was fitted with more powerful engines and was capable of carrying an increased bomb load of up to 1,448 lb. It equipped three squadrons from October 1929 and continued in the heavy bomber role until October 1935. This Hinaidi II serial K1075 was on the strength of 99 Squadron.

Philip Jarrett collection

The de Havilland 60M Gipsy Moth entered RAF service in 1929 as a two-seat *ab initio* trainer and light communications aircraft. Its use was widespread in flying training schools up to the beginning of the Second World War, and it also appeared in formation aerobatics at the RAF's Hendon displays. This Gipsy Moth serial K1200 was photographed in Iraq.

J.M. Bruce/G.S. Leslie collection

This Blackburn Iris serial N185 was built with a wooden hull as the prototype for the Iris with a metal hull which entered service with 209 Squadron when it was re-formed at Mount Batten at the beginning of 1930. The flying boats continued with the squadron until April 1934, when they were replaced with Perths.

Aeroplane Monthly

The Hawker Demon was a two-seat fighter variant of the Hart light day-bomber. The first conversions entered service on an experimental basis in March 1931. It was armed with twin Vickers guns firing forward through the propeller arc and a single Lewis gun in an adapted rear cockpit which gave an improved field of fire. From October 1936 some Demons were also fitted with a hydraulic turret in the rear cockpit. Demons were on the strength of thirteen squadrons, at home and abroad, continuing until shortly before the outbreak of the Second World War. These Demons were photographed at Mersa Matruh in Egypt, with serials K4523 and K4511 in the foreground.

G.R. Pitchfork collection

The Fairey Gordon was an adaptation of the Fairey IIIF, with a Panther IIA radial engine replacing the Napier Lion. A two-seat day bomber, it first entered RAF service in April 1931. Gordons continued overseas until the outbreak of the Second World War. The example in this photograph, serial K3481, served in the Fleet Air Arm and was known as the Seal.

Aviation Bookshop

'FIRST IN SERVICE' by Charles J. Thompson

One of the most successful aircraft produced for the RAF in the inter-war years was the Hawker Hart day-bomber, which entered squadron service in January 1930. It was a two-seater, armed with a Vickers gun firing forward and a Lewis gun in the rear cockpit, and could carry 500 lb of bombs. Fast and manoeuvrable, it handled well and was adaptable. Some continued in squadron service up to 1939. A trainer version was produced in 1933 and also continued up to 1939. This Hart I, serial K2443, was the first to be delivered to the RAF. It arrived in January 1930 at Eastchurch in Kent for 33 Squadron.

The Short Rangoon was a general reconnaissance flying boat which entered squadron service in April 1931. It carried a crew of five and was armed with three Lewis guns in the bow and amidships. The bomb load was 1,000 lb. Only six were built, serving with two squadrons, the last being withdrawn in July 1936. Serial S1433 in this photograph was the prototype; it also served with 203 Squadron in Iraq.

Philip Jarrett collection

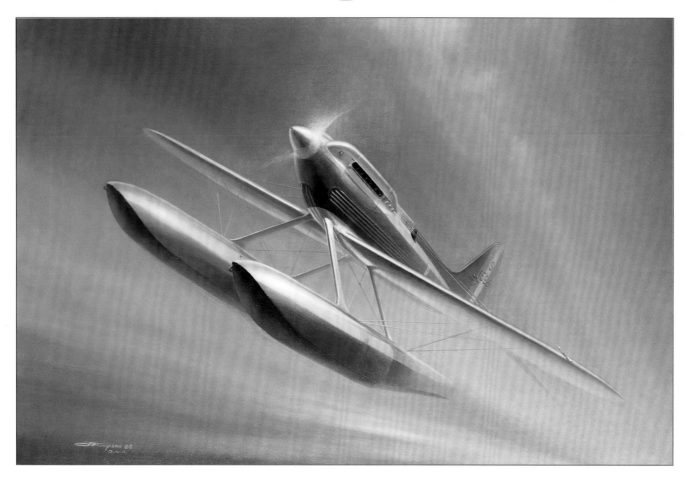

'SUPERMARINE'S SPEED MACHINE' by Charles J. Thompson

Supermarine S.6B serial S1595 was flown in the Schneider Trophy Contest on 13 September 1931 by Flt Lt J.N. Boothman of the RAF's High Speed Flight at an average speed of 340 mph, winning for Great Britain the third successive victory in five years and thus securing the trophy in perpetuity. On 29 September the same aircraft was flown by Flt Lt G.H. Stainforth at a speed of 407.5 mph. This was the first aircraft to exceed 400 mph and gained the world speed record for Great Britain. The design of this splendid machine was continued with the development of the Spitfire.

'ADVANCED TRAINER'
by Charles J. Thompson
The Hawker Audax entered squadron service in February 1932 as the army co-operation version of the Hart day-bomber. It was a two-seater, with one gun firing forward and another aft, and was fitted with a message-collecting hook on the undercarriage. Some continued in squadron service overseas until May 1941. This Audax, serial K7404, was on the strength of No. 12 Elementary Flying Training School in 1938.

The Westland Wallace was a development of the Wapiti, with a more powerful engine, which entered squadron service in January 1933. Like its predecessor, it was a two-seat, general-purpose aircraft, fitted with a Vickers gun firing forward and a Lewis gun firing aft, and with a bomb-carrying capacity of 580 lb. The example in this photograph, serial K3562, was the first to have been converted from the Wapiti, and it was followed by many others as well as newly built machines. Some continued in service until May 1937.

Philip Jarrett collection

The Fairey Long-range Monoplane was designed for the purpose of securing the World Long-distance Record for Great Britain, with the phenomenal range of 5,000 miles. Only two were built. The first, serial J9479, made an unsuccessful attempt in 1929 and crashed later in the year, killing both crew members. The second, serial K1991, seen here, took off from Cranwell in Lincolnshire on 6 February 1933 and secured the record by arriving in Walvis Bay in South West Africa after a flight of 57 hours 25 minutes.

Philip Jarrett collection

The Saro Cloud was an amphibian introduced in August 1933 as a trainer for flying boat crews. It had a crew of two and could seat eight trainees, with provision for bomb-racks and two gun positions. Only sixteen were built, entering service with the Seaplane Training Squadron at Calshot and the School of Air Pilotage at Andover, both in Hampshire. For a few months in 1936, several were on the strength of 48 Squadron at Manston in Kent.

Philip Jarrett collection

The Handley Page Heyford followed the Hinaidi and other heavy night-bombers, entering squadron service from November 1933. It was armed with three Lewis guns in nose, dorsal and ventral positions and could carry up to 3,500 lb of bombs. It equipped eight squadrons and a few continued until July 1941, being the last of the RAF's heavy biplane bombers.

Philip Jarrett collection

The Avro Tutor was a two-seat *ab initio* trainer which began to replace the Avro 504N in 1933. In that year, and subsequently, Tutors of the Central Flying School delighted the public with aerobatics at the RAF's Hendon displays. The upper surfaces of their wings were painted with red and white 'sunburst' stripes, as on the inverted Tutor, serial K3240, in this photograph. Tutors continued until 1939, a few remaining afterwards.

Philip Jarrett collection

The Boulton Paul Overstrand began to replace the Sidestrand in January 1935. It was a five-seat day-bomber, with three Lewis guns in front, dorsal and ventral positions, and could carry up to 1,600 lb of bombs. Only 101 Squadron was equipped with Overstrands, although some were loaned to 144 Squadron for a few weeks in early 1937. They were withdrawn from front-line service in August 1938.

Philip Jarrett collection

The Blackburn Perth replaced the Iris with 209 Squadron from January 1934. With more powerful engines, it was the RAF's largest flying boat in its day. Only four were built, such as serial K4011 in this photograph, and these continued with the squadron until May 1936, when they were replaced with Short Singapores.

Aeroplane Monthly

The Singapore III was the last in the line of the Short flying boats, entering service in January 1935. It carried a crew of six, was armed with three machine-guns and could carry up to 2,000 lb of bombs. Eight squadrons were equipped with Singapores and a few machines continued in front-line service until 1941. This machine was photographed in 1935 while on the strength of 230 Squadron at Pembroke Dock.

Author's collection

The Hawker Hardy was a two-seat general-purpose aircraft supplied to two overseas squadrons from April 1935. It was armed with a forward-firing Vickers gun and a Lewis gun in the rear cockpit, and could carry up to 224 lb of bombs. The Hardy was employed mostly on reconnaissance and ground support duties, some continuing until the early months of the Second World War. These were on the strength of 30 Squadron when it was based in Iraq.

Philip Jarrett collection

The Supermarine Scapa, an improved version of the Southampton, first entered service in May 1935 and continued until December 1938. This Scapa, serial K4200, served with 202 Squadron in Malta.

Aeroplane Monthly

The Gloster Gauntlet was another single-seat fighter, armed with two Vickers guns, which entered squadron service from May 1935. It eventually equipped fourteen squadrons. Although most were replaced by 1938, a few saw action in 1940 against the Regia Aeronautica in East Africa. These Gauntlets were photographed while rehearsing for the RAF Hendon display of 1937, with machines of 213 Squadron in the foreground.

Philip Jarrett collection

The Vickers Vildebeest, originally designed in 1928, was the only torpedo-bomber available to the RAF in the years immediately before the Second World War. It carried a crew of either two or three and was armed with a Vickers gun firing forward and a Lewis gun firing aft. Of course, it was extremely vulnerable to enemy monoplane fighters. This Vildebeest III, serial K4608 of 22 Squadron, was photographed at Hal Far in Malta, where the squadron was based for a year from October 1935.

J.M. Bruce/G.S. Leslie collection

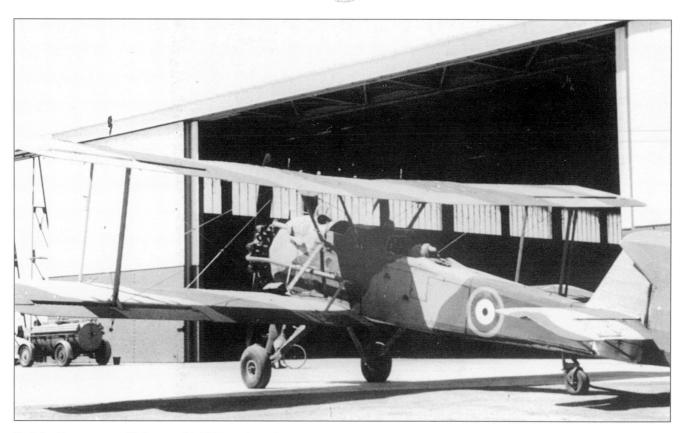

The Vickers Vincent was a modified version of the Vildebeest, designed to succeed the Wapiti, and entered service in July 1935. It carried a long-range fuel tank in lieu of the torpedo, and gave good service in the Middle East until the arrival of new monoplanes. Some continued until January 1943. This camouflaged Vincent of 47 Squadron was photographed at Khartoum in 1938.

47 Squadron Archives

The Vickers Valentia was a development of the Victoria troop-carrier, with a crew of two and provision for twenty-two passengers. Some were converted from Victorias, fitted with more powerful engines, while others were newly built. They first entered service in September 1935 and equipped three squadrons, serving in Iraq, Egypt and India. A few continued until May 1944. The example in this photograph is serial K2343 of 216 Squadron.

Philip Jarrett collection

The Saro London entered service in April 1936, eventually equipping four flying boat squadrons. With a crew of six, it was armed with three machine-guns and could carry up to 2,000 lb of bombs. Some continued in front-line service until June 1940.

Aeroplane Monthly

The Handley Page Harrow was one of Britain's first monoplane heavy bombers when it entered squadron service in January 1937, under the RAF's Expansion Scheme intended to counter the threat posed by German militarism. With a crew of five, it was fitted with power-operated turrets in nose, dorsal and tail positions, containing four machine-guns in all, and could carry up to 3,000 lb of bombs. However, Harrows were converted to the transport role on the outbreak of war and some served in that capacity up to VE-Day.

Philip Jarrett collection

'HAWKER FURY' by Charles J. Thompson

This interceptor was faster than any other RAF fighter when it entered squadron service in 1931. Armed with twin Vickers guns synchronized to fire through the propeller arc, it was much admired for its clean lines, aerobatic performance and response of controls at high speed. This example, serial K5673, was on the strength of 1 Squadron, which was equipped with these machines from February 1932 to November 1938.

The Fairey Hendon was a heavy night-bomber which entered service in November 1936. It was armed with three Lewis guns in nose, dorsal and tail positions and could carry up to 1,600 lb of bombs. Only fourteen were built and all of them, such as serial K5085 in this photograph, were supplied to 38 Squadron, although some were later detached to form the new 115 Squadron. Hendons continued in service until replaced by Wellingtons in July 1939.

Philip Jarrett collection

RAF armoured cars, adapted by Rolls-Royce from their famous Silver Ghost model and fitted with a turret, were employed by the RAF in areas of the Middle East. They helped maintain control over vast stretches of desert which formed part of the British Empire between the wars. This armoured car was photographed at Heliopolis in Egypt.

G.R. Pitchfork collection

The Vickers Wellesley, a two-seat aircraft with two machine-guns and a bomb-carrying capacity of 2,000 lb, was introduced in April 1937. It became famous the following year when two Wellesleys broke the World Long-distance Record, flying non-stop from Egypt to Australia. Some Wellesleys continued with 47 Squadron in Egypt up to March 1943, employed on reconnaissance work.

Author's collection

The Supermarine Stranraer first entered service with 228 Squadron at Pembroke Dock in April 1937. It was larger than its predecessor, the Supermarine Scapa, although the range, armament and bomb load remained the same. Some continued until April 1941, when they were replaced with Catalinas. This example, serial K7292 on the strength of 228 Squadron, was photographed at Pembroke Dock in 1939, with a Sunderland in the background.

Aviation Bookshop

The Hawker Hector entered squadron service in May 1937 as an army co-operation two-seater. Armed with one Vickers gun forward and a Lewis gun aft, it carried a bomb load or containers up to 224 lb. It was replaced by the Westland Lysander in 1939, but some Hectors saw active service during the German Blitzkrieg of May 1940. This Hector, serial K8108, was on the strength of 13 Squadron at Odiham in Hampshire.

Aeroplane Monthly

CHAPTER THREE

BATTLES LOST AND WON

The air raid sirens which accompanied Britain's declaration of war turned out to be a false alarm. In some ways, this was characteristic of the following months, which became known as the 'phoney war' by the Western powers. The powerful Wehrmacht crushed the desperate resistance of the Poles, who were stabbed in the back by the Russian troops advancing across their eastern border from 17 September by pre-arrangement with Hitler. The hapless country was divided by the two great powers and suffered long years of subjugation and cruelty.

The armada of German bombers expected over London did not arrive. The respite was a godsend to the country, which was able to build up its anti-aircraft defences, including shelters, balloons and searchlights, as well as to complete mobilization. Ten squadrons of Fairey Battles had been sent to France on 2 September to form an Advanced Air Striking Force. They were soon joined by five squadrons of Bristol Blenheims, four of Hawker Hurricanes and five of Westland Lysanders, to form the Air Component of the British Expeditionary Force on the left flank of the French defences. This was not a very formidable force to face a powerful enemy, but few military experts seemed to realize the fighting potential and tactics of the Wehrmacht. The French Air Force, although numerous, was equipped with only a few modern machines. A hundred RAF squadrons remained at home, together with the Balloon, Reserve, Training and Maintenance Commands. Of these squadrons, the Blenheims of No. 2 Group in England were placed under the operational control of the RAF's Advanced Air Striking Force in France. There were twenty-two more squadrons in more distant parts of the world.

President Roosevelt had already appealed to the belligerents, asking them to refrain from bombing targets which might result in civilian deaths. The War Cabinet was informed that Germany possessed about 3,600 front-line aircraft and was thus superior to the RAF and the French Air Force combined. This report was exaggerated, but the fear of massive air attacks and the resulting civilian panic persuaded the British and the French to agree to the President's earnest request. Hitler also agreed, but only after the campaign in Poland had been won, and without any intention of keeping his word.

With this major restriction, Bomber Command was given two objectives. One was to hunt and attack German warships, which were of course legitimate

'FAIREY BATTLE' by Charles J. Thompson
Although the Fairey Battle entered squadron service in May 1937, it was already obsolescent when the Second World War broke out. Intended as a light bomber for tactical work, carrying 1,000 lb of bombs and armed with two machine-guns, it proved no match for German fighters when the Blitzkrieg began in the West. Most of the remaining aircraft were turned over to training duties. This painting is of a Battle of 12 Squadron, based at Amifontaine in France in May 1940.

military targets, and to drop leaflets on Germany. On the day war was declared, a Blenheim, 18 Hampdens and 9 Wellingtons hunted off Wilhelmshaven without success. During the night, ten Whitleys dropped leaflets on Germany cities, in an attempt to persuade civilians of the folly of waging war. There were no losses and the leaflets had no effect, but the raid did demonstrate that the RAF was capable of penetrating German air space and also provided the aircrews with operational experience. However, subsequent leaflet raids resulted in a high loss rate of 6 per cent.

Then, on 4 September Bomber Command despatched 15 Blenheims and 14 Wellingtons in daylight against German warships in harbour. Seven aircraft were lost for meagre results, in spite of the bravery and determination of the crews. Subsequent sorties of this nature resulted in heavy losses, so that it became apparent that daylight bombing sorties were extremely unprofitable. The RAF had no long-distance fighters capable of escorting the bombers, while the power-operated turrets which had carried such high hopes proved of only limited effectiveness against enemy fighters, even when the bombers flew in tight formation.

At home and in France, RAF fighters patrolled the skies but found few targets other than the occasional reconnaissance aircraft. One development of significance was the formation of the Heston Flight of reconnaissance aircraft under F. Sidney Cotton, an entrepreneur who was given the rank of wing commander. This clandestine unit, equipped with a handful of Blenheims, Hudsons and Spitfires, which was renamed No. 2 Camouflage Unit on 1 November 1939 and then the Photographic Development Unit on 17 January 1940, expanded into an organization that supplied British Intelligence with vital photographic records throughout the war, at home and abroad.

Coastal Command was at full stretch from the beginning of the war, although it was the most neglected of the three operational Commands. It was equipped mainly with Avro Ansons, which by then were obsolescent, but there was also a handful of Hudsons, Sunderlands and other flying boats. There were also twelve ancient Vildebeest torpedo-bombers overdue for retirement. The Command's strength lay in the pilots and crews, who were highly trained and proficient. Of course, attacks on enemy warships were permitted, but only one small vessel was sunk before the Germans attacked in the West. One U-boat was sunk, but that victory was shared with HM ships. Attacks against enemy merchant vessels were prohibited, unless it was clear that they were connected with German surface raiders. Meanwhile the squadrons provided convoy escorts and reconnaissance, the crews watching helplessly while many Allied merchant ships were sunk by mines and U-boats.

The Bristol Blenheim I was hailed as a remarkable advance on light bomber biplanes when it entered squadron service in March 1937, for it could cruise at about 200 mph. With a crew of three and a bomb-carrying capacity of 1,000 lb, it was armed with a single machine-gun firing forward and another in the mid-upper turret. This became known as the 'short-nose' Blenheim when the 'long-nose' Blenheim was introduced in March 1939. The Blenheim I in this photograph was on the strength of 45 Squadron in the Middle East and was employed on photo-reconnaissance.

The Medmenham Club

The German invasion of Norway and Denmark came as no surprise to British Intelligence. Hitler had cast covetous eyes on Norway since the Russian invasion of Finland at the end of November 1939, partly to secure supplies of high-grade iron ore from Sweden which passed through that country to feed the German war machine, and partly to forestall any Allied attempt to send troops to assist the Finns or provide a flanking movement against Germany. The main question was whether the Allies could help the Norwegians resist the invasion, and in the event their efforts proved fruitless. Mines were laid in Norwegian waters on 8 April 1940 to hinder the German invasion force which was known to have set sail. The day before, Blenheims of Bomber Command had bombed these vessels, but without scoring any hits. Thereafter, bad weather prevented any sightings. German parachutists descended on Norway on 9 April, supported by swarms of aircraft, and secured important airfields. German troops entered Denmark on the same day and soon occupied that almost defenceless country.

An Allied expeditionary force was sent to northern Norway. Landings were made at Namsos on 14 April, followed by more at Aandalsnes and Narvik. They were supported by carrier-borne FAA aircraft but were bombed by the Luftwaffe and there were no airfields on which the RAF could land. On 24 April a squadron of RAF Gladiators from an aircraft carrier landed on a frozen lake in an attempt to give support, but conditions were too cold for take-off and most of the machines were destroyed by bombing. The remainder returned to the UK. Two landing strips were constructed north of Narvik and the re-equipped Gladiator squadron landed there on 24 May. They were followed by a Hurricane squadron two days later. By then, the Wehrmacht had thrust its way through the Low Countries and France. It was decided to withdraw from Norway, where the situation had become untenable. By 7 June the surviving Gladiators and

Hurricanes had landed on the deck of the aircraft carrier HMS *Glorious*, but tragically this warship was sunk the following day by the battleships *Scharnhorst* and *Gneisenau*. Only two survivors were picked up by a fishing vessel.

The German attack in the West began on 10 May 1940 when Hitler's Panzer divisions crossed the frontiers of the Low Countries. They were supported by Junkers Ju87 Stuka dive-bombers, while other bombers attacked airfields, Junkers Ju52 transports dropped parachutists over key positions and other troops landed in gliders. The strength of the Luftwaffe was overwhelming. It consisted of 1,300 long-range bombers, 380 dive-bombers, 1,150 fighters, 640 reconnaissance aircraft, 475 transport aircraft and 45 gliders. From the beginning, the Germans ruled the skies over their chosen battlegrounds.

As with Norway, the attack came as no surprise to British Intelligence. By pre-arranged plan, Anglo-French forces moved into Belgium to support the troops of that country, who were making a fighting retreat. What was not fully anticipated was the astonishing co-ordination and firepower of the attacking forces, nor the extent of their mobility. The sight and sound of a Stuka dive-bomber, coming down at an angle of about 60 degrees with its wind-driven 'screamer' switched on, unnerved the troops below before the bombs exploded with high accuracy on the pilot's chosen target.

The RAF did its best to support the ground forces, from both French and English bases. On the first day Lysanders from France were sent out on reconnaissance, escorted by Hurricanes. However, thirty-two Battles sent to bomb the German columns from low level met with disaster. A storm of fire from ground positions shot down thirteen aircraft and damaged all the remainder. Thirty-three Blenheims sent out from England to attack Dutch airfields and German transport aircraft scored considerable successes for the loss of three of their number. Bomber Command had intended to attack the Ruhr at night, but this plan was vetoed by the French for fear of retaliation against their cities. Only a handful of Whitleys were sent to bomb road bridges leading into Holland, while Wellingtons bombed a Dutch airfield. There were no losses.

On the next day Blenheims from England and France delivered attacks but suffered losses and damage. The crews of the Battles continued their heroic efforts but of eight despatched only one returned. Hampdens and Whitleys attacked road and rail communications at night, losing three aircraft. Meanwhile, the inadequately equipped Belgian forces were unable to withstand the onslaught of the Panzers and Stukas, which tore narrow gaps through their defences.

On the third day the Anglo-French forces reached their chosen battle lines. Nine Blenheims of the Advanced Air Striking Force were despatched to attack a German column but came into combat with fighters and only two returned. The Germans poured over bridges across the Albert Canal and five Battles were sent in a fruitless attempt to destroy these with their light bombs. They caused minor damage but all five were shot down by flak. Meanwhile forty-two Blenheims were sent from England to bomb bridges in Holland and eleven were lost. A handful of Wellingtons and Whitleys bombed road junctions that night, without loss.

The British and French forces took the full impact of the German Blitzkrieg and gaps were torn in their lines, through which the Panzers streamed, turning to attack from the rear. Split from each other, the armies of both countries began to retreat and before long were in chaos, destroying or abandoning their out-dated equipment. The Dutch capitulated on 14 May, on the day German bombers made a devastating attack on Rotterdam, killing almost a thousand civilians, rendering thousands more homeless and destroying swathes of buildings. This cynical disregard of the pledge to President Roosevelt released the British from their obligation, and Bomber Command began to attack the Ruhr on the night of 14/15 May.

At the outset of this assault, there were 135 Blenheims and Battles in France. By the end of the third day, this number was reduced to 72. This rate of attrition could not be sustained, but more was expected of the survivors. On 14 May, 71 aircraft took off to attack the advancing Germans but 40 did not return. The RAF in France was thus almost wiped out. On the same day, Blenheims of Bomber Command lost six of their number over Holland. On 17 May, twelve aircraft from one squadron of home-based Blenheims were sent to attack German troops but eleven were shot down and the single remaining aircraft crash-landed in England. The Hurricanes in France fared somewhat better and in fact scored numerous victories, but their mobile radar stations were soon destroyed and their airfields were being bombarded and overrun. On 19 May all the remaining serviceable aircraft were flown to England, to operate from more distant airfields.

By this time the Allies were in full retreat and it was almost every man for himself. The British were told to make for Dunkirk and await rescue, but the docks were being smashed by German bombers. The soldiers converged on the port, protected by screens of gallant defenders, and began to form up in columns on nearby beaches. They were pounded by dive-bombers and strafed by fighters, while only limited protection could be given to them by RAF fighters operating from England. At the same time RAF bombers attacked German troops out of sight of the hapless men on the beaches. Belgium had no alternative but to surrender on 27 May.

The Royal Navy began its herculean efforts to evacuate the troops from Dunkirk, as well as others at ports in western France. In response to public appeal, a huge flotilla of little ships sailed to Dunkirk, most of them manned by

The Westland Lysander, nicknamed the 'Lizzie', entered the RAF in May 1938 as an army co-operation aircraft, with very short landing and take-off distances. Lysander squadrons went to France in September 1939 as part of the Air Component of the British Expeditionary Force. Most Lysanders were withdrawn from front-line service by 1942 but some continued on special duties and on invaluable air-sea rescue work. The Lysanders in this photograph were on the strength of 225 Squadron when engaged on training exercises with the army. The undercarriages were fitted with racks for small bombs or containers of food, water and ammunition.

Author's collection

civilian volunteers. In some ways the small ships were more useful, for the beaches were too shallow for warships. With the columns of soldiers up to their shoulders in water, many of these little ships returned again and again to ferry the exhausted men out to the warships, while other soldiers kept fighting to prevent the Germans from reaching the beaches. The SS later murdered some of these last-ditch defenders. French as well as British were rescued. By 4 June the miraculous total of over 335,000 men had reached English ports, and nothing more could be done. The defeated soldiers expected to be treated with ignominy but instead they were welcomed as heroes.

France was still at war when Italy invaded through the Alps on 10 June. Whitleys of Bomber Command raided Turin on the night of 11/12 June. A force of Wellingtons was sent to the Toulon area and bombed Genoa on 15/16 June. These raids were not very effective, but the Italians were given a foretaste of a very unpleasant future. France agreed to an armistice on 22 June and hostilities ceased three days later, when the country was partitioned into German-occupied and nominally French-controlled zones. By this time, the RAF had lost almost a thousand aircraft in the campaign.

The shock and incredulity felt by the British people at this unparalleled defeat were soon replaced by a steely resolve and optimism known as the 'Dunkirk spirit', inspired by the new and indomitable Prime Minister, Winston Churchill, who had taken over from Neville Chamberlain on 11 May. The whole country came alive with preparations for continuing and winning the war, and nowhere was this energy more pronounced than in the expansion and re-equipment of the RAF. Overtures from Germany for accepting armistice terms were met with contempt.

The greatest need was to build up Fighter Command, for the prelude to any airborne and seaborne invasion of Britain would be an attempt by the Luftwaffe to wrest control of the skies from the RAF. To this end, Churchill had already appointed the dynamic and ruthless newspaper proprietor, Lord Beaverbrook, to head a new Ministry of Aircraft Production formed from various departments of the Air Ministry. Beaverbrook had the authority to direct production and establish an order of priority for the aircraft types. In doing so he disorganized production flows but also galvanized the factories into greater efforts. One of his moves was to insist on rebuilding slightly damaged aircraft using parts taken from those more seriously damaged, instead of allowing them all to moulder in dumps. His tenure in office was short and certainly controversial, but it is a fact that the number of fighters available to RAF squadrons at the outset of the Battle of Britain was much the same as when it ended.

Merchant convoys around the coasts of Britain were protected by the RAF's Mobile Balloon Barrage Flotilla, to help deter Junkers Ju87 Stuka dive-bombers.

Author's collection

On 30 July 1940 Hitler ordered Reichsmarschall Hermann Goering to prepare for the 'great air battle of the Luftwaffe against England'. In spite of its victory in the West, the Luftwaffe had lost 40 per cent of its aircraft and had needed time to recover. The date for the commencement was eventually set as 5 August 1940. After achieving air superiority over the RAF and destroying the British aircraft industry, the Luftwaffe was to continue by attacking harbours concerned with food importation, other than those needed for German seaborne landings. Meanwhile the RAF had also been able to recoup its strength and engage the enemy during his attacks against coastal convoys and airfields. Successes were scored against the detested Stukas, which became favoured targets for Spitfires and Hurricanes.

When the postponed assault began, on *Adlertag* 13 August, the Luftwaffe could muster in France, Belgium, Denmark and Norway a combat strength of 1,370 twin-engined bombers, 406 dive-bombers, 319 twin-engined fighters and 813 single-engined fighters. The Germans estimated that the RAF possessed only about 500 fighters and that the monthly replacement rate was about 200. In fact, the Commander-in-Chief of the RAF's Fighter Command, Air Chief Marshal Sir Hugh Dowding, had at his disposal about 1,100 fighters, although only about 750 were manned by pilots trained for operational flying. The squadrons were also dispersed, some of them as far away as Scotland. The monthly production of new fighters was actually over 400. Backing the Hurricanes and Spitfires were the radar stations, the Observer Corps, the Balloon Command and the Anti-aircraft Command, all under the operational control of Fighter Command, which had developed a highly efficient system of gathering instant information and issuing orders, one vital link being the defence teleprinter network.

This strange aircraft, Westland Lysander serial K6127, was fitted with twin fins and a mock-up of a four-gun turret. It was tested at the RAF's Aeroplane and Armament Experimental Establishment at Boscombe Down in Wiltshire, and was intended to strafe German troops on the beaches in the event of an invasion.

Aeroplane Monthly

What followed was a war of attrition. On the day before *Adlertag*, Stukas attacked the radar stations in the south-east of England. All save one station were back in action after hasty repairs. The stations were not easy to knock out, for pinpoint bombing was required, the attacking Stukas were vulnerable to Hurricanes and Spitfires, the open-work structures of the towers were seldom damaged by blast, and mobile stations were available in emergencies.

For the next three-and-a-half weeks, the Luftwaffe concentrated on airfields. Although there were casualties to RAF personnel and many hangars and buildings were destroyed or damaged, most airfields continued to operate. Orders from Fighter Command Headquarters at Bentley Priory in Middlesex ensured that most aircraft were in the air before each attack, so that fewer than twenty fighters were destroyed on the ground in this period. Each RAF airfield covered a large area and it was very difficult to put one out of action for more than a few hours. Casualties were dealt with first, then fires were extinguished, telephone lines restored and craters on the runways filled up, while fighters continued to land and take off from grass areas. The emergency services, both RAF and civilian, were among the heroes of the hour. If buildings such as the operations room were seriously hit, as happened at RAF Manston, the fighters operated from another airfield. In the belief that all available RAF fighters were concentrated in the south-east, on 15 August Goering despatched about 150 aircraft from Norway and Denmark against targets in north-east England.

'THE VERY FIRST OF THE FEW'
by Charles J. Thompson
The first Spitfire I to enter squadron service was serial K9789, flown to 19 Squadron at Duxford in Cambridgeshire by Geoffrey Quill on 4 August 1938. Powered by a Merlin engine of 1,030 hp and armed with eight Browning machine-guns, or later four machine-guns and two 20 mm cannons, the Spitfire combined with the Hurricane to bring victory to the RAF in the Battle of Britain.

RAF fighters pounced on them and destroyed fifteen and damaged many more, for no losses. In fact the Luftwaffe lost seventy-five aircraft on this day, the highest in the whole campaign. The Germans never repeated this tactic.

Meanwhile, Bomber Command continued its night attacks against German cities, including Berlin on 3/4 and 4/5 September. Hitler was furious and ordered Goering to switch his attacks to London by day and night. These raids began on 7 September but proved to be tactical errors, for they enabled the RAF to rebuild its stations in the south-east and also brought the attackers within easier range of the Hurricanes and Spitfires stationed to the north-east of London. Most of the bombs were dropped on London docks, but the people did not panic or rebel, as German Intelligence hoped.

Both air forces had suffered heavily from casualties by this time. Between 19 August and 6 September Fighter Command had lost 290 aircraft and 97 pilots, while the Luftwaffe had lost 375 aircraft and 678 men. Of course, the German aircraft did not usually go down over friendly territory. Moreover, Dowding rotated his squadrons, allowing some to move away from the main battle area for short periods, but the Luftwaffe crews had no such respite. They could not understand why Spitfires and Hurricanes kept coming at them with no diminution of strength or determination, instead of being whittled down to almost nothing as they had expected. It was reported that when Goering asked the German fighter ace Adolf Galland what he required to eliminate the RAF, he received the reply 'Give me a squadron of Spitfires!'

However, there is no doubt that the RAF was losing many of its best and

'BURGESS vs HINTZE' by Charles J. Thompson
During an air battle over Kent in the afternoon
of 29 October 1940, Sgt John H.H. Burgess in
Spitfire I serial P9318 of B Flight, 222 'Natal'
Squadron, based at Hornchurch in Essex,
engaged Messerschmitt Bf109E-4/B
Werkenummer (works number) 2024 of
3/Erprobungsgruppe 210, flown by Oberleutnant
Otto Hintze from the advanced airfield at
Calais-Marck. Closing up with the enemy,
Burgess fired a seven-second burst with his
eight Browning machine-guns, hitting the
German aircraft's engine and causing it to lose
speed. Hintze jettisoned his cockpit hood and
Burgess watched as he managed to bale out
without turning the aircraft on its back, possibly
by pushing the control column forward and
'bunting' the fighter into an inverted loop so
that he was thrown out of the cockpit. His
parachute opened and he landed safely while his
aircraft crashed at Sheerlands Farm, Buckley, in
Kent. Hintze spent the remainder of the war as
a PoW and Burgess also survived the war.

most skilled pilots. Others were coming through the training system but they
lacked operational experience and needed further instruction at squadron level.
The Luftwaffe was suffering from the same problem. It was a matter of which
side could hold out longer. The climax came on 15 September when Goering
made a maximum effort attack, with wave after wave of aircraft directed in
daylight against London. They were met with the usual attacks by RAF fighters
and at the end of the day it was claimed that 180 of the enemy had been shot
down. The true number was 59, for the loss of 26 from Fighter Command, but
this was enough to convince the Germans that the prospect of victory had
vanished.

Two days later Hitler postponed the invasion and the fleet of barges and
warships of the Kriegsmarine which had been assembled was dispersed. Some
daylight attacks continued until the end of the month, with the Luftwaffe still
losing a high proportion of those despatched. The Luftwaffe had lost 1,339
aircraft and Fighter Command 723 aircraft during the months of August and
September. Goering decided to switch to night attacks and the Battle of Britain
was over.

Fighter Command's Headquarters at Bentley Priory, Stanmore, in Middlesex, where reports from radar stations and the Observer Corps were received and incoming enemy aircraft plotted on a huge board. Orders for interception were sent out to fighter groups, who in turn passed them on to stations and then to squadrons. The procedure was extremely swift and effective.

Author's collection

The celebrated Hawker Hurricane I shared with the Spitfire the honours for the RAF's victory in the Battle of Britain and in fact shot down more enemy aircraft. First entering service in December 1937, it was a robust aircraft armed with eight .303 inch machine-guns. This Hurricane of 32 Squadron was photographed at Hawkinge in Kent.

Author's collection

Pilots of 32 Squadron photographed in July 1940 at Hawkinge in Kent, in front of one of their Hurricane Is.

Author's collection

Pilots of 601 (County of London) Squadron, which was engaged in the Battle of Britain from airfields in the south-east, south and south-west of England. Ten of the squadron's pilots had been awarded the DFC at the time this photograph was taken. They are beside one of their Hurricane Is showing the squadron's distinctive winged sword emblem on the tail fin.

Author's collection

Dornier Do17M, unit code A5+EA, of the Geschwaderstabstaffel of Sturzkampf-geschwader 1, flown by Unteroffizier Lengenbrink, was shot down on 25 July 1940 by Spitfire Is of 152 Squadron based at Warmwell in Dorset, while on a reconnaissance mission. The pilot was killed and the other two crew members were captured, one wounded.

Author's collection

Junkers Ju88A-1, unit code 9K+CL, of 3/Kampfgeschwader 51, flown by Obergefreiter Dickel, was shot down on the night of 12/13 August 1940 while on a bombing raid. It crashed near Godstone in Surrey and broke up, with the tail section falling some distance from the rest of the aircraft. The pilot was killed but the other three crew members baled out and were wounded when captured.

Author's collection

'ADLERTAG' by Charles J. Thompson
'Adlertag', or 'Eagle Day' was 13 August 1940, the day the Germans considered that the Battle of Britain began, although there had been considerable activity the day before. The main targets of the bombers, many of which were escorted by fighters, were RAF airfields in the south and south-east of England. This painting depicts Dornier Do17Zs of 9/Kampfgeschwader 2, without fighter escorts, under attack by Hurricane Is of 111 Squadron based at Croydon in Surrey, while over Sheerness in Kent.

This Dornier Do17Z, unit code U5+DS, of 7/Kampfgeschwader 2 was shot down on 13 August 1940 by Hurricane Is of 111 Squadron based at Croydon, while on a bombing mission against RAF Eastchurch in Kent. It crashed on mud-flats at Seasalter near Whitstable in Kent and broke up. Two of the crew were killed and the other two captured.

Author's collection

The final dive of a Dornier Do17Z-2 with its starboard engine on fire, photographed from the ground on 18 August 1940. It was probably one of the Dorniers of 9/Kampfgeschwader 76 which were shot down during their attack on Kenley airfield.

Author's collection

Dornier Do17Z-2, unit code F1+DT, of 9/Kampfgeschwader 76 was flown by the Staffelkapitän, Hauptmann Roth, on 18 August 1940, during the height of the Battle of Britain. Hit by ground fire from RAF Kenley in Surrey and further damaged by two Hurricanes of 111 Squadron from RAF Croydon, it crash-landed at Leaves Green near Biggin Hill in Kent. Much of the machine burnt out but the five crew members got out and were captured.

Author's collection

Junkers Ju88A-5, unit code
4D+AD, of Stab III/Kampf-
geschwader 30 (Adler
Geschwader) was flown by the
Gruppenkommandeur, Major
Hackbarth, during an attack on
London docks in the late
afternoon of 9 September 1940.
It was shot down by RAF fighters
and crashed on the beach at
Pagham, near Bognor Regis, in
Sussex, and became a total loss.
The pilot and one crew member
were captured but the other two
were killed.

Author's collection

Heinkel He111H-3, unit code 1H+GP, of 6/Kampfgeschwader was flown by Unteroffizier Niemeyer on 23 September 1940 during a night attack on London. It was shot down
by anti-aircraft fire and crashed at 01.37 hours near Gordon Boys Home at Chobham in Surrey, bursting into flames. The pilot and two crew members were killed but a fourth
baled out and was captured.

Author's collection

'A FIELD OF HUMAN CONFLICT' by Charles J. Thompson
Inspired by the immortal words of Winston Churchill at the end of the Battle of Britain, this painting shows a Spitfire I of 54 Squadron, based at Hornchurch in Essex, attacking a formation of Heinkel He111s.

A flying legend in the form of Spitfire IXc, serial MH434 (G-ASJV). The photograph was taken on 23 May 1997.

British Crown Copyright/MOD/Sgt Rick Brewell

A Gefreiter (Leading Aircraftman) being led away to captivity. The opened parachute pack carried by the soldier indicates that the young Luftwaffe airman had baled out. His shoes and socks had been temporarily taken off him, to prevent any attempt at escape.

Author's collection

Oberleutnant Karl Fisher of 7/Jagdgeschwader 27 attempted to force-land his Messerschmitt Bf109E-1, white 9, near Queen Anne's Gate in Windsor Great Park on 30 September 1940, after combat with RAF fighters when escorting a bomber formation. His machine overturned but Fisher remained unharmed and was taken prisoner. The Messerschmitt was righted by the RAF and put on display in the local high street for fund-raising.

Author's collection

German aircraft shot down by fighters or anti-aircraft fire, collected at a dump in an RAF station. Identifiable are the fuselage of a Junkers Ju87 Stuka, the fuselages of two Dornier DO17Z-2s and part of the tail fin of another Do17Z-2.

Author's collection

A batch of Luftwaffe prisoners, shot down in the Battle of Britain, being taken by coach to a prisoner-of-war camp.

Author's collection

CHAPTER FOUR

OVER TO THE OFFENSIVE

The victory in the Battle of Britain gave an enormous boost to the morale of the British people. They had seen that a handful of young pilots, some still in their late teens, could defeat the mighty Luftwaffe, provided they flew modern machines and were backed by a superb organization. The myth of the invincible German war machine had been exploded. It had been beaten once and could be beaten again. On 25 October 1940 Air Chief Marshal Sir Charles Portal took over from Sir Cyril Newall as Chief of Air Staff, and continued the task of expanding and modernizing the RAF.

One method of striking back at Germany had been devised soon after Dunkirk. This was the formation of the Special Operations Executive (SOE), a body of men and women trained to foster armed resistance movements and begin sabotage in the countries occupied by German forces. With the coastlines under enemy control, the best method of taking in and bringing out these clandestine units was by air. A special flight, equipped with a handful of Lysanders capable of short take-offs and landings, together with a few Whitleys, had been set up in August 1940. Plans were afoot for the expansion of this small unit, which eventually grew into a squadron and had another squadron added to it. The aircraft were sometimes crewed by nationals of the occupied countries who had joined the RAF, while members of the SOE landed or dropped by parachute were often of the same nationality.

The autumn of 1940 was a proud time for the men and women in RAF uniform, but there were grim nights for many civilians. The weight of the Luftwaffe bomber force fell on the cities, and it was London which first experienced onslaught from 7 September 1940. In reasonable weather the area was easy to pick out from the air, with the silvery Thames winding down to the sea. Only a few of the heaviest anti-aircraft guns were effective up to 25,000 ft while searchlights could not illuminate above 12,000 ft. The RAF's night-fighter force was inadequately equipped at this time. Hurricane and Spitfire pilots relied solely on visual observation, but some Blenheims were fitted with rather rudimentary air interception radar. The two-seat Defiant was also adapted to this night-fighter role, pending the arrival of the Beaufighter which was coming into service with more effective air interception radar and very powerful armament.

For purposes of navigation in cloudy conditions, and especially for locating targets further inland, the Luftwaffe made use of its *Knickebein* blind-flying

Left: In the closing months of 1940, a force of about fifty Fiat CR42 'Falco' fighter biplanes formed part of the Corpo Aero Italiano operating over England from Maldegen near Brussels. On 11 November 1940, while escorting some Fiat BR20 'Cicogna' bombers on a raid on Harwich, they were intercepted by Spitfires and Hurricanes and lost heavily, without loss to the RAF. One of the fighters, flown by Sergente Salvadori of 95° Squadriglia 18° Gruppo, force-landed with a fractured oil pipe at Orfordness, as shown here. This Fiat is now on display in the Battle of Britain section of the RAF Museum at Hendon. (*The Aviation Bookshop*) Right: One of the Italian prisoners, who was fortunate enough not to be injured, arriving in London by train. (*Author's collection*)

equipment. A ground transmitter sent out a broad beam at about 30 megacycles per second along which the bomber flew. This gave out a series of dots and dashes on either side of a line, which merged into a single note in the receiver when the aircraft was flying in the centre. When this signal crossed another beam, the crew knew that the bombs should be dropped over the intended target. The system was accurate enough for 'area bombing', but fortunately Dr R.V. Jones, a brilliant young British scientist attached to MI6, was able to identify it and devise a method of distorting the beams so that they were no longer effective.

London bore the brunt of the Blitz until the middle of November 1940, when Goering, disappointed at the stoicism of the civil population, who had proved far more resilient than he had expected, switched some of the bombers to industrial centres and ports. Goering and Hitler hoped that these attacks, in combination with an intensified U-boat campaign, would starve Britain of essential war materials and food, bringing the country to its knees.

Another radio aid, requiring more specialist training than the *Knickebein* system, was adopted by *Kampfgruppe 100*, the Luftwaffe's specialist 'pathfinder' unit which marked targets with flares and incendiaries for the main bomber stream. Known as 'X-Gerät', it utilized a frequency of about 75 megacycles per second. A narrow director beam was sent out, crossing other beams at obtuse angles. With the navigator using a stopwatch, this gave a very precise position for releasing the bombs. It was used over Coventry on the night of 14/15 November

1940, with devastating effect. Fortunately, Dr Jones was also able to identify this system and develop jamming apparatus.

The British were not idle in devising other counter-measures. Dummy towns and airfields were constructed, and a fair proportion of the enemy's bombs fell on these when decoy fires were lit. More heavy anti-aircraft guns came into service. The new Beaufighter scored its first night-fighter success on 19 November 1940 and thereafter began to take an increasing toll of the German bombers, which hitherto had suffered a nightly loss of only about 1 per cent.

Another success, which would have seemed incredible to the Germans if they had known about it, was the ability of the Government Code and Cypher School at Bletchley Park in Buckinghamshire to decrypt the Luftwaffe's coded 'Enigma' signals, with increasing speed and accuracy. By the latter part of 1940 British Intelligence were aware of the Luftwaffe's 'order of battle' as well as its operational instructions, signals between aircraft and ground, and such matters as aircraft serviceability on the station. This intelligence was gathered alongside the results of the Photographic Reconnaissance Unit (PRU), as the Photographic Development Unit had been renamed on 8 July 1940, when newly commanded by Wing Commander G.W. Tuttle and placed under the control of Coastal Command. This became No. 1 PRU on 16 November 1940, in preparation for a

The Blenheim IF night-fighter came into service with 25 Squadron in December 1938 and continued during the Blitz of 1940/1. The Blenheim I was normally armed with one gun firing forward and another in the turret, but the night-fighter version was among those additionally fitted with a four-gun pack under the fuselage. From July 1940 these Blenheims were equipped with the first airborne interception radar, although it was the Beaufighter that later became better known for this equipment.

Author's collection

similar unit being set up in Egypt. By this time the Spitfires, fitted with extra fuel tanks instead of armament, were ranging far and wide over enemy territory and bringing back astonishing photographs from both high and low level.

One outcome of all this intelligence was the employment of heavy bombers at night against the Luftwaffe's airfields in France and the Low Countries in the early part of the winter of 1940/1. Some Blenheims were transferred to the role of 'intruders' and began to harry these airfields and the enemy bombers at night. Other Blenheims of Bomber Command began daylight 'Circus' operations in January 1941 against targets close to the coasts of north-west Europe. They were escorted by large numbers of fighters, with the intention of drawing the Luftwaffe into combat and winning a war of attrition. It has to be said that these operations proved quite costly, partly because damaged RAF fighters suffered the same problem as the Luftwaffe in the Battle of Britain; they were over enemy territory when the pilots needed to bale out or force-land.

The heavier bombers continued night attacks. It was intended that they would concentrate on synthetic oil plants from mid-January 1941, since oil was known to be the Achilles heel of the Germany war machine. However, the combination of winter weather and inadequate navigational equipment hindered this plan. By mid-February, many of the heavy bomber attacks were directed against ports in Germany and France, in an attempt to restrict the U-boat campaign which was assuming worrying proportions. Some of the Blenheim squadrons were diverted to daylight attacks at low level against shipping along the Dutch and German coasts, mainly since Coastal Command was still inadequately equipped for this task. The crews flew into the face of withering flak from escort vessels and merchant ships, and lost heavily. Although they believed that they had sunk many ships with their light bombs, an examination of German records after the war revealed that there were very few successes.

One of the roles of the ubiquitous Beaufighter was that of a night-fighter, the first being equipped with air interception radar from September 1940. This Beaufighter was on the strength of 125 Squadron, which was engaged on home defence with these machines from February 1942 to February 1944. The photograph was taken at 02.00 hours, preparatory to take-off.

Author's collection

By the spring of 1941 about 40,000 civilians had been killed in Britain and 46,000 injured, mostly in London, and the country was clamouring for strong retaliation against Germany. Bombing also seemed to be the only way that Britain, standing with its Empire against a powerful enemy, could hope to achieve victory. The seeds of the whirlwind which would later devastate Germany were sown in this period. The Blitz against British targets continued until the night of 10/11 May 1941, when London endured its last heavy attack, and then miraculously died away. This was puzzling to many people, but not to British Intelligence, which had been aware well in advance that Germany was preparing to attack in the East and needed to withdraw many Luftwaffe units for this purpose. The British warnings to Josef Stalin went unheeded.

Hitler had promised his generals that when the Wehrmacht attacked Russia 'we have only to kick in the door and the whole rotten edifice will tumble'. He had miscalculated again, although the unprepared Russian forces fell back in some disorder from the onslaught which began on 22 June 1941. In spite of Stalin's suspicions that Britain was in league with Germany, the RAF did its best to help its new ally. On 9 July 1941 Bomber Command was directed to concentrate its efforts on the German transportation system, in the belief that this would hinder the supply of troops and stores to the Eastern Front as well as to the Mediterranean war zone. By this time Bomber Command consisted of about a thousand aircraft within forty-nine squadrons, but eight of these squadrons were equipped with Blenheims capable of carrying only a light bomb load for a limited range. The Blenheims continued daylight 'Circus' operations and scored some successes but at the heavy cost of about 7 per cent per sortie. Of the other squadrons, four were still working up to operational readiness while some of the others were equipped with new heavy bombers, the twin-engined Avro Manchester and two four-engined machines, the Short Stirling and the Handley Page Halifax. The casualty rate among the night-bombing squadrons was about half that of the Blenheim squadrons, but a menace was beginning to appear in the form of enemy night-fighter squadrons over Germany, equipped and trained in the use of special radar apparatus.

The future of the night-bombing force was cast into serious doubt on 18 August 1941 when a survey conducted by D.M.B. Butt of the War Cabinet Secretariat was completed. This had been requested by Winston Churchill's scientific advisor, Lord Cherwell, previously Professor Sir Frederick Lindemann, who wielded considerable influence. With the aid of the RAF's Photographic Interpretation Unit, Butt examined numerous photographs taken with the aid of flares by cameras fitted to bombers in a hundred night raids on twenty-eight targets during the previous June and July. He found that only about one in four crews who claimed success in raids against German targets dropped their bombs within 5 miles of the targets. In the Ruhr, where the targets were often obscured by industrial haze and there were very strong defences, the proportion was only one in fourteen. On the other hand, when attacks were made against French ports, the proportion rose to two in three. Not unexpectedly, Churchill raised strong doubts when it was proposed on 2 September to increase the bombing force to 4,000.

The problem was primarily one of navigation. The bombers were not equipped with any special instruments to enable them to find the targets with certainty. Navigation depended primarily on 'dead-reckoning', a form of calculation based on the aircraft's compass course and airspeed, plus estimates of wind speed and direction. Wireless bearings were not effective unless the aircraft was close to the transmitting station. In order to check positions, the crew looked below and tried to pick out landmarks, but this was not easy at high level over a blacked-out countryside. Coastlines, lakes and rivers could be identified in clear weather, but otherwise celestial navigation was attempted with the use of a bubble sextant. This was a lengthy procedure and at best gave accuracy to within about 5 miles, and only when the calculations were complete and the aircraft had passed well beyond the position where the observations were taken. Without the help of new navigational equipment, the bombing of targets in the German heartland was proving to be wasteful of crews and materiel, producing little effect.

The course of the war was changed dramatically on 7 December 1941 at 07.50 hours local time, when carrier-borne Japanese aircraft bombed and torpedoed the American Pacific Fleet at Pearl Harbor in Hawaii. Hitler had unwisely assured Japan that he would side with her in the event of war with the USA and the British Empire. The ultimate defeat of his Third Reich was thus ensured.

Up to this time RAF aircraft had been manned almost entirely by pilots and crews who had been trained in Britain. Further increase in the striking power of the service would not have been possible without an enormous increase in training. Facilities for instruction in technical subjects for ground personnel were being

On 22 May 1941 this Heinkel H-8 of 4/Kampfgeschwader 27 hit a mist-covered hill near Lulworth Cove in Dorset and skidded to a halt without serious damage. It was fitted with a fender designed to cut or deflect balloon cables but this was very heavy and also required a counterbalancing weight in the tail. It soon proved impracticable and the remaining aircraft were modified as target tugs, designated He111H-8/R2s.

Author's collection

'EAGLE LANDING' by Charles J. Thompson
A Hurricane I of 71 'Eagle' Squadron preparing
to land at Kirton in Lindsey.

increased rapidly, the courses having been shortened and made more intensive. The
main problem was how to train more aircrews, for the whole country had become
a battle zone and the vagaries of the climate imposed limitations on flying.
Fortunately a most successful organization, the Empire Air Training Scheme, had
been devised shortly after the outbreak of war when Canada, Australia, New
Zealand and Southern Rhodesia offered to train their own nationals to fly
alongside the RAF. South Africa soon joined in the project. This scheme was now
extended to include aircrew trainees from Britain, who were sent out in escorted
convoys. Aircraft were supplied from Britain, together with RAF instructors who
had completed an operational tour or had shown a special proficiency in their own
training. Elementary Flying Training Schools, Service Flying Training Schools,
Bombing and Gunnery Schools, Air Observer Navigation Schools and Wireless
Schools were set up rapidly, and other specialist schools soon followed.

The first overseas training courses began in April 1940, and the rate of
expansion was remarkable. By the middle of 1942 the Empire Air Training
Scheme was capable of turning out 11,000 pilots and 17,000 other aircrew
each year, and these numbers continued. Yet another scheme began in the
Southern States of the USA in June 1941, following a generous offer by
General Henry A. 'Hap' Arnold, the Chief of the USAAF, to train RAF pilots
alongside his own men. This was arranged before the USA entered the war, and
training continued until February 1943, by which time 4,370 RAF pilots had
graduated.

Those men who returned home with their wings or brevets, or were sent to

'NIGHT FIGHTER' by Charles J. Thompson
A Defiant night-fighter of 256 Squadron, based
at Catterick in Yorkshire, in December 1940.

the Middle East, required further training in local conditions, such as at
Advanced Flying Units, Operational Training Units or Heavy Conversion Units.
They were joined by many men from the Dominions and the occupied countries,
who then flew either in RAF squadrons or in squadrons under the operational
control of the RAF. The men who were trained overseas formed the majority of
the RAF crews who were to help bring Germany, Italy and Japan to their knees
in the next few years, led by those who had flown in the earlier part of the war.
However, the crews who manned Bomber Command in December 1941 were
still awaiting the new equipment which would enable them to find their targets
at night.

The first 'Eagle' squadron of the RAF was formed at Church Fenton in Yorkshire on 19 September 1940 and was manned by American personnel, some of whom had already been in combat in the Battle of Britain. This was 71 Squadron, which had served during the First World War, mainly with Australian pilots. Brewster Buffalos were used in training but Hurricane Is arrived by November 1940 and the squadron was operational on defensive duties from Kirton in Lindsey in Lincolnshire.

Author's collection

The Hurricane II was fitted with a Merlin XX engine of 1,280 hp, replacing the Merlin II of 1,030 hp. The Mark IIA, which retained the eight .303 inch machine-guns, entered squadron service in September 1940. The Mark IIB, shown here, was armed with four 20 mm guns and first operated in April 1941.

Author's collection

Some Hurricane IIBs were converted into fighter-bombers, carrying two 250 lb bombs under the wings. These 'Hurribombers' came into service in September 1941 and were employed in the Mediterranean and Burma theatres as well as at home. The load was later increased to two 500 lb bombs.

Author's collection

The Bell Airacobra equipped only 601 Squadron, replacing Hurricanes from August 1941. It was employed in the ground attack role but there were continual problems with serviceability and it was taken off operations by the end of the year, to be replaced by the Spitfire.

Author's collection

On 7 September 1941 Hurricane IIBs of 81 Squadron and Hurricane IIAs of 134 Squadron, forming No. 151 Wing, took off from the aircraft carrier HMS *Argus* and landed at Vaenga in North Russia, to act as escorts for Soviet bombers operating over the area of Petsamo. Other Hurricanes were sent in crates, making up the number to thirty-nine in all. The RAF men were received enthusiastically by the Russians.

Author's collection

The Hurricane pilots flew numerous sorties, claiming sixteen enemy aircraft for the loss of one of their number. Lack of spare parts prevented the Mark IIBs from having extra armament and they flew with the eight guns of the Mark IIA. The squadrons handed their aircraft to the Russians in October and the men returned to Britain the following month. This Russian officer was photographed watching an RAF pilot clip on his parachute harness.

Author's collection

Some Hurricane IIBs were converted to fighter-bomber duties, carrying two 250 lb bombs, and began cross-Channel operations in October 1941. These Hurribombers were on the strength of 175 Squadron, which was formed at Warmwell in Dorset on 3 March 1942. The pilots were photographed walking back to their hut after a raid.

Author's collection

The Westland Whirlwind was the first twin-engined fighter employed by the RAF when it was first introduced into squadron service in December 1940. Armed with four 20 mm cannon in the nose, it had considerable fire-power to add to a useful range when escorting Blenheim light bombers. It could also carry four 250 lb bombs, as shown in this photograph. Whirlwinds continued in front-line service until December 1943.

Author's collection

The Spitfire VB, powered by a Merlin engine of 1,440 hp and armed with two 20 mm cannon and four .303 inch machine-guns, entered squadron service in February 1941. This example, serial AD185 of 19 Squadron based at Matlaske in Norfolk, was photographed over the North Sea on 27 November 1941. It was flown by a Czechoslovakian in the RAF, Sgt Sokol, when his squadron was acting as rear cover for three Beauforts of 217 Squadron from Thorney Island, escorted by Spitfires of 152 Squadron from Coltishall in Norfolk, which were attacking shipping off the Hook of Holland, with the author navigating the formation.

Author's collection

The Spitfire XII, fitted with a Griffon engine of 1,735 hp, was designed for low-altitude combat and came into service in the spring of 1943, primarily to counter Focke-Wulf Fw190s which were making daylight attacks along the south coast of England. The armament consisted of two 20 mm cannon and four .303 inch machine-guns, and it could also carry two 250 lb bombs. Its distinguishing features were a pointed rudder, clipped wings and a nose of different shape.

Author's collection

The Miles Magister was the first monoplane trainer in the RAF when it was introduced in September 1937. It was used in Elementary Flying Training Schools throughout the war, becoming known affectionately as the 'Maggie'. Many wartime volunteer pilots trained in this aircraft, doing 'circuits and bumps' and aerobatics.

Aeroplane Monthly

The Airspeed Oxford was an advanced monoplane trainer which first entered RAF service in November 1937. It was used mainly for pilot training, such as serial HN386 in this photograph, but some were fitted with dorsal turrets for gunnery training. Oxfords served in several countries under the Empire Air Training Scheme and some continued in communications duties after the war.

Aeroplane Monthly

The de Havilland Tiger Moth entered service with the RAF in 1932 as an *ab initio* trainer and continued in this role throughout the Second World War and beyond. During this period, most RAF pilots trained on this delightful machine, which still has its devotees. This photograph was taken by the author on 25 July 1995, when twelve RAF and FAA veterans were flown in formation by pilots of the de Havilland Moth Club from the RFC airfield at Rendcomb to the International Air Tattoo at RAF Fairford. The veterans later had the honour of taking the salute at the fly past, which commemorated the 50th anniversary of VE-Day.

Author's collection

The two-seat Hawker Henley was intended as a fast light bomber, but its role was changed to that of a target-tug on anti-aircraft co-operation duties when it was introduced in November 1938. Henleys continued in this undramatic but necessary role almost to the end of the Second World War.

Philip Jarrett collection

A large draft of aircrew volunteers leaving Britain for training in Canada in their various specialisms.

Author's collection

The North American Harvard became a standard aircraft for sixteen years with RAF Flying Training Schools after its introduction in December 1938. It also served in Canada and Southern Rhodesia. These Harvards were photographed at No. 20 Service Flying Training School at Cranbourne in Southern Rhodesia, where the author was the Station Navigation Officer in 1943/4. The Harvard was a particularly noisy aircraft which could be identified by the rasping note of its direct-drive propeller with high tip speeds.

Author's collection

Trainee flight mechanics of the WAAF working on advanced rigging maintenance with a Westland Lysander.

Author's collection

WAAF flight mechanics on duty servicing Miles Masters at the Advanced Training Unit at Montrose in Scotland, during practice night flying. The Master was introduced early in the Second World War as a two-seat advanced trainer and continued in RAF service up to 1950.

Author's collection

The Miles Martinet was designed as a target-tug, entering service in 1942 to replace obsolete but unsuitable aircraft such as the Battle which had been converted to this role. It was a two-seater, similar to the Master but with a longer nose to compensate for the weight of the towing apparatus in the rear cockpit. The crew had to hope that the gunners under training would concentrate their fire on the drogue and not on the towing aircraft. Martinets continued with this essential task for several years after the end of the war.

Philip Jarrett collection

Paratroops were trained from the summer of 1940 at No. 1 Parachute Training School at Manchester's Ringway Airport, under joint RAF and Army control. The men in this photograph were making practice jumps from the ventral opening of a Whitley fuselage, after the 'dustbin' turret had been removed.

Author's collection

The Armstrong Whitworth Whitley, with a crew of five, was withdrawn from Bomber Command in April 1942, but meanwhile some had been allocated to training duties. Six were allocated to No. 1 Parachute Training School at Ringway and the first jumps were made on 12 July 1940. At first the men jumped from a platform which replaced the rear turret and opened their parachutes by pulling ripcords manually. This method was changed to jumping through the hole created by the removing of the 'dustbin' turret, with the parachutes opening from a static line in the aircraft.

Author's collection

CHAPTER FIVE

HOSTILE WATERS

Coastal Command had begun the war with only 183 aircraft, of which 135 were obsolescent Avro Ansons, 12 were obsolete Vickers Vildebeests, 9 were Lockheed Hudsons recently arrived from the USA, and the remainder were flying boats, of which some were also obsolescent. After the fall of France, the Command faced a problem that seemed almost insuperable. Suddenly, it was presented with an enemy coastline which had expanded from Germany's short North Sea littoral to one which stretched from the North Cape of Norway to the Franco-Spanish border, covering thousands of miles. Along this vast coastline were numerous Norwegian fjords and harbours where enemy warships and merchant vessels could shelter, in addition to the ports of Holland, Belgium and France. From these, enemy U-boats could cause havoc with the Atlantic convoys. The surface warships of the Kriegsmarine were also formidable, with great battleships, cruisers, destroyers, torpedo boats, minesweepers and smaller vessels. Yet, from necessity during Britain's immediate plight, Coastal Command was the most neglected of all three operational Commands in the home-based RAF, in terms of new equipment.

Iceland became a new base for the Command after British troops landed there in May 1940 to deny the island to the Germans. Gibraltar was handed over to its authority soon after Italy entered the war. This provided additional bases for operating over the Atlantic, but the U-boat war against the convoys began to go very badly for the British merchant fleet. There was a stretch in mid-Atlantic where the U-boats could operate unmolested by any land-based aircraft, and the sinkings soon reached appalling levels. The U-boat crews named this the 'happy time' and Winston Churchill confessed after the war that their sinkings were the most worrying matter he had experienced, causing him to wonder if Britain could prevail. Of course the British convoys were escorted by warships but there were too few of them and they were not yet equipped with radar. In addition, the Royal Navy was at full stretch covering other oceans and the Mediterranean Sea.

There were a few modest improvements in Coastal Command's equipment by the end of 1940. More Hudsons had arrived to replace the Ansons, with their better armament, longer range and heavier bomb-carrying capacity, although these aircraft were not ideally suited to the anti-shipping war. More Sunderlands had been built to replace obsolete flying boats, and these aircraft proved excellent

The Avro Anson first entered squadron service in March 1936 and became the standard reconnaissance aircraft in Coastal Command up to the outbreak of the Second World War. It had a limited range, a very low bomb-carrying capacity, and was armed with only one machine-gun firing forward and another in the turret, but it was also a highly reliable aircraft which became known as 'Faithful Annie'. In various roles it continued in RAF service until June 1968. This example was on the strength of 502 Squadron at Aldergrove in Northern Ireland, which was equipped with Ansons from January 1939 to November 1940.

Author's collection

as convoy escorts and in the anti-submarine war, within the limits of their range. Some squadrons were equipped with Blenheim IVs, which were being slowly phased out of Bomber Command. A few Whitleys and Wellingtons were also transferred from the same source. Some Swordfish from the Fleet Air Arm were placed under the control of Coastal Command. The new Beaufort torpedo-bomber had arrived, and its initial technical problems had been overcome. Even more promising, a single squadron had been equipped with the new Beaufighter IC for long-distance escort work. This was the aircraft that would ultimately transform the war against Germany's coastal traffic. Many photo-reconnaissance Spitfires had been added to No. 1 PRU, which was carrying out superb work.

The strength of Coastal Command stood at 554 aircraft in January 1941, but these were not sufficient to meet the tasks it faced. Perhaps its greatest asset lay in the pilots, who were also highly trained as navigators and were capable of flying over vast stretches of ocean with confidence. A stream of wartime volunteers was coming through Training Command to share the burdens they shouldered.

Daylight attacks by the new Beauforts were proving extremely costly. The Germans had been able to acquire a huge merchant fleet from the occupied countries and these plied along the coasts, principally bringing war materials from Narvik via Rotterdam. These were then taken by barge down the Rhine to the Ruhr, and coal was exported to Sweden in return. The German convoys, which included Swedish ships, were escorted by armed trawlers and covered by fighters of the Luftwaffe. On the other hand, magnetic mines dropped at night by Beauforts and other aircraft at the entrances to enemy harbours were far more 'cost-effective', sinking a number of vessels for proportionately fewer losses.

However, in 1941 the squadrons desperately required better equipment and improved intelligence, and here British science was coming to their aid. Some of the aircraft such as the Wellingtons were being fitted with the new Air to Surface

Vessel (ASV) radar, which gave the approximate distance and direction of a ship on its screen. The first instrument was still rather experimental, but better equipment was being devised. The anti-submarine bombs which the aircraft carried at the beginning of the war had proved almost totally ineffective in practice, even when scoring direct hits, but they were being replaced by a new and powerful depth-charge. The Government Code and Cypher School at Bletchley Park was beginning to decrypt the wireless traffic of the Kreigsmarine in home waters, giving information about U-boats and coastal traffic. A Coastal Command Development Unit had been set up in November 1940 and was carrying out trials on aircraft and new equipment.

These were the 'dark days' for Coastal Command, but there were a few successes. A single Beaufort torpedoed and badly damaged the battleship *Gneisenau* outside Brest harbour on 9 April 1941, before being blown out of the sky. The pilot was awarded a posthumous VC. Another Beaufort torpedoed and put out of commission the cruiser *Lützow* off south-west Norway on 13 June 1941. But up to the middle of 1941, the Command had sunk only two U-boats in the entire war, and these victories were shared with warships. All this began to change slowly when new aircraft, long-range Catalinas and Liberators, arrived from the USA. These new arrivals were closing the Atlantic Gap by operating from Iceland. Meanwhile, unarmed Mosquitos were added to the strength of No. 1 PRU, and photo-reconnaissance of the results of Bomber Command's attacks could cover the whole of Europe.

The Lockheed Hudson began to replace the Avro Anson in May 1939 and was also employed as a strike aircraft. With seven machine-guns and more than twice the range of the Anson, it gave good service for several years, including use in air-sea rescue squadrons. These Hudsons were on the strength of 48 Squadron, which was equipped with variants of these machines from September 1941 to February 1944.

Author's collection

By the end of 1941 the strength of the Command stood at 633 aircraft. There was, however, a humiliation for the country when two German battleships and a heavy cruiser, escorted by destroyers, left Brest in February 1942 and made their way up the English Channel to home waters, damaged only by magnetic mines dropped by the RAF. The anti-shipping war was also disrupted the following month when events in the Mediterranean and the Far East necessitated the withdrawal of all the Beaufort torpedo-bomber squadrons to these theatres. Their role was partly filled by Hampdens which were no longer required by Bomber Command and had been converted into the torpedo-carrying role. Although these aircraft were not entirely suitable for this task, the crews carried out some noble work in daylight off Norway, operating over such long distances that fighter escort was not possible. They also dropped magnetic mines near harbour entrances. In September 1942 their numbers were reduced when two squadrons were flown to North Russia to protect Allied convoys taking supplies to Murmansk from attacks by German battleships sheltering in Norway. Some were lost en route and then, on completion of their detachment, the surviving Hampdens were handed over to the Russians.

Meanwhile, Beaufighters arrived in larger numbers to equip the anti-shipping squadrons. The first Strike Wing, consisting of one anti-flak squadron and one torpedo-carrying squadron, was formed in November 1942 at North Coates in Lincolnshire. The Blenheims had been phased out while most of the Hudsons had been turned over to air-sea rescue work, a task which the squadrons performed admirably in combination with high-speed launches. Some of the Whitleys still continued, on shorter-range sorties over the Bay of Biscay, while the Sunderlands soldiered on with their indispensable convoy escort and anti-submarine work. The number of Spitfires and Mosquitos within No. 1 PRU had grown so rapidly that on 19 October 1942 the unit was disbanded and the aircraft formed into five separate squadrons, each with a specific area of operations, although these sometimes overlapped.

One great difficulty which the anti-submarine squadrons had faced was the fact that the U-boats surfaced only at night on their passages to and from mid-Atlantic, enabling them to move faster and recharge their batteries. Although blips sometimes appeared on the ASV radar, which by 1942 was vastly improved, the aircrews could seldom identify the targets and by the time they had decided to attack, the U-boats had dived. This began to change on 4 June 1942, when an Italian submarine was brilliantly illuminated by a Wellington fitted with the new Leigh Light and then subjected to an attack with depth-charges. The submarine escaped on that occasion, although it was badly damaged, but the attack heralded a new era in the anti-submarine war. Before long, the hunters became the hunted.

In January 1943 Coastal Command possessed 858 front-line aircraft and was beginning to gain ascendancy over the enemy. By this time British Intelligence was aware of the positions of U-boats in the North Atlantic, with considerable accuracy. The 'very long-range' aircraft, mostly Liberators and Catalinas, had closed the Atlantic Gap. A single squadron of Halifaxes and one of Fortresses were added to the Command. Wellingtons and Liberators were fitted with Leigh Lights when desirable, and all aircraft were equipped with advanced ASV. The effect on the U-boats was dramatic. In the twelve months ending June 1943, Coastal Command sank seventy-one U-boats or Italian submarines operating in the Atlantic, and damaged many more. This success was coupled with a much improved rate of sinkings by British escort vessels. The Kriegsmarine was unable to sustain such a rate of losses and their head, Grand Admiral Karl Doenitz,

'SEA EAGLE' by J.S. Bailie
The first attack with the aid of a Leigh Light took place in the early morning of 4 June 1942 when Wellington VIII serial ES986 of 172 Squadron, flown by Sqn Ldr Jeaffreson H. Greswell from Chivenor in North Devon, was hunting off the north coast of Spain. The Italian submarine *Luigi Torelli* from Bordeaux, commanded by *Tenente di Vascello* Augusto Migliorini, was suddenly lit up and then badly damaged by four depth-charges. The submarine ran aground near Cape Peñas in Spain but was eventually freed. It was damaged further on 7 June by Sunderlands in a daylight attack. After beaching at Santander in Spain, it underwent temporary repairs and returned on the surface to Bordeaux on 14 June, escorted by relays of German aircraft.

ordered the remains of his U-boat fleet to move south for the time being. Other U-boats were more heavily armed and were ordered to remain on the surface by day during their passages through the Bay of Biscay in order to fight it out with the attacking aircraft. Needless to say, they were pounced on and suffered further losses, although they brought down some aircraft.

The German coastal trade also experienced some extremely unpleasant surprises in 1943. British Intelligence was able to determine the times of sailing of enemy convoys, their composition and even their cargoes, from a combination of decrypts of Kriegsmarine signals and photographs brought back by Spitfires and Mosquitos. The North Coates Strike Wing was reinforced with a third squadron and its attacks were supported by swarms of Spitfires, with the pilots of Fighter Command eager for combat with the Luftwaffe. Sinkings of enemy vessels suddenly increased and the rate of success improved further when the anti-flak squadrons became adept with the new rockets from April 1943 onwards. A blast from a single rocket-firing Beaufighter was estimated to be equivalent to a broadside from a destroyer, and these aircraft did in fact sink such warships, both off north-west Europe and in the Mediterranean.

The Germans increased the number of escort vessels and fitted extra armament to their merchant ships, but more Strike Wings were formed and sinkings increased. At the same time, Bomber Command made heavy attacks on enemy ports and also dropped hundreds of magnetic mines in enemy waters, including the Baltic Sea. During the year the destruction of the German merchant fleet began to exceed the capacity of the enemy ship-building programme to provide replacements. The sinkings also affected the Swedish shipping companies, which had profited greatly from the trade in their vessels from Narvik to Rotterdam. They began to refuse to sail on this coastal route but the alternative, from their Baltic ports to Emden in north Germany, was closed by ice for much of the year.

By the middle of 1943 Coastal Command had become a formidable force and was growing further. More squadrons converted on to 'very long-range' aircraft and new squadrons were formed. The Whitleys and the Hampdens were phased out. By then, all the equipment was modern and the crews were in good heart, backed by their efficient ground staff, knowing that they were defeating the enemy. The new

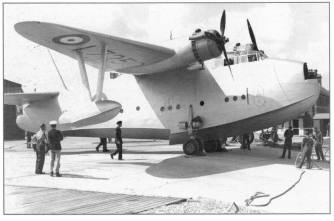

The Saro Lerwick followed the Sunderland as the second monoplane flying boat in the RAF, entering service with 209 Squadron in December 1939. Only twenty-one were built and these did not have a very long operational life, being withdrawn from squadron service in October 1942 in favour of Catalinas.

Aeroplane Monthly

Beaufighter TFX, fitted with more powerful engines and other improvements, began to replace older variants. Mosquito VI fighter-bombers and Mosquito XVIII 'Tsetses' joined the anti-shipping squadrons. The latter were Mosquitos equipped with anti-tank guns as their primary weapons. The Wick Strike Wing was formed in October 1943, followed by another at Leuchars in March 1944, both covering the Norwegian coastline. Yet another was formed at Davidstow Moor in Cornwall during June 1944, consisting of Mosquitos, to range along the French coast. Sinkings of enemy vessels intensified along every coast occupied by the enemy, at a much faster rate than new ships were being built. Many other vessels were seriously damaged but managed to return to ports. However, the repair yards could not keep pace with the work involved. The number of merchant ships and escort vessels available to the enemy went into serious decline.

In the anti-submarine war the Germans devised new equipment to counter the RAF's radar, but British scientists consistently moved ahead with new devices. Coastal Command was able to use a new base in the Azores from October 1943, after the Portuguese agreed to provide facilities. This provided additional coverage of the Atlantic, both to the north and south. From the beginning of July 1943 to D-Day, 6 June 1944, Coastal Command sank the astonishing total of 114 U-boats and damaged many more. At the same time the Royal Navy increased its rate of sinkings. Although the Germans had increased production by building new U-boats in sections in inland areas away from the bombing, and then assembling them in the ports, they could not train crews fast enough to make good their losses. Some of the U-boats were going to sea with hastily trained and inexperienced crews, and suffered accordingly. On the other hand the aircraft available to Coastal Command had increased to 889 at the end of 1944, and more were being added every month.

Everyone in Britain knew that it was only a matter of time before the 'Second Front' opened in north-west Europe and that the strength of the RAF was being built up for this purpose. Coastal Command stood ready to play its part in that great enterprise.

Coastal Command employed Bristol Blenheim IVs as long-distance fighters, fitted with a gun pack containing four machine-guns under the fuselage, in addition to the normal twin machine-guns in the turret. These Blenheims were on the strength of 254 Squadron, which was equipped with these machines from January 1940 to June 1942.

Author's collection

Coastal Command received its first Bristol Beaufighters ICs in December 1940 when they arrived with 252 Squadron at Chivenor in North Devon. Fitted with two Hercules engines of 1,400 hp and armed with four 20 mm cannon and six .303 inch machine-guns in the wings, the Beaufighter soon proved a very formidable long-distance fighter.

Author's collection

The Bristol Beaufort first entered service in November 1939 as a replacement for the Vildebeest biplane. It carried a crew of four and was armed with a single machine-gun firing foward and another in a mid-upper turret. Able to carry an 18 inch torpedo or a bomb load of up to 2,000 lb, it was considered the fastest torpedo-bomber in the world. Although a sturdy machine, it was difficult to fly on one engine and at first was plagued with engine problems. It was also employed on low-level bombing and mine-laying. This photograph of serial N1041 of 217 Squadron was taken in mid-1941 off the north coast of Cornwall.

Author's collection

This Beaufort of 217 Squadron, at St Eval in Cornwall, was hit by flak while mine-laying off the west coast of France in the early morning of 26 June 1941.

Author's collection

On 13 June 1941 several Beaufort Is of 42 Squadron were despatched from Leuchars in Fifeshire to hunt the German heavy cruiser *Lützow* (sometimes called a pocket battleship), which was known from Enigma intercepts to be off the coast of south-west Norway. One of the Beauforts, serial L9939, flown by Flt Sgt Ray H. Loveitt, came across the warship escorted by destroyers and made a surprise attack. The torpedo scored a hit and put the warship out of action for several months. Loveitt was awarded a DFM. He is shown here, fourth from left, while another torpedo is being loaded on his Beaufort.

Author's collection

The Blackburn Botha torpedo-bomber was supplied only to 608 Squadron, in June 1940, but it proved to be dangerously underpowered and was withdrawn from front-line service five months later, after patrols over the North Sea. The machines were transferred to training duties, primarily for air gunners and wireless operators, but were always disliked. A few continued until September 1944.

Philip Jarrett collection

The German heavy cruiser *Admiral Hipper* in dry dock at Brest, photographed by a Spitfire of the Photographic Reconnaissance Unit from St Eval in Cornwall on 26 January 1941. The warship entered the French port with machinery defects and slight damage from British cruisers after commerce raiding in the Atlantic. Photo-interpreters ascertained that the hull, funnels and bridge were dazzle-painted (to break up the outline) and the hangar for three aircraft was open.

Author's collection

The Consolidated Catalina I, known as the PBY-I in the USA, began to enter service with Coastal Command squadrons in March 1941 and continued to the end of the war. With a crew of up to nine and an armament of six machine-guns in four positions, it had a remarkable endurance which could be increased to about 24 hours with extra fuel tanks. Catalinas gave excellent service in RAF squadrons from home bases and in the Indian Ocean.

Author's collection

The Supermarine Walrus entered service with the Fleet Air Arm but was adopted by the RAF from October 1941 onwards as an air-sea rescue machine. Known somewhat indecorously as the 'Shagbat', it rescued hundreds of airmen downed in the sea around Britain as well as in the Mediterranean and the Indian Ocean. This Walrus I serial W3026 was on the strength of 276 Squadron, which was the first to be equipped with these machines when based at Harrowbeer in Devon. A Lysander can be seen flying in the background.

Author's collection

This German Würzburg radar at St Bruneval, near Cap d'Antifer on the north coast of France, was photographed on 5 December 1941 by Flt Lt A.E. 'Tony' Hill of No. 1 Photographic Reconnaissance Unit based at Benson in Oxfordshire, flying Spitfire VD (later designated PR IV) serial R7044. The building behind the radar dish was a sanatorium before the war. From this and other photographs, the Model Section of the RAF's Photographic Reconnaissance Unit at Medmenham in Buckinghamshire constructed an accurate model for study by paratroops, commandos and RAF aircrews and technicians.

Author's collection

A combined operation against St Bruneval took place on the night of 27/28 February 1942. A company of paratroops and an RAF radar mechanic were dropped by Whitley Vs from Dishforth in Yorkshire led by Wg Cdr P.C. Pickard. They were supported by commandos landed from the sea. After the assault, all save fifteen casualties were brought out by the Royal Navy. In this photograph, Pickard is examining a German helmet.

Author's collection

Two German prisoners were brought back from the raid. The man on the left is an infantryman, being searched by a paratrooper with a German rifle over his shoulder, while the other is a Luftwaffe radar operator. The raiding party also brought back the receiver of the Würzburg, the amplifier, the pulse generator, the transmitter and details of the operating method.

Author's collection

The Consolidated Liberator I, known in the USA as the B-24, began to arrive at Prestwick in Ayrshire during March 1941, flown across the Atlantic by ferry pilots. Some were diverted to transport work but most entered service with Coastal Command.

Author's collection

An RAF Liberator over a tanker in the North Atlantic, part of a convoy bringing supplies to Britain.

Author's collection

The first unit to receive the new Consolidated Liberator was 120 Squadron at Nutts Corner in Northern Ireland. The machine carried four .50 inch machine-guns, operated manually, in the nose, tail and waist positions, as well as a gun pack beneath the fuselage. It was also fitted with the new Air to Surface Vessel radar, with aerials mounted above the fuselage. The Liberator was destined to be the major land-based aircraft which closed the Atlantic Gap, where hitherto U-boats had been able to operate with impunity from air attack.

Author's collection

The Boeing B-17 Fortress entered service with the RAF in May 1941 as a day-bomber but did not continue in this role. In January 1942 the remaining Fortresses were transferred to Coastal Command as 'very long-range' aircraft, partly to help close the gap in mid-Atlantic where U-boats were operating unhindered by land-based aircraft. Modified versions continued until July 1945. This Fortress serial FK197 of 251 Squadron was photographed in 1945, at a time when the squadron was based at Reykjavik and was engaged on meteorological and air-sea rescue duties.

G. Flowerdale via A.S. Thomas

This remarkable close-up of the German battleship *Tirpitz* was taken in the late morning of 28 March 1942 by Flt Lt Alfred F.P. Fane. He was streaking over Aasfjord near Trondheim in Spitfire PR Type D serial R7044 of C Flight, No. 1 Photographic Reconnaissance Unit, stationed at Wick in Caithness.

Author's collection

The de Havilland Mosquito VI fighter-bomber entered service with Coastal Command as a strike aircraft. It was armed with four 20 mm cannon and four .303 inch machine-guns, and could also carry either eight rockets or two 500 lb bombs. The cannon in some of these Mosquitos were removed and replaced with a single Molins anti-tank gun protruding underneath the nose. These were known as Mark XIIIs or Tsetses, as the example in this photograph.

Author's collection

The Mosquito VI fighter-bomber was armed with four 20 mm cannon and four .303 inch machine-guns in the nose, and it could also carry two 500 lb bombs in the fuselage. Two more 500 lb bombs could be carried under the wings, although long-range tanks were sometimes fitted as an alternative.

Author's collection

The Molins anti-tank gun, firing six-pounder shells, fitted in the belly of a Tsetse. Although this gun replaced the four 20 mm cannon, the four .303 inch machine-guns in the nose were retained.

Aeroplane Monthly

The RAF's air-sea rescue launches saved the lives of many airmen, enemy as well as Allied. Their length was 63 ft and they were capable of 35 knots. With a crew of nine, they could stay at sea for a considerable time.

Author's collection

The launches were fitted with a turret which carried a Vickers K machine-gun.

Author's collection

The Vickers Warwick, designed as a heavier version of the Wellington, proved unable to carry a useful load when it was produced in the summer of 1942. Some were assigned to BOAC for transport work, such as G-AGFK in this photograph, but were found to be unsuitable and were re-assigned to the RAF. Some Warwicks were employed as RAF transports but their most successful role was in air-sea rescue, carrying airborne lifeboats.

Author's collection

The Beaufighter VIC was introduced into Coastal Command in June 1942. It was fitted with more powerful engines as well as a dihedral tailplane for better stability at low level. The forward armament remained the same as in the Beaufighter IC, but the navigator was equipped with a backward-firing Vickers gun.

British Aerospace

Rockets with 25 lb solid-shot warheads being slotted into rails under the starboard wing of a Coastal Command Beaufighter. The aircraft could carry eight of these deadly weapons, which were aimed into the sea immediately in front of a vessel so that they penetrated below the waterline.

Author's collection

The effect of an enemy 20 mm cannon shell on the armoured windscreen of Beaufighter TFX serial JM343 of 248 Squadron on 2 August 1943. The pilot was blinded temporarily by dust and splinters but managed to land the aircraft back at Predannack in Cornwall.

Author's collection

Damage to Beaufighter IC serial X8037 of 236 Squadron after an air battle with Messerschmitt Bf109s during an attack by the North Coates Strike Wing off the Dutch coast.

Author's collection

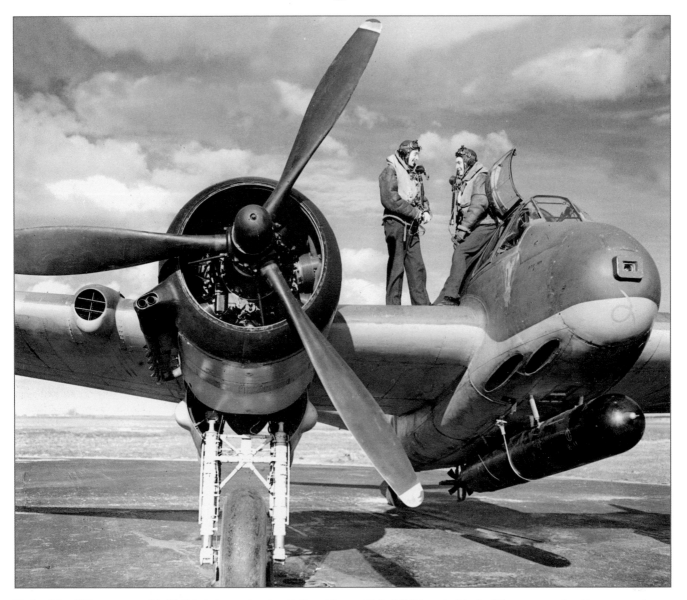

The Beaufighter TFX was a version of the Mark VI which entered service with Coastal Command in April 1943. It retained the four 20 mm cannon and could carry a torpedo (when it was known as the Torbeau), or bombs or rockets, and proved a very formidable aircraft.

Author's collection

The first successful attack by the North Coates Strike Wing took place on 18 April 1943, when twenty-one Beaufighters of 143, 236 and 254 Squadrons, escorted by Spitfires, attacked a German convoy off IJmuiden. The Norwegian merchant ship *Hoegh Carrier* was torpedoed and sunk, while several escorting minesweepers were damaged. No aircraft were lost. This photograph shows a Beaufighter flying over an M-class minesweeper.

Author's collection

On 2 August 1943 the North Coates Strike Wing despatched 36 Beaufighters, escorted by 51 Spitfires, to attack a large convoy off the Dutch island of Texel. The Beaufighters attacked with rockets, cannon and torpedoes, sinking the German merchant ship *Fortuna* of 2,700 tons and the flak ship *Vp1108* of 314 tons (shown here) as well as damaging several other vessels. All aircraft returned although several were damaged.

Author's collection

The Supermarine Sea Otter was an amphibian built to succeed the ageing Walrus for air-sea rescue duties, having a more powerful engine and a longer range. It carried a crew of up to four and was armed with a Vickers gun in the bows and two amidships. Sea Otters entered service in April 1944 and continued for several months after the war. The example in this photograph, serial K8854, was the prototype.

Philip Jarrett collection

This Type VIIC U-boat, *U-625*, commanded by Oberleutnant zur See Siegfried Straub, left Brest on 29 February 1944 but was attacked ten days later in the North Atlantic by Sunderland serial EK591 of 422 (RCAF) Squadron flown from Castle Archdale in Northern Ireland under the captaincy of Flt Lt S.W. Butler. The U-boat and the Sunderland exchanged fire and both were hit. Butler then dropped six depth-charges which straddled the U-boat, as shown here. The U-boat then submerged but resurfaced a few minutes later and actually signalled to the flying boat congratulating the men on their bombing accuracy. It sank over an hour later, leaving some of the crew in dinghies, but none survived.

Author's collection

On 29 March 1944 the North Coates Strike Wing despatched 29 Beaufighter TFXs to attack a German convoy off Borkum. The force consisted of 9 aircraft from 254 Squadron, 6 of which were armed with torpedoes, 10 from 236 Squadron armed with rockets and cannon, and 10 from 143 Squadron armed with cannon. The convoy consisted of 16 merchant vessels escorted by 3 minesweepers and a *Sperrbrecher* (a heavily armed and converted merchant vessel). One Beaufighter was shot down but two German merchant vessels were torpedoed and sunk, *Hermann Schulte* of 1,305 tons and *Cristel Vinnen* of 1,894 tons. Many other vessels were damaged by rockets and cannon fire.

Author's collection

The Consolidated Liberator VI entered Coastal Command in the summer of 1944, joining earlier variants of this highly successful 'very long-range' aircraft. It was better armed, with twin .50 inch machine-guns in nose, dorsal and tail turrets, as well as one in a ventral turret and another in each waist position. This Liberator VI was also fitted with a Leigh Light under the starboard wing, for illuminating U-boats at night.

Author's collection

This photograph, showing the effectiveness of a Leigh Light fitted to a Liberator of Coastal Command, was not released until October 1944.

Author's collection

CHAPTER SIX

ENEMY TERRITORY

The future of Bomber Command remained in doubt for several months after the Butt Report of 18 August 1941. Operations continued until it became known that in the four months preceding 10 November 1941 the Command had lost 526 bombers by night and day, almost equivalent to the whole of its average front-line strength. The evidence of the attacks shown in the report did not seem to justify such heavy expenditure of aircrews and aircraft. On 13 November the Commander-in-Chief, Air Marshal Sir Richard Peirse, was ordered to carry out only limited operations while the future of his Command was being debated.

These restrictions remained in being for the next three months, which saw the entry of the USA into the war, the initial successes of Japan in the Pacific and South-East Asia, and the see-saw battles in North Africa. Peirse was removed from his position on 8 January 1942 and his place was taken over on a temporary basis by Air Vice-Marshal J.E.A. Baldwin. Meanwhile, the War Cabinet was busy considering the order of priorities to be given to the country's limited resources. Eventually it was decided that the only way Britain could bring the war to the heart of Germany and help the Russians on the Eastern Front was to build up Bomber Command but to change the strategy. A great force of 4,000 bombers would be gathered as rapidly as possible for this purpose, but instead of attempting precise attacks against military targets, forty-three German industrial cities would be razed to the ground by a method which became known as 'area bombing'. The War Cabinet was aware that a new navigational device would shortly bring much-needed assistance to the bomber crews for this task. It was thought that the morale of the German civil population would collapse about six months after this new strategy was fully implemented, leading to the end of the war. Churchill assured Stalin that this new offensive would begin in strength as soon as the winter weather abated.

The new directive was issued to Bomber Command on 14 February 1942, and the man who would implement the new policy was chosen. Eight days later, Air Chief Marshal Sir Arthur Harris was appointed as the new chief of Bomber Command. He was known for his dynamism and trenchant manner, a man who would stick to his purpose and overcome all odds to achieve his goal. The directive accorded exactly with his views as to the best conduct of the war.

The force Harris inherited was not huge, consisting of only about 550 front-line aircraft. About 75 were day-bombers, mainly Blenheims but with a few

The room at Bomber Command Headquarters in High Wycombe, Buckinghamshire, where operations were planned.

Author's collection

Douglas Bostons sent over from the USA. Wellingtons, Hampdens and Whitleys still dominated the night-bombing force, and there were a few of the disappointing Manchesters. More significant, however, were the four-engined bombers coming into service, the Halifaxes and Stirlings, while the new Lancasters were nearing the end of their production lines. These carried a far greater weight and were classed as heavy bombers, while the twin-engined night aircraft were relegated to 'medium' bombers. The Blenheims became 'light' bombers, but they were being phased out and replaced with one of the most successful aircraft of the war, the remarkable Mosquito light bomber, as well as Bostons brought from America.

Harris set about his task with a will, at a time when the strength of the Command was growing. He increased the number of incendiary canisters in bomb loads, knowing that fires in combination with lateral blast maximized the destructive effect in built-up areas. Whenever possible, he concentrated his night-bombing force on a single target each night. It was to his advantage that the new navigational aid, known as GEE, had entered its trials in July 1941 and indeed had been tested by two aircraft on an operational flight over the Ruhr on 11 August. One of these aircraft failed to return on another test the following

The Short Stirling I is renowned as the first four-engined bomber to enter service with the RAF, in August 1940. First to receive the new aircraft was 7 Squadron at Leeming in Yorkshire, as shown by this photograph of serial N3641. With a crew of up to eight, a maximum bomb load of 14,000 lb and an armament of eight machine-guns in three positions, it became one of the RAF's main heavy bombers until the middle of 1943.

Author's collection

day but fortunately it seemed unlikely that the device had been captured by the Germans.

The first GEE radar aids employed two transmitters emitting a train of pulses which were picked up on a screen by the aircraft's navigator, who was able to plot the position lines on a special GEE chart. The range of the system was affected by the curvature of the earth and thus depended on the altitude of the aircraft, but it could give the position of the aircraft with an accuracy of about 6 miles when 400 miles away, or a greater accuracy when closer to the transmitters. It was easy to operate and could be used in all weathers. Harris employed it for the first time on the night of 3/4 March 1942 when he despatched 235 aircraft to bomb the Renault factory at Billancourt, to the west of Paris, which was making about 18,000 trucks per year for the German forces. Some 40 per cent of the buildings were destroyed, production was halted for a month and final repairs took several more months to complete. Only two aircraft were lost. However, British scientists were aware that the Germans would eventually capture a GEE set and devise counter-measures.

Essen in the Ruhr felt the weight of Bomber Command five nights later, as well as the two subsequent nights. Attention was then turned to Kiel, followed by Cologne on 13/14 March. Then the bombers went back to Essen on 25/26 and 26/27 March. A very destructive raid took place against Lübeck on 28/29 March, when about 30 per cent of the buildings in the old city were razed to the ground, mainly by fire, and many people were killed or injured. This attack is known to have enraged Hitler, but worse was to follow with a series of raids on Rostock in the latter part of April which resulted in the destruction of 60 per cent of the main town area, again mainly by fire sweeping through ancient buildings.

These attacks continued on a major scale and with increased accuracy until the first 'Thousand Bomber Raid', against Cologne on 30/31 May 1942. This effort, which astounded the British people, was achieved by sending every serviceable

The Vickers Wellington, known to RAF aircrews as the 'Wimpy' after the character J. Wellington Wimpy in the Popeye cartoons, was designed by Barnes Wallis and the prototype first flew in June 1936. The Wellington entered squadron service in the autumn of 1938 and continued as one of the mainstays of Bomber Command until late 1942. The Mark IC was armed with twin machine-guns in nose and tail turrets, with two more in beam positions, and could carry 4,500 lb of bombs. This example was on the strength of 75 Squadron.

Author's collection

aircraft in Bomber Command, plus over 350 from the Operational Training Units (OTUs) and even 4 from Flying Training Command, giving a total of 1,047 despatched. Forty-one aircraft were lost, but immense damage was done, with many people killed or injured and over 45,000 bombed out. It was estimated that over 150,000 people fled the city after the raid.

Meanwhile, another part of the strategic bombing offensive designed to cripple Germany began to reach fruition. The first elements of the newly formed US Eighth Air Force had begun to reach Britain and the first, very minor, operation took place on 4 July 1942 when six American crews took off in Bostons borrowed from the RAF, on a daylight raid against Dutch airfields. Two did not return, but the raid marked the beginning of a force which would join the RAF in a massive assault on the German heartland. It would be equipped mainly with B-17 Flying Fortresses and B-24 Liberators, together with fighter escorts which improved steadily in range and effectiveness, all designed solely for daylight operations.

In the early morning of 19 August 1942, a combined raid took place on Dieppe, when Canadian regiments and Commandos were landed by the Royal Navy under a strong cover from fighters and light bombers of the RAF, together with a handful of B-17 Fortresses and some Spitfires of the US Eighth Air Force. It was classed as a large-scale raid with limited objectives, providing an experiment before the eventual opening of the Second Front. The assault was repelled with heavy casualties amounting to over 4,000 men, while the RAF lost 106 aircraft in the air battles with the Luftwaffe, which lost fewer than half that number. The experiment must be classed as a failure, although it was asserted at the time that valuable lessons were learnt in the process.

A more encouraging development took place that month, with the formation of the RAF's Pathfinder Force (PFF) under Gp Capt. Donald C.T. Bennett. It had become recognized that even with the aid of GEE, Bomber Command was not producing sufficiently accurate results on all occasions. For several months it had been argued that some of the best crews should be gathered into a special unit which would locate each target and guide the main bomber stream to it with the use of flares. This move was strongly resisted by Sir Arthur Harris, who felt that the best crews should be retained in the squadrons as examples to the others. Eventually he was overruled by Sir Charles Portal and the order to establish the PFF was issued on 11 August 1942. The first operation took place on the night of 18/19 August against Flensburg on the Baltic coast but German records show that the target was not hit at all. A raid against Frankfurt on 24/25 August produced meagre results and it was not until three days later, over Kassel, that the new PFF began to achieve the accuracy for which it became famous.

The night operations continued, but in the latter part of the year another radar service was introduced as a navigational aid. This was code-named *Oboe* and employed two transmitters, one at Dover and the other near Cromer, which sent out a stream of pulses to a receiver-transmitter in a PFF Mosquito. The ground operator was able to determine the precise distance of the aircraft from his station and guide the crew along a path to the target. When the ground operator at Cromer saw that this path crossed the line of his pulses, he told the navigator to release the bombs.

Crews of 149 Squadron walking out to their Wellington Is at Mildenhall in Suffolk, in early 1940.

Rick Chapman

Hopes were raised high when the Handley Page Hampden entered RAF service in August 1938. A twin-engined bomber with a crew of four, it was armed with four machine-guns, could carry a bomb load of 4,000 lb and had a remarkable maximum speed. However, the defensive armament proved inadequate in daylight raids and it was eventually surpassed in performance by four-engined bombers. The Hampden was withdrawn from Bomber Command squadrons in September 1942 but found a new role as a torpedo-bomber with Coastal Command. This aircraft was on the strength of 185 Squadron, which was based at Thornaby in Yorkshire at the outbreak of war.

Author's collection

This system was tested with bombs over a power station at Lutterade in the Netherlands on the night of 20/21 December 1942 and appears to have achieved an accuracy of about a mile and a half. However, another test over Essen on 23/24 December resulted in the bombs falling smack in the centre of the Krupps factory. The device thus proved extremely accurate but there were drawbacks since only a single aircraft could be employed at any one time while the range was limited to a maximum of 270 miles if the aircraft flew at 28,000 ft. Its use was thus confined to PFF Mosquitos, but it remained effective up to the end of the war.

Another device came into service in January 1943. It was code-named H_2S and consisted of a small radar transmitter in the aircraft which emitted signals to the ground beneath. These were reflected back and displayed on the screen of a cathode ray tube about 5 inches in diameter, around which a trace revolved, followed by an image of the ground. The early version of this instrument produced only indistinct images but it was usually possible to pick out a river, coastline and the rough shape of a town. As with other radar devices, it was not affected by the weather. Perhaps more importantly, it could be carried by all bombers and the enemy could not jam it.

In February 1943 Franklin D. Roosevelt and Winston Churchill met at Casablanca in Morocco, together with their Chiefs of Staff, to formulate plans for the future conduct of the war. One of the results was an instruction to Bomber Command requiring the destruction of the German military, industrial and economic system, with priorities to be given to U-boat and aircraft construction, oil plants and targets in 'enemy war industry'. Harris had already been ordered during the previous month to devote much of Bomber Command's efforts to the French ports of Lorient, St Nazaire, Brest and La Pallice during the winter months of 1942/3, in an attempt to disrupt the operations of the U-boats which were sinking so many ships in the Atlantic convoys. By March 1943, however, attention was turned primarily to the Ruhr. By then, the Command had grown into seven Groups with about 700 aircraft, of which the majority were the new four-engined types carrying far greater bomb loads. Moreover, more of these were being produced at a fast rate. At the same time, the US Eighth Air Force had become more powerful, so that 'round the clock' bombing of Germany was feasible with the combined day and night forces.

The Germans did not stand still under the resultant hammering. General Josef Kammhuber had been appointed by Goering as early as July 1940 to set up a night-fighter force. By the middle of the following year he had begun to install a radar chain and a belt of searchlights across the path of bombers approaching Germany from England. Night-fighters, controlled from ground stations, were fitted with efficient airborne radar by mid-1942 and thereafter took an increasing toll of RAF bombers. About two-thirds of the RAF aircraft that failed to return fell to these night-fighters, but in the same year British scientists had devised a novel but simple method of jamming the ground stations. This was achieved by dropping strips of aluminium foil which interfered with the frequency of the ground stations and clouded the radar screens. It was code-named *Window* but its use was at first vetoed, for fear that the Germans would soon emulate the system and employ it against the British radar chain.

On the night of 16/17 May 1943 the newly formed 617 Squadron breached the Möhne and Eder dams in the Ruhr. Nineteen modified Lancasters were despatched, each carrying the remarkable 'bouncing bomb' devised by the British scientist and aircraft designer Barnes Wallis. Eight aircraft failed to return from the low-level attack, but the resulting flood caused widespread flooding and disruption of communications, as well as about 1,250 fatal casualties. The extent of the damage to the economy of the Ruhr was exaggerated at the time, but there is no doubt this astonishing achievement produced an electrifying effect on the morale of the RAF and the British people generally. It will forever occupy a foremost place in the annals of RAF history.

On 1 June 1943 the whole of No. 2 Group, consisting of squadrons equipped with Ventura, Boston, Mitchell and Mosquito light bombers left Bomber Command to form part of the 2nd Tactical Air Force. This was set up under Fighter Command in advance of the forthcoming Second Front and included the fighters, fighter-bombers and tactical reconnaissance aircraft of No. 83 Group, as well as the troop-carrying and glider-towing aircraft of No. 38 Group. However, the status of this new formation would change and expand within the next few months as the invasion plans matured.

The sting in the tail of a Whitley was a turret equipped with four Browning machine-guns. After withdrawal from service with Bomber Command, some Whitleys were employed on gunnery training.

Author's collection

Hamburg was subjected to an enormous series of attacks at the end of July 1943. Bomber Command despatched 791 aircraft on the night of 24/25 July, with the PFF aircraft using *H2S* to identify and mark the aiming point. Enormous damage was caused by the main force, which used *Window* for the first time and rendered useless the German radar stations and the radar-controlled searchlights. The US Eighth Air Force despatched 123 B-17 Fortresses the next day and 121 more on the following day. However, an attack by 787 aircraft of Bomber Command on 27/28 July resulted in terrible destruction. A huge and uncontrollable firestorm was created during a dry night of high temperature, sucking in air and raging for three hours. Over 60 per cent of the city's living accommodation was destroyed, 41,800 people were killed and 38,000 injured. Two-thirds of the population, approximately 1,200,000 people, fled what was left of the city in fear of more raids to come, and indeed these took place on the nights of 29/30 July and 2/3 August.

The combined attacks against Germany continued with almost unabated fury throughout the remainder of the summer of 1943. Northern Italy also received attention from Bomber Command in early August, and it is believed that the resultant damage helped to persuade the unhappy people of that country to agree to an armistice with the Allies on 8 September. On 17/18 August Bomber Command made its historic raid with 596 aircraft against Peenemünde on the Baltic coast, where the V2 rocket research establishment had been identified from air photographs. Forty aircraft were lost, mainly to German night-fighters, some of which were fitted with new upward-firing cannon known as *Schräge Musik*. The raid set back the German programme by about two months and also caused a dispersal of the experiment establishment.

The Allied Expeditionary Air Force was created on 15 November 1943 under Air Marshal Sir Trafford Leigh-Mallory. This consisted of the 2nd Tactical Air Force which had been formed the previous June, the US Ninth Air Force equipped with tactical aircraft such as Lightnings, Mustangs, Thunderbolts, Marauders and Dakotas, and the whole of Fighter Command, which was renamed Air Defence of Great Britain. General Dwight Eisenhower was chosen by the Combined Chiefs of Staff as the overall commander of the great Allied force which would eventually land in Europe. His deputy was an Englishman in the RAF, Air Chief Marshal Sir Arthur Tedder.

Sgt John Hannah was only eighteen when he won the VC for an operation on the night of 15/16 September 1940. He was a wireless operator/air gunner in a Hampden I of 83 Squadron based at Wyton in Huntingdonshire, which was attacking invasion barges in the docks at Antwerp when the aircraft was hit by an incendiary shell and set on fire. The rear gunner was forced to bale out but Hannah, in spite of exploding ammunition, put out the fires with two extinguishers, burning himself badly in the process. The navigator had also baled out, but Hannah crawled forward and helped guide the pilot, Plt Off C.A. Connor, back to base.

Author's collection

Bomber Command remained under Sir Arthur Harris, although he was aware that eventually his aircraft would have to play their part in the enterprise, as would the bombers of the US Eighth Air Force. During the winter of 1943/4 Harris directed his force mainly against the prestigious target of Berlin and other cities deep in enemy territory. This part of the campaign cannot be classed as the most successful. Berlin certainly suffered badly but it was outside the range of *Oboe* and the German night-fighters took an increasing toll of the attackers.

By the end of March 1944 the impending invasion of Normandy necessitated a change of targets, although Harris was loath to suspend, or even reduce, his programme of destroying every major German city in turn. In the new campaign the heavy aircraft of Bomber Command were joined by the Allied Expeditionary Air Force, by now under the command of Air Marshal Sir Arthur Coningham, and the US Eighth Air Force. It was evident to the planners that the success of the first Allied bridgeheads on the coast would depend on reinforcements and supplies being brought in more rapidly than those of the defenders. Thus the enemy transport system in northern France and Belgium had to be obliterated if possible. For over two months, railways, bridges, rolling stock, maintenance and repair facilities were targets for the combined air forces, in spite of the inevitable casualties which were caused to some civilians in the occupied regions. Continuous tactical photo-reconnaissance brought back the results of this colossal assault. Enemy airfields were also subjected to overwhelming attacks, while the Luftwaffe fighters were brought to battle by the Allies operating in far greater strength. In the closing days before D-Day, the enemy radar system along the entire coast of Belgium and northern France was almost destroyed. On the south coast of England, a huge force was waiting for the greatest invasion in history.

A Wellington damaged by enemy action being repaired in an RAF depot. If beyond repair, such aircraft were dismantled and used as spare parts for other aircraft.

Author's collection

On 12 August 1941 fifty-four Blenheims, each carrying two 500 lb bombs, were despatched on a daylight raid on two power stations in Cologne. They were escorted by Whirlwind fighters. The Blenheims went in at low level, and ten were shot down by flak or fighters. The Blenheim in this photograph, flying through flak, was on the strength of 114 Squadron based at West Raynham in Norfolk. Whirlwinds continued in front-line service until December 1943.

Author's collection

The ill-starred Avro Manchester entered service with 207 Squadron in November 1940 and subsequently was on the strength of eight other squadrons. Armed with eight guns in three positions and carrying over 10,000 lb of bombs, it suffered frequent failures with its two Rolls-Royce Vulture engines. All Manchesters were withdrawn from operational work by June 1942. However, the design of this medium-heavy bomber led to the famous Lancaster heavy bomber.

Author's collection

This damage was sustained on the night of 9/10 April 1941 by Wellington IC serial T2739 of 99 Squadron, flown by Flt Lt Harvey. The squadron, based at Waterbeach in Cambridgeshire, was raiding Berlin. Harvey attacked the target at 00.32 hours, dropping six 500 lb general purpose bombs from 10,000 ft. Shortly afterwards, the Wellington was in combat with a night-fighter, which was seen to go into a steep dive after being hit several times by gunfire from the rear turret.

Author's collection

The crew of a Short Stirling I receiving their final briefing.

Author's collection

The view from the nose of a Stirling, with the bomb aimer looking through a course-setting bombsight, which was standard equipment in the RAF at the time the aircraft came into service.

Author's collection

A Short Stirling I of 7 Squadron being bombed up.

Author's collection

The seven crewmen of a
Stirling being debriefed by an
intelligence officer in the
operations room, after
returning from the raid
on Berlin on the night of
23/24 August 1943.

Author's collection

The first combined operation
of the war took place on
27 December 1941 when
Commandos landed on the
Norwegian island of Vaasgö.
Bomber Command provided
19 Blenheims and
10 Hampdens for supporting
operations. Of these,
13 Blenheims of 114
Squadron made a low-level
attack on the fighter airfield
at Herdla, near Bergen, as can
be seen in this F24 mirror
photograph showing a tail
wheel, bomb bursts and two
Messerschmitt BF109s taking
off. Two Blenheims collided
and the crews were killed.

Author's collection

The Handley Page Halifax entered squadron service in September 1940 as the RAF's second four-engined monoplane bomber, following the introduction of the Stirling a few weeks before. It was armed with two guns in the nose turret and four guns in the tail turret, with provision for beam guns, and could carry up to 13,000 lb of bombs. Various marks of the Halifax continued in RAF front-line service throughout the war. This Halifax I serial L9530 was on the strength of 76 Squadron.

Author's collection

The first pilot (right), second pilot (left) and wireless operator (below) in a Halifax, photographed in October 1941. The heavy bomber carried a crew of seven.

Author's collection

LACW W.D. Hughes of the WAAF backing a tractor with a trolley containing 1,000 lb medium capacity bombs towards a Halifax, while mechanics check the engines preparatory to a night raid.

Author's collection

Halifaxes over the port of Brest on 18 December 1941. They were part of a force of forty-seven Halifaxes, Stirlings and Wellingtons which were despatched on a daylight raid against the battleships *Scharnhorst* and *Gneisenau* that were sheltering there, together with the cruiser *Prinz Eugen*. They met intense flak and a smokescreen and the warships were not hit although six bombers were lost.

Author's collection

The Douglas DB-7 first entered RAF squadron service in July 1941 and was named the Boston III. It was a light bomber used mainly for daylight operations, escorted by Spitfires. Armed with four machine-guns in the nose and two more in each of the ventral and dorsal positions, it could give a good account of itself in combat. The Boston was unusual since it was the only aircraft in the RAF in which the pilot was not expected to be the last to bale out, the rear gunner being equipped with sufficient controls to keep the aircraft steady while he avoided the high tail. This Boston was photographed dropping bombs over Charleroi in Belgium.

Aeroplane Monthly

The navigator/bomb aimer's position in the nose of a Boston III.

Author's collection

On 8 March 1942 twelve Boston IIIs of 88 and 226 Squadrons, strongly escorted by Spitfires of Fighter Command, attacked the Ford Truck factory at Poissy, near Paris. They scored many hits, but one Boston crashed after the attack.

Author's collection

Bombs dropped by Bostons scoring hits on the docks of Le Havre during a daylight raid on 26 March 1942. One Boston was lost from the twenty-four despatched. The photo-interpreters picked out a system of bomb shelter trenches around the central dock.

Author's collection

The Lockheed Ventura was similar to the Hudson supplied to Coastal Command but was intended as a light bomber for Bomber Command, first entering RAF squadron service at the end of May 1942. The armament was quite heavy, with two .50 inch and two .303 inch machine-guns in the nose, up to four .303 inch machine-guns in a dorsal turret and two more in a ventral position. The bomb load was up to 2,500 lb. Venturas in Bomber Command were engaged primarily on daylight raids and scored some successes at the expense of heavy casualties. They were withdrawn from Bomber Command in September 1943 but some served on meteorological duties in Coastal Command and others on maritime reconnaissance in the Mediterranean.

Philip Jarrett collection

The four-engined Avro Lancaster occupied the premier place among the heavy bombers of Bomber Command during the Second World War. Developed from the unsuccessful twin-engined Manchester, it began to enter squadron service in December 1941. The Mark I had a crew of seven and was armed with ten machine-guns in four positions, and normally carried up to 14,000 lb of bombs. This Lancaster I, serial R5852, was on the strength of 83 Squadron.

Author's collection

Avro Lancasters nearing the end of a production line. The machine in the foreground is being lifted by cranes to enable the undercarriage to be fitted.

Author's collection

A young aircraft worker, Miss Elsie Yates, busy in the nose of a Lancaster on the assembly line.

Author's collection

A 4,000 lb 'blockbuster' bomb being loaded on a Lancaster prior to take-off from a snow-covered airfield. Lancasters frequently carried this cylindrical bomb, which was sometimes called a 'cookie' since it was often dropped when incendiaries tumbled out of large canisters carried by the same aircraft. The lateral blasts of the bombs combined with fires from the small incendiaries were considered the most effective method of laying waste to built-up areas.

Author's collection

News of the RAF's new 12,000 lb bomb was released to the British public on 13 March 1944, with a photograph comparing the weapon with earlier bombs. The new bomb was carried only by Lancasters.

Author's collection

The invention of FIDO (Fog Investigation and Dispersal Operation) saved the lives of many aircrews returning to England. Developed by the Petroleum Warfare Department, it consisted of petrol burners along both sides of the runway, which guided the aircraft to their landing place and burnt away the fog. FIDO was installed initially at three emergency airfields, Carnaby in Yorkshire, Woodbridge in Suffolk and Manston in Kent. This Lancaster was photographed while landing.

Author's collection

The North American B-25, a medium bomber with a crew of five, was armed with six .50 inch guns in four positions and could carry up to 6,000 lb of bombs. It was first supplied to RAF squadrons in September 1942 and was known as the Mitchell. This Mitchell II, serial FL218, was on the strength of 180 Squadron, which received these machines in September 1942 while based at West Raynham in Norfolk. Mitchells are remembered mainly for their role in the 2nd Tactical Air Force.

Author's collection

The de Havilland Mosquito IV light bomber, with a crew of two and no armament, first entered squadron service in November 1941. It was capable of carrying 2,000 lb of bombs at high altitude and at an airspeed that could outdistance enemy fighters. Equally importantly, it was later equipped with advanced radar which enabled it to locate targets with accuracy. These Mosquito IVs were on the strength of 139 Squadron, which formed part of the Pathfinder Force from July 1943 onwards.

Author's collection

A German gun on a flak tower firing at Mosquito IVs during a low-level attack on 20 January 1943 against engineering works at Hengelo in the Netherlands. There is flying debris from exploding bombs in the foreground. None of the eight Mosquitos was lost in this operation, which must have caused consternation among the passengers of the coaches drawn by a locomotive of the 3900 Class which happened to be passing. The photograph was taken from a Mosquito of 105 Squadron based at Marham in Norfolk.

Author's collection

On 23 March 1943 fifteen Mosquitos of Bomber Command were dispatched on a daylight raid against the St Joseph locomotive works at Nantes, led by Wg Cdr W.P. Shand. They attacked in two waves, the first at 50 ft and the second at 1,000 ft. Direct hits were scored and all aircraft returned safely.

Author's collection

Halifaxes of Bomber
Command's No. 6 (Canadian)
Group preparing to take off for
the great raid against Hamburg
on the night of 27/28 July 1943.

Author's collection

Hamburg photographed after the great
raid and firestorm of 27/28 July 1943,
when 40,000 people were killed, many
injured, and about 1,200,000 fled the
city for fear of more raids.

Author's collection

The Eder Dam photographed on 13 May 1943 by Fg Off G.W. Puttick in Spitfire PR XI serial BS502 of 542 Squadron based at Benson in Oxfordshire. A patch of cloud is covering part of the basin below the dam.

Author's collection

This almost identical photograph of the Eder Dam was taken on 18 May 1943 by Fg Off D.G. Scott in Spitfire PR XI serial EN411 of 542 Squadron. Water is still pouring through the breach, about thirty hours after the attack by 617 Squadron.

Author's collection

The Möhne Dam was photographed by Fg Off F.G. Fray, flying Spitfire PR XI serial EN343 of 542 Squadron, a few hours after the attack by 617 Squadron on the night of 16/17 May 1943. Water was still pouring through a breach over 200 ft wide, and foam was covering the power station.

Author's collection

Fg Off Scott continued to Kassel, 20 miles below the Eder Dam and an important centre for the manufacture of aircraft, locomotives and U-boat engines. The swollen Fulda River had swamped the district of Unter Neustadt and affected many of the town's services.

Author's collection

Fg Off Fray continued to Fröndenburg, 13 miles downstream from the Möhne Dam. Two vertical photographs were combined to show a submerged road, a destroyed railway bridge, wrecked railway coaches, submerged railway sidings and an electricity works isolated by flood waters.

Author's collection

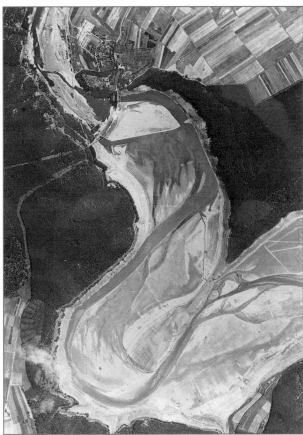

The Eder Dam photographed on 17 July 1943 by Flt Lt G.B. Singleton in Spitfire PR XI serial MB793 of 542 Squadron. Two months after the dam was breached, the dry reservoir could be seen, with the water of the Eder River being drained through No. 2 power house. A light railway had been built to the dam wall, with huts for workmen.

Author's collection

The first North American Mustang, such as serial AM148 of 26 Squadron in this photograph, was fitted with Allison engines and employed on armed tactical reconnaissance at low level from January 1942 onwards. The Mustang III, or P-51B, was powered by the Rolls-Royce Merlin 61 engine and fitted with long-range drop-tanks. It first went into action in December 1943 with the US Eighth Air Force.

Aeroplane Monthly

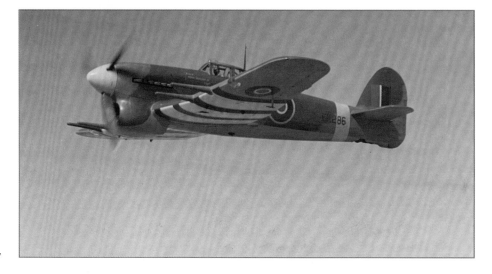

The Hawker Typhoon achieved fame as a fighter-bomber in the 2nd Tactical Air Force, especially during the Allied advances through France, Belgium and Holland after D-Day. It cleared a way for the armies by use of the 'cab rank' method of circling and waiting for instructions to attack targets on the ground with its four 20 mm cannon and either two 1,000 lb bombs or eight rocket projectiles with 60 lb high-explosive warheads. The Typhoon in this photograph, serial EK286, is painted with black and white invasion stripes.

Aeroplane Monthly

The Hawker Tempest V, a single-seat fighter-bomber developed from the Typhoon, first entered squadron service in January 1944. It was armed with four 20 mm guns in the wings and could carry rocket projectiles of up to 2,000 lb of bombs. The Tempest V of the 2nd Tactical Air Force, such as this example painted in invasion stripes, proved a formidable aircraft in the last years of the war in Europe. A tropicalized version, the Tempest VI, appeared after VE-Day and a long-range version, the Tempest II, entered service in August 1945. Some of the latter continued in Malaya until 1951.

Philip Jarrett collection

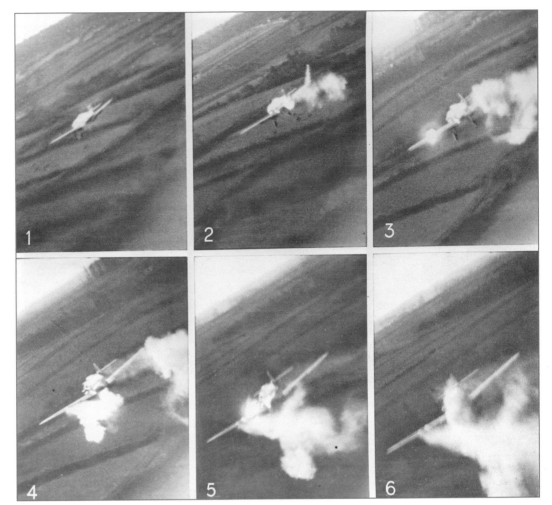

The destruction of a Messerschmitt Bf109G in the afternoon of 21 January 1944 by Typhoon IB serial JP846 flown by Sqn Ldr P.W. Lefebre, who led the Harrowbeer Wing on that day. It was spotted approaching Lannion airfield on the north coast of Brittany, with its wheels down. Lefebre opened fire at 175 yd and closed to 75 yd, capturing this sequence of photographs on the Typhoon's G45 ciné camera. With its engine and port wing burning, the Messerschmitt struck the perimeter track and exploded. A second Bf109G was shot down by other Typhoon pilots.

Author's collection

On 11 April 1944 six Mosquito VIs of 613 Squadron from Swanton Morley in Norfolk, part of the 2nd Tactical Air Force, attacked a five-storey building in The Hague where records used by the Gestapo were housed. Bombs went through the front door and two windows, wiping out almost all the files, while a German barracks nearby was also destroyed.

Author's collection

The Gnome and Rhône factory at Limoges, manufacturing aero-engines, photographed before an attack on the night of 8/9 February 1944.

Author's collection

The results of the attack of 8/9 February 1944 on the Gnome and Rhône factory. Only twelve Lancasters took part, from 617 Squadron based at Woodhall Spa in Lincolnshire. They were led by Wg Cdr Leonard Cheshire, who marked the target when flying at low level. Each Lancaster dropped a 12,000 lb bomb, and ten of these hit the factory, causing great destruction.

Author's collection

The airfield at Tours in France photographed in April 1944,
showing the main station building, barracks, hangars, other
buildings and aircraft. The Allies decided to obliterate this airfield.

Author's collection

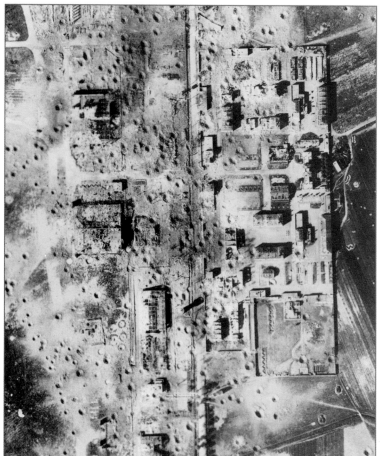

The airfield at Tours after a series of small but very accurate attacks.
On 28 April 1944 45 P-38 Lightnings of the US Eighth Air Force
dropped 1,000 lb bombs for the loss of one aircraft. Two days later,
44 Lightnings attacked without loss. The heaviest attack was on the
night of 7/8 May 1944 when 53 Lancasters and 8 Mosquitos of Bomber
Command destroyed most of the remaining buildings, for the loss of
two aircraft.

Author's collection

'PEDAL POWER' by Charles J. Thompson
The seven-man crew of a Lancaster, dressed in flying kit and carrying parachute packs, pedalling to a misty dispersal point at a Bomber Command airfield before entering their aircraft.

On 12 April 1944 the 2nd Tactical Air Force dispatched eight Mosquito VIs of 107 Squadron from Hartfordbridge in Hampshire and six of 613 Squadron from Swanton Morley in Norfolk to attack the railway yards at Hirson in north-east France. Escorted by Typhoons, the Mosquitos made diving attacks which caused extensive damage to locomotive sheds, repair shops and railway tracks. All aircraft returned, with only one Mosquito damaged.

Author's collection

An ammunition works and depot at Salbris, south of Orleans, photographed in early May 1944.

Author's collection

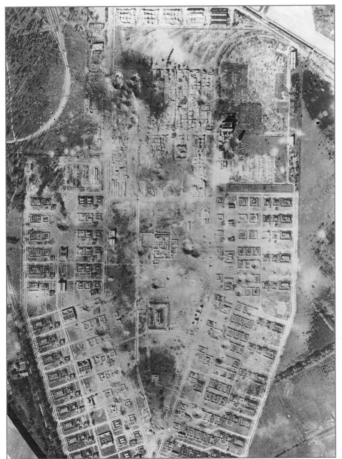

The ammunition works and depot at Salbris after an attack by 58 Lancasters and 4 Mosquitos of Bomber Command on the night of 7/8 May 1944. The bombing was remarkably accurate but 7 Lancasters were lost.

Author's collection

CHAPTER SEVEN

UNDERBELLY OF THE AXIS

When the dictator Benito Mussolini decided to join in the spoils of Germany's victory in the West, by attacking southern France on 11 May 1940, his Regia Aeronautica numbered some 1,700 aircraft. Most were based in Italy but about 500 were stationed in Libya, East Africa and the Dodecanese. To face these, the RAF possessed about 300 aircraft. These were widely dispersed over Egypt, the Sudan, Kenya, Palestine and Gibraltar, although the latter was soon passed to the control of Coastal Command. Moreover, the force consisted of an odd miscellany of aircraft. There were some fairly modern Blenheims, Sunderlands, Bombays and Lysanders but others were Gladiators, Battles and Wellesleys, with an assortment of older aircraft. On 11 June 1940 all these forces were brought under the operational control of RAF Middle East in Egypt, commanded by Air Chief Marshal Sir Arthur Longmore.

Il Duce dreamed of creating an Italian empire that would cover most of the Mediterranean and its islands, as well as southern France, Greece, Tunisia, Egypt and the British possessions in East Africa, but his military ambitions were not crowned with success. The RAF went into immediate attacks in the Western Desert and caused some havoc. However, reinforcement of their scanty forces was essential. Twin-engined aircraft could fly out from Cornwall to Gibraltar and then via Malta to Egypt, although some of these suffered technical problems en route or were subject to air attack. Others were crated ready for assembly but the sea route through the Mediterranean was perilous, with the over-stretched resources of the Royal Navy and the unexpected loss of the French Fleet, while the journey round the Cape was too lengthy.

Fortunately another plan had been visualized and went into operation from 24 August 1940, even though this was a period when the RAF was fighting desperately against the might of the Luftwaffe in the Battle of Britain. Crated aircraft were sent by sea to Takoradi in the Gold Coast and after assembly were fitted with long-range tanks if necessary. RAF ferry pilots, with the help of BOAC, then flew them across Nigeria and French Chad to the Sudan and then up to Egypt, refuelling at staging posts en route. This method, although not without its hazards over part of the terrain, proved remarkably successful up to the end of the war in Africa.

The air defence of Malta was in a parlous state when Italy entered the war.

The Gloster Gladiator was the last biplane fighter to enter RAF squadron service, in February 1937. A single-seater armed with four .303 inch machine-guns, it was manoeuvrable but outclassed in speed and altitude by the new monoplane fighters. Nevertheless, Gladiators served in the Air Component of the British Expeditionary Force which went to France on the outbreak of war. Others went to Norway and the Middle East. One squadron at home was still equipped with Gladiators during the Battle of Britain. Three machines, nicknamed 'Faith', 'Hope' and 'Charity', bore the brunt of the initial attacks on Malta by the Italian Air Force in June 1942. This Gladiator I, serial K7974, was on the strength of 112 Squadron at Helwan in Egypt during October 1939.

A.J. Thorne via A.S. Thomas

There were five target-towing Swordfish used for anti-aircraft gunnery practice, which were turned over to reconnaissance work. The only fighters capable of tackling bombing raids by the Regia Aeronautica were three Gladiators, originally belonging to the FAA. Flown by RAF pilots, they carried out sterling work until joined by four Hurricanes at the end of the month and seven more in July. This tiny force confronted 200 Italian aircraft in Sicily, with considerable success. Twelve more Hurricanes were flown off a carrier on 2 August and a squadron of Sunderlands arrived on 13 September. Three Marylands flown out from England in September were formed into a reconnaissance flight. Apart from these, there were always several Wellingtons at Malta, en route to Egypt, and some of these carried out bombing raids against Italian ports. Sixteen Wellingtons were formed into a squadron on 14 December and bombed airfields in Italy, Sicily and Malta.

Enemy troops in Abyssinia, Eritrea and Italian Somaliland outnumbered the British in East Africa by more than ten to one, although the opposing aircraft were roughly equal at about 150 each. The Italians attacked a small force of defenders in British Somaliland and forced them to retreat across to Aden on 18 August 1940. The British were also on the defensive in Kenya and the Sudan. But this state of affairs did not last for long. Troop reinforcements began to arrive and, protected by a makeshift collection of RAF aircraft and squadrons of the South African Air Force (SAAF), began to raid Italian territory. Enemy airfields were attacked frequently. More troops arrived and in January 1941 began to invade Italian territory from Kenya, the Sudan and British Somaliland. In one of the lesser-known campaigns of the war, they made progress everywhere and by early April were approaching the port of Massawa. Four Italian destroyers were sunk in the Red Sea by the RAF and the FAA, and two more were scuttled. Victory was assured when Addis Ababa was entered on 6 April but a lengthy mopping-up operation was required in the vast mountainous terrain and the last Italian troops did not surrender until the following November.

Meanwhile, events began to move quickly in the Balkans. German troops entered Romania unopposed on 7 October 1940 and began to occupy the country, securing much-needed supplies of oil from the Ploesti region. Mussolini had seized Albania in April 1939 and, not to be outdone by Hitler's latest move, began to invade Greece from that country on 28 October 1940. With only about 75 aircraft in the Royal Hellenic Air Force, the Greek government requested help from Britain. In response, three Blenheim and three Gladiator squadrons were sent from Egypt to airfields near Athens, from where they provided air defence and bombing attacks against enemy airfields. The Greek Army proved far too tough and experienced in mountain warfare for the Italians, who suffered humiliating reverses in the next few months.

The British launched an attack in the Western Desert on 9 November 1940, supported by the RAF in Egypt. This had been reinforced by two squadrons of Wellingtons and one of Hurricanes, while another Hurricane and three Blenheim squadrons had been transferred from the Canal Zone. The campaign was astonishingly successful. By February 1941 the British and Commonwealth troops had advanced over 600 miles, past Benghazi as far as the Gulf of Sirte, had destroyed the last Italian armoured division and taken about 130,000 prisoners. There seems little doubt that if this campaign had been allowed to continue, the troops would have reached Tripoli and cleared the Italians out of North Africa. But there was a sharp reversal after the first units of the Deutsches Afrika Korps, led by the brilliant General Erwin Rommel, landed in Tripoli in February 1941. By the time this Korps was ready to advance, on 1 April 1941, the Germans had entered Bulgaria and were threatening Greece. The over-stretched British forces in North Africa had been weakened by the need to switch Army and RAF units to counter this move. In any event, they could not withstand Rommel's Blitzkrieg. Although the Germans had no experience of desert warfare, their tactics worked perfectly. Speed, continuous pressure and the superb co-ordination of armour, infantry and aircraft drove the British back to Egypt within two weeks, leaving only an enclave at Tobruk to hold out against the onslaught.

The Bristol Bombay was introduced into RAF service as a long-range troop-carrier and bomber/transport in November 1939, serving in the Middle East and the UK. It was armed with two Vickers machine-guns in the nose and tail and could carry 2,000 lb of bombs. Bombays carried out night raids against Italian positions in the early part of the war in the Western Desert and Eritrea, and thereafter served as transports, until August 1944.

Author's collection

While these reverses were taking place, Malta underwent an intensified bombardment from the air. In early January 1941 there were some 250 aircraft available to the Axis in Sicily, mostly German machines of Fliegerkorps X, while Malta could muster only a single squadron of fighters among the sixty aircraft it possessed. Aircraft were being destroyed on the ground as well as in the air. Six Hurricanes were flown over from Gazala in Libya to help relieve the situation, but these were all that could be spared.

Developments elsewhere were even worse for the British. The Wehrmacht invaded Yugoslavia and Greece on 6 April 1941 with the overwhelming strength of twenty-seven divisions supported by 1,200 aircraft. The British element which opposed them consisted of six Commonwealth divisions which landed in Greece,

The Short Sunderland, which first entered service in June 1938, proved a great success with Coastal Command and maritime squadrons in the Middle East, during the war and later. Usually armed with six machine-guns and capable of carrying 2,000 lb of bombs or depth charges for about thirteen hours, it gave an excellent account of itself in the anti-shipping war. These Sunderland Is of 230 Squadron, based at Alexandria, were photographed during the British withdrawal from Greece in April 1941.

Author's collection

plus three squadrons of Hurricanes, Lysanders and Gladiators and two detachments of Wellingtons. The outcome was inevitable. The Royal Yugoslav and Royal Hellenic Air Forces were soon eliminated and after nine days of warfare only forty-six RAF aircraft remained serviceable, while the troops were forced into a fighting retreat. On 20 April 1941 the survivors were withdrawn by sea to Crete, leaving most of their equipment behind, and the remaining RAF aircraft flew to the island.

There was a respite of several weeks but then, on 20 May, the full force of Germany's airborne units fell on Crete. About 650 aircraft covered some 700 transports or gliders for the operation, which carried 15,000 men. The defenders were more numerous but lacked equipment and there were only twenty-four Hurricanes, Gladiators and Fulmars to cover them, for the distance from Egypt was too great for other air support. The German airborne troops overcame the defenders, although it was a close-run thing and they suffered such severe losses that Germany never again attempted a similar operation. It is believed that the depletion of this force was one of the reasons why an airborne invasion of Malta was never attempted. Half the Commonwealth troops in Crete were evacuated to Egypt by the Royal Navy, at the cost of three cruisers and six destroyers.

These German victories stirred up trouble in Iraq, where Britain was responsible for security under the Regency. A *coup d'état*, led by the Iraqi politician Rashid Ali, took place on 3 April 1941. British Intelligence knew that he was sympathetic to the German cause and that Hitler harboured plans to advance through Syria and Iraq in order to seize the Persian oil wells. This would enable the Wehrmacht to advance on Egypt from a new direction, eventually linking up with the Deutsches Afrika Korps in the west, thus occupying the Suez Canal and imperilling the British positions in India and Africa. From the end of April 1941 about 9,000 Iraqi troops laid siege to RAF Habbaniya, about 55 miles from Baghdad, and opened artillery fire on the defences. This was a flying school, but Gladiators and Audaxes took off and strafed the insurgents, while Wellingtons from RAF Shaibah in the Persian Gulf bombed Iraqi positions. By the end of May the Iraqis retired in some dismay to Baghdad, where they were defeated by a British column. The previous government was restored and the British then entered Syria, which was defended by Vichy French forces and about a hundred aircraft. After a difficult campaign for both sides, the Vichy forces capitulated on 14 July.

On 1 June 1941 Air Marshal Sir Arthur Tedder took over as Air Officer Commanding-in-Chief of RAF Middle East. This was the time when the Luftwaffe was beginning to withdraw some of its units for the forthcoming invasion of Russia. At the same time, the RAF was steadily building up its strength, with aircraft arriving from the Takoradi route or from Gibraltar. By November 1941 the RAF and FAA consisted of about 660 aircraft in the Western Desert and 120 in Malta.

The Curtiss P-40 Tomahawk was a single-seat fighter supplied to the RAF in February 1940 and employed on low-level tactical reconnaissance at home and on ground attack in the Western Desert. It was replaced by the Mustang in England and Kittyhawks in the Middle East.

Author's collection

The Axis possessed some 540 aircraft in North Africa, but suffered from problems with serviceability with its extended lines of communication and supplies. By then British Intelligence was able to decrypt all German signals relating to the order of battle of the Deutsches Afrika Korps and the dates of sailing of Italian and German convoys as well as the contents of their cargoes. Photo-reconnaissance aircraft from Malta verified the exact position of these convoys which were then attacked by anti-shipping aircraft and by submarines of the Royal Navy. In November 1941 14 of the 22 supply ships sent from Italy were sunk. The need for supplies, particularly fuel, was Rommel's Achilles heel.

On 18 November 1941 the reinforced British and Commonwealth troops opened an offensive in the Western Desert, following a bombardment of enemy positions by the RAF, in which strafing attacks by Beaufighters were particularly effective. The beleaguered garrison in Tobruk was relieved and the Axis forces fell back as far as Agedabia in Libya, although not in disorder. But in December two large convoys succeeded in reaching Tripoli, enabling Rommel to go over to the offensive with his Panzerarmee Afrika, as the Axis forces had been renamed. By 6 February 1942 the British had retreated to Gazala, west of Tobruk.

In January 1941 400 German aircraft arrived in Sicily, under the command of Generalfeldmarschall Albert Kesselring, and Malta came under an intense and prolonged bombardment. A few Spitfires arrived to defend the island but by the following March only six serviceable fighters remained, together with a few bombers. The situation became critical and forty-seven Spitfires were flown off the US carrier *Wasp* on 20 April but most were destroyed on the ground the following day. Meanwhile, supplies poured across the Mediterranean from Italy to Tripoli, almost unimpeded by the RAF.

Rommel was able to open another offensive on 26 May 1942. It was the most successful part of his campaign, for he captured about 45,000 prisoners and vast supplies of fuel, as well as taking Tobruk. It seemed that on this occasion he would reach Cairo but the British managed to stall the long advance at El Alamein, a little-known village on the north-west coast of Egypt. A period of stalemate followed, while the British were able to build up their ground forces in Egypt and a steady stream of new aircraft and crews arrived. All the Beaufort squadrons in the UK were posted to the Far East but were halted in Malta and pressed into service against the Axis convoys. Two other Beaufort squadrons were already in Egypt. Escorted by Beaufighters, they sank ship after ship, although their own losses were extremely heavy. Wellingtons fitted with ASV radar attacked at night and also sank Axis vessels. Royal Navy submarines took an increasing toll. Once again Rommel began to run short of fuel and military supplies, while those being brought to the front line were subjected to continual attack from the air.

This was the time when the string of German victories in the war came to an end. The Wehrmacht was being bled to death on the plains of Russia while a whole army, consisting of 278,000 men, was stalled at Stalingrad and would soon be encircled and eventually forced to surrender. By October 1942 the RAF controlled ninety-six operational squadrons in Egypt, including thirteen of the USAAF, amounting to about 1,200 aircraft. There were 300 more in Malta. Under 700 aircraft supported Rommel in North Africa.

On 23 October 1942 the British opened their offensive at El Alamein and on this occasion could not be halted. Almost every Italian supply vessel which attempted to cross the Mediterranean was sunk by Beauforts, Bisleys or Wellingtons in this crucial period. The Axis forces retreated in good order but they suffered heavy losses and this time did not stop until they reached Tunisia. Here an unpleasant surprise was sprung on 7 November, in the form of the Anglo-American landings at Oran and Algiers, commanded by General Dwight Eisenhower.

From this time, the Axis forces had to fight on two fronts in north-west Africa, but their supply position improved temporarily. The Axis forces responded to the Allied landings by occupying Vichy France, securing numerous merchant vessels and setting up bases in Tunisia. With only 100 miles separating Sicily and Tunisia, supplies began to pour across by sea. At the same time, the Luftwaffe increased its transport machines in Sicily from 250 to about 750, which flew supplies and troops to the beleaguered Panzerarmee Afrika.

Wellingtons of 38 Squadron, based in Egypt, flying over the Western Desert in vee formation.

Author's collection

On 17 February 1943 Air Marshal Sir Arthur Tedder was appointed as Air Officer Commanding the new Mediterranean Air Command, integrating the air operations of both the British and Americans throughout the entire region but with responsibility to Eisenhower for operations in Tunisia and to the British Chiefs-of-Staff for operations in the Middle East. This partnership worked well. A continuous air offensive was mounted against the Tunisian ports, the supply vessels and the air transports, causing enormous destruction. The Axis forces put up a skilled and determined resistance against the air and ground assaults but all remaining units were forced to surrender by 14 May 1943. The Allies took about 250,000 German and Italian prisoners in the Tunisian campaign.

The next stage of the Allied assault on the Axis underbelly was a combined assault on Sicily. Airfields, ports and industrial targets on the island, as well as those on Sardinia and southern Italy, were subjected to continuous air attacks.

Airborne troops were towed in gliders to Sicily on 10 July 1943, while others descended by parachute. On the same day, a colossal convoy of 2,000 vessels arrived off the southern shore of the island, under strong air cover. The troops landed, in some places against fierce opposition, and enemy airfields were rapidly secured and restored for the arrival of Allied fighters from Malta. The Allied forces fought their way across the island, capturing many Italian prisoners, but the Germans retreated in good order to the Strait of Messina and withdrew to the mainland on 17 August. About 1,000 wrecked Axis aircraft were left on Sicily.

Meanwhile, some of the cities in northern Italy came under air attack and it was evident that the Italian people had had enough of the war. Mussolini was deposed by the Fascist Grand Council on 25 July and placed under arrest. He was rescued in a skilful operation by German paratroops on 12 September from imprisonment near the San Grosso mountain and formed a puppet government in Germany. When the first British troops crossed the Strait of Messina on 3 September and landed on the toe of Italy, the country was anxious for peace. The terms of an Armistice were agreed on 8 September, the day before American troops landed at Salerno in Campania, and the Italian Government declared war on Germany five days later.

By then, the Luftwaffe in Italy had been almost obliterated, but the German troops still resisted strongly and skilfully. A hard and bloody slog up the peninsula lay ahead for the Allied troops. They were supported by the 'cab-rank' system which was later to be used with great effect in Normandy. Allied fighters patrolled the skies, waiting to be called upon to strafe enemy strongpoints with bombs, cannons and rockets. This method saved many Allied casualties on the ground.

The British met with a reverse in the Aegean in this period. Their purpose was to seize the Italian Dodecanese Islands and then to invade Greece. This strategy might have had the political motive of forestalling the Russians, who could advance through Romania and bring Greece under Communist control. The British held Cyprus and bypassed Rhodes, which was strongly defended by the Germans. On 13 September 1943 they landed on the island of Kos, while paratroops were dropped from Dakotas. The island of Leros was also occupied on the following day, and Samos on 17 September.

The Italian garrisons welcomed the new arrivals, but there were no airstrips where RAF fighters could land. The Luftwaffe had far shorter lines of communication. German aircraft were brought in from other areas and began to strafe the British positions. Although the Greek airfields were bombed by the RAF, the only direct support of the British troops was from Beaufighters based on Cyprus. These operated at the limit of their range and were no match for German single-engined fighters. On 3 October German troops landed on Kos by sea and air, retaking the island. Leros fell to them on 12 November and Samos ten days later. The whole episode was another demonstration that large combined operations were impossible without adequate air cover.

On the Italian peninsula the RAF and the USAAF were able to establish themselves around the area of Foggia in Apulia from 28 September 1943. The airfields were used as bases to bomb the vital oil installations around Ploesti in Romania, Germany's main source of natural oil. The winter of 1943/4 was unusually wet and operations against the strong defensive lines established by the Germans across the peninsula were extremely difficult. One development was the formation of the Balkan Air Force in early June 1944, formalizing the command of squadrons which had been supporting partisan operations in Yugoslavia for several months. By this time, it consisted of sixteen squadrons and two flights,

The Martin Maryland, a reconnaissance bomber with a crew of four, was supplied by the US under contracts originally placed by the French and was employed by the RAF from October 1940. Armed with four machine-guns in the wings and two more in dorsal and ventral positions, it could carry 2,000 lb of bombs. It saw service mainly in the Middle East. These Marylands of 12 (SAAF) Squadron were photographed taking off from a landing ground in the Western Desert.

Author's collection

equipped with Halifaxes, Dakotas, Spitfires, Hurricanes, Mustangs, Baltimores, Venturas and Beaufighters, as well as several Italian fighters and bombers, manned by men from five nations. These gave continuous assistance to the partisans who were holding down many German divisions in Yugoslavia.

The British and American armies struggled up the Italian peninsula against fierce opposition, and finally captured Rome on 4 June 1944. However, this important event was overshadowed in the world news during this momentous period by the D-Day landings in Normandy two days later. The push northwards continued and the Americans entered Florence on 4 August. Then many of these American troops were withdrawn for the invasion of southern France, which took place on 14/15 August.

In the eastern Mediterranean the RAF in Egypt continued its attacks against Crete and the Aegean islands held by the Germans, as well as the vessels trying to supply them. The garrison in Crete was in a parlous state by the end of May 1944, but a determined attempt to re-supply it with a convoy from Greece was almost obliterated by the RAF and SAAF. In August 1944 the Russians were advancing through Romania and the Germans realized that their positions in the islands and in Greece itself were untenable. They began to evacuate the islands and withdraw northwards, leaving pockets of men to surrender to British landing forces.

On 14 October 1944 British advance parties crossed from Piraeus to Athens, and the RAF also arrived. Unhappily, the British were caught up in a civil war which broke out six weeks later and Beaufighters were called upon to make rocket attacks against the positions of left wing rebels. These operations continued until a ceasefire was agreed on 12 January 1945.

In Italy the RAF continued to attack German positions in the north of the country as well as longer range operations against Germany itself. The Germans were steadily pushed back into the Po valley. Mussolini was captured by Italian partisans and executed on 28 April. The fighting remained bitter until the German armies finally surrendered on 2 May 1945.

A Martin Maryland being
bombed-up in the Western
Desert.

Author's collection

Explosions from bombs dropped by a Maryland of the SAAF,
with black smoke rising from two Axis vehicles which had
been hit.

Author's collection

Blenheim IV serial T2177 of 11 Squadron, wrecked at Larissa in Greece. The squadron was based there from 26 February to 15 March 1941, during the period when Italy tried unsuccessfully to invade Greece and before Germany joined in the attack on 6 April. The squadron was based at other airfields in Greece until 16 April. A wrecked Henschel He126 is in the background.

Rick Chapman

One of the many RAF Hurricanes found by the Germans when they occupied Larissa airfield in Greece. It probably belonged to 33 Squadron, which was based there from 4 March to 17 April 1941, or to 113 Squadron, which was based there from 29 March to 3 April 1941.

Rick Chapman

A leading aircraftman of the RAF examining a Fiat Cr42 'Falco' which had come to grief when landing with one wheel shot away at Fort Capuzzo, near Bardia in Libya, before the airfield was captured by the British.

Author's collection

Flares from attacking aircraft and searchlight beams from the defenders light up the night sky during a raid on Malta in March 1941.

Author's collection

Sunderland I, serial L5807, of 228 Squadron, burning in Kalafrana seaplane base in Malta after strafing by Messerschmitt Bf109s on 27 April 1941.

Author's collection

The German airborne assault on Crete, which was defended by ill-equipped British and Dominion troops, supported by only a handful of Hurricanes, began on 20 May 1941. Nevertheless the outcome of the battle remained in doubt while many of the attackers were wiped out, such as this Junkers Ju52 going down in flames near Heraklion. The German paratroops and airborne soldiers finally prevailed, in spite of huge losses, and many of the defending forces were withdrawn by the end of the month.

Author's collection

From May 1941 Beaufighter ICs were sent to the Middle East, flying out from Cornwall via Gibraltar and Malta. They served as long-range fighters and gave an excellent account of themselves with their enormous fire-power. The example here is serial T3316.

Author's collection

Bombs exploding on Valletta during a daylight attack on 21 January 1942.

Author's collection

Spitfire pilots sprinting from a bullet-blasted building to their aircraft for a quick take-off, evidently amused by the presence of a photographer. Most of the fighter aircraft were based at Hal Far in Malta.

Author's collection

The Curtiss P-40D Kittyhawk was a more powerful version of the earlier Tomahawk, and entered service with the RAF in the Middle East during December 1941 as a fighter-bomber. It later served in Italy, where it was also engaged on tactical reconnaissance. This Kittyhawk I of 112 Squadron was photographed at Kabrit in Egypt on 18 December 1942.

Aeroplane Monthly

On 9 October 1942 this Axis train was attacked by four Beaufighter ICs of 252 Squadron from Edku in Egypt and three Bisleys of 15 (SAAF) Squadron from Maryut in Egypt. The engine and many of the trucks were destroyed by cannon fire and bombs.

T. Armstrong

The Martin Baltimore replaced the Maryland, manufactured to British specifications with more powerful engines and better crew communication. It entered RAF service in January 1942, armed with four .303 inch machine-guns in the wings and up to six more in a dorsal turret and a ventral position. This Baltimore IIIA, serial FA342, was photographed taking off from Luqa in Malta to bomb enemy positions in Sicily.

Author's collection

The last of the Blenheim family was the Mark V, or Bisley. It had more powerful engines than its predecessors and was fitted with increased armour protection as well as two machine-guns in a nose blister, firing backwards. Most of its operations were carried out as a light bomber in the Mediterranean theatre but its performance proved inadequate. The Bisley in this photograph is serial DJ702, which was on the strength of No. 12 Advanced Flying Unit based at Spittlegate in Lincolnshire.

Aviation Bookshop

'ROMMEL'S LAST TANKER' by Charles J. Thompson
On 26 October 1942 the Italian tanker *Proserpina* of 4,869 tons was part of a convoy which attempted to reach Tobruk to bring vital fuel to the Panzerarmee Afrika, which was fighting desperately at El Alamein. It was hit by a torpedo dropped by a Beaufort of 47 Squadron flown by a Canadian in the RAF, Plt Off Ralph R. Manning, and also hit by bombs dropped by a Bisley flown by Maj Douglas W. Pidsley of 15 (SAAF) Squadron, both from Gianaclis in Egypt. The tanker sank, destroying Rommel's last hopes of sustaining his armour at El Alamein. Manning's Beaufort is in the foreground of this painting, which is now the property of 47 Squadron at Lyneham.

Living conditions for the aircrews of 252 Squadron in the Western Desert in late 1942. Left to right: Sgt Gordon Nettleship of the RCAF; Sgt Stan Kernaghan of the RCAF; Sgt Archie Powell of the RAF. One of the squadron's Beaufighters is in the background.

S.J. Kernaghan

An Italian bomber deliberately set on fire by British sappers on a captured airfield. Such enemy aircraft, left behind when the British 8th Army advanced, often contained booby-traps.

Author's collection

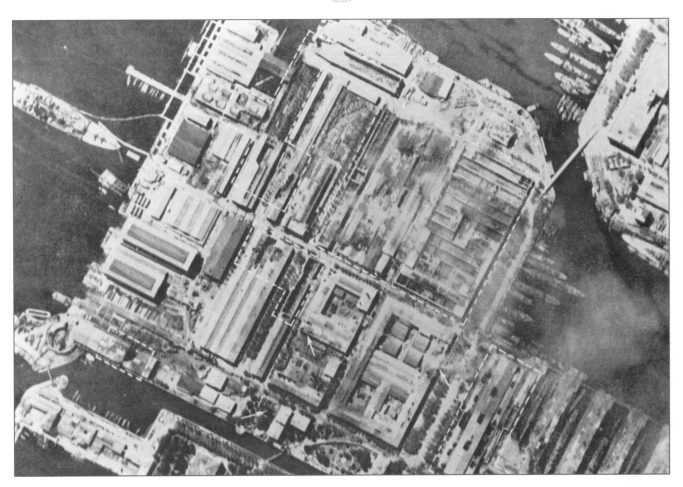

Bomber Command made attacks on La Spezia in north-west Italy on 13/14 and 18/19 April 1943, despatching 389 Lancasters and Halifaxes on the two raids. Five aircraft were lost but others in difficulties landed at airfields in North Africa. Sheds, warehouses and workshops were destroyed or damaged. These attacks by heavy bombers played a major part in the Italian decision to surrender the following September.

Author's collection

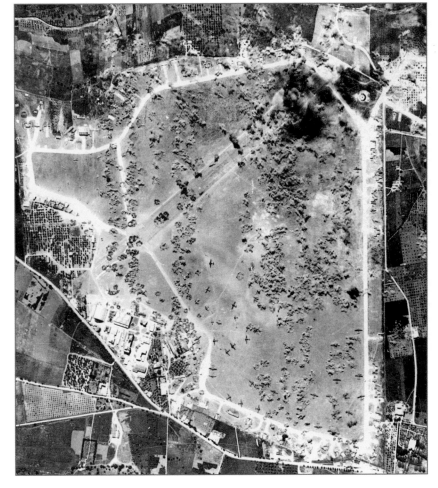

The airfield at Milo in Sicily under attack by B-17 Fortresses of the Northwest African Air Forces on 5 April 1943. Bombs can be seen exploding among the enemy aircraft, mostly Junkers Ju52s.

Author's collection

The Italian cruiser *Trieste* of 10,500 tons anchored inside torpedo nets at La Maddalena in Sardinia on 10 April 1943, with bombs from B-17 Flying Fortresses of the USAAF falling towards her. Bombs hit her bridge and also holed her underwater. Attempts at salvage failed and she turned over and sank 90 minutes after being hit.

Author's collection

Cactus trees shielding Spitfires at a forward airfield in Tunisia, a few weeks before the last of the Axis forces in North Africa were finally mopped up on 14 May 1943.

Author's collection

The Spitfire VIII was designed to take the Merlin 61 engine of 1,560 hp and a four-blade propeller. Armament consisted of two 20 mm cannon with either four .303 inch machine-guns or four more 20 mm cannon, and it could also carry 1,000 lb of bombs. It was tropicalized for duties in the Mediterranean and Burma theatres of war, and first reached 145 Squadron in Italy during June 1943, as shown in this photograph of serial JF509.

Author's collection

Sticks of bombs exploding as Martin B-26 Marauders of the USAAF attack Alghero airfield in Sardinia on 25 May 1943. This destruction of enemy aircraft and airfield installations was a prelude to the invasion of Sicily on 10 July 1943.

Author's collection

A photographic mosaic of the British 8th Army – the Desert Rats – invading the coast of the Gulf of Noto in the south-east corner of Sicily on 10 July 1943. The US 7th Army went ashore further to the west. The landings were successful everywhere.

Author's collection

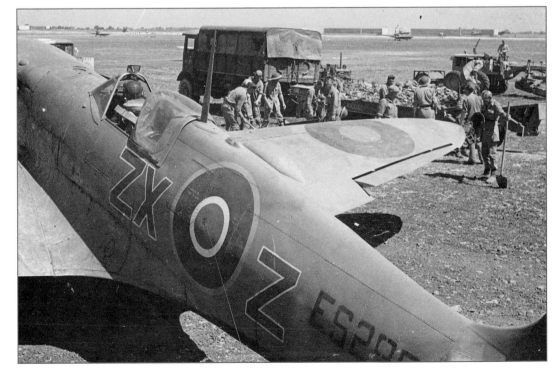

Spitfire VCs of 145 Squadron from Luqa landed at Pachino in Sicily on 13 July 1943, only three days after the Allied invasion. Although the entire airfield had been ploughed up by the Axis forces, the RAF's Servicing Commandos and the Royal Engineers cleared it up rapidly, as shown in this photograph of the men loading stones in a tank transporter.

Author's collection

Abandoned Messerschmitt Bf109s on Comiso airfield in Sicily, which was captured by the British 8th Army a few days after the Allied invasion of 10 July 1943.

Author's collection

A Messerschmitt Me323 *Gigant* under attack with cannon fire in August 1943 off Cap Corse, Corsica, by a Marauder flown by Wg Cdr W. Maydwell of 14 Squadron, based at Protville in Tunisia and part of 328 Wing, 242 Group, Northwest African Coastal Air Force. With three of its six engines put out of action, it turned towards the coast and made a forced landing.

Author's collection

On 3 September 1943 the British 8th Army made the first Allied landings on the continent of Europe by crossing the Strait of Messina and going ashore on the beaches of Calabria. Italy surrendered four days later.

Author's collection

Two battleships, five cruisers and four destroyers of the Italian Navy, commanded by Admiral de Zara, entered Grand Harbour in Malta on 10 September 1943, after Italy had surrendered. However, a radio-controlled bomb dropped by the Luftwaffe sank the battleship *Roma* while she was en route to surrender.

Author's collection

The port of Messina under heavy air bombardment, with smoke rising from rolling stock maintenance yards and goods stations. By 14 August 1943 this was the last town in Sicily held by the Axis forces. They completed their retreat to the Italian mainland three days later.

Author's collection

Kittyhawk pilots of 3 (RAAF) Squadron relaxing in the barn that served as their crew operations room when based at Agnone in Sicily from 2 August to 13 September 1943, while engaged on tactical support for the British 8th Army. A dispatch rider's motor bicycle is in the barn, melons are ripening on the wall and there is a Kittyhawk on the airfield beyond. The squadron moved to Grottaglie in Italy on 14 September, after the invasion of the mainland.

Author's collection

A German escort vessel in the eastern Mediterranean, under attack on 17 September 1943 by cannon-firing Beaufighter TFXs of 252 Squadron from Berka in Libya.

Author's collection

Bullock power for the RAF. A local farmer helped to clear and prepare Serreterre airfield, near Naples, after its capture by the Allies. The Spitfire XIs were on the strength of 232 Squadron, which arrived there on 23 September 1943.

Author's collection

Containers with supplies for the Yugoslav Partisan Army being dropped by the RAF. In February 1944 Winston Churchill announced that this force was holding down fourteen German and six Bulgarian divisions.

Author's collection

The German minelayer *Drache* (formerly Greek) of 1,870 tons, under attack on 26 September 1943 by three Beaufighter VIs of 252 Squadron and one of 227 Squadron, all from Lakatamia in Cyprus, while in harbour in the island of Siros. The vessel was damaged by cannon and machine-gun fire but the bombs overshot. She was finally sunk on 22 September 1944 by Beaufighters of 252 and 603 Squadrons at Port Vathi in Samos.

D.O. Butler

In the afternoon of 14 November 1943 four Beaufighter VIs of 46 Squadron and four of 227 Squadron took off from Lakatamia on a sortie to the island of Leros. Two of the 46 Squadron aircraft, flown by Flt Lt D.J.A. Crerar and Fg Off B.F. Wild chased a Heinkel He111 and shot it down in the sea, as shown in this photograph. Two Messerschmitt Bf109s then appeared and shot down two Beaufighters of 46 Squadron, the crews being killed. The remainder of the formation escaped by flying over the Turkish coast.

D.O. Butler

The German armed merchant vessel *Gertrud* of 1,960 tons, part of a convoy trying to bring supplies to Crete, under rocket attack on 1 June 1944 by a Beaufighter TFX of 252 Squadron flown by Fg Off William Davenport from Mersa Matruh in Egypt. She was badly hit but was towed into Heraklion, where she blew up the following day after being hit by bombs dropped by Baltimores of 15 (SAAF) Squadron from LG07 in Egypt.

G.G. Tuffin

Bostons of the SAAF flying over enemy positions near the town of Frosinone. In May 1944 this area of Italy was occupied by German troops fighting against the Allies advancing on Rome.

Author's collection

In the early evening of 4 July 1944, two Beaufighter TFXs of 603 Squadron, flown from Gambut in Libya by WO L.F. Sykes of the RCAF and Flt Sgt E.F. Rennie of the RAF, came across this Junkers Ju52 floatplane flying low near the island of Siros in the central Aegean. The German machine turned towards a layer of fog but the Beaufighters closed astern and hit it in the starboard engine and mainplane.

D.O. Butler

The Ju52 floatplane, already on fire, alighted near the island and burst into flames from end to end. Survivors were seen swimming in the water by the crews of the Beaufighters as they left.

D.O. Butler

In August 1944, 16 (SAAF) and 19 (SAAF) Squadrons were equipped with Beaufighter TFXs and operated over Yugoslavia from Biferno in Italy, as part of the Balkan Air Force which had been formed the previous June. The SAAF Beaufighters in this photograph were making rocket attacks against German positions in the town of Zuzemberk.

Author's collection

The Martin B-26 Marauder was supplied to RAF and SAAF squadrons in the Mediterranean theatre from August 1942 onwards. A medium bomber with a crew of six, it was well-armed and could carry up to 4,000 lb of bombs. This RAF Marauder was photographed while bombing a railway bridge over the River Asino at Chiaravalle, near Ancona on the Adriatic coast. The Allies entered Ancona on 18 July 1944.

Author's collection

British troops disembarking at Piraeus in early October 1944, watched by crowds of Greeks, after the German withdrawal.

Author's collection

A Beaufighter TFX participating in a Victory Parade over Athens at the end of the war.

D.O. Butler

CHAPTER EIGHT

THE GREAT INVASION

On the night of 5/6 June, an Allied invasion fleet of about 6,500 ships and landing craft formed up near Littlehampton in Sussex, before setting off due south for the beaches of Normandy. The landings had been postponed for twenty-four hours as a result of bad weather, but further delays were not practicable even though conditions did not improve as much as hoped. As it happened, the timing caught the Germans by surprise, for they did not believe that a fleet would sail in such weather.

D-Day is rightly remembered primarily for the airborne soldiers who descended on France before the landings and the men who stormed the beaches under fire. But the RAF and the USAAF also played their part on that momentous day. The beaches had been covered assiduously by photo-reconnaissance aircraft, so that the troops in each landing craft carried clear photographs showing precise landing points and the objectives they were to secure. Bomber Command had delivered attacks on coastal batteries on the previous night.

The initial task of the 6th Airborne Division was to secure the eastern flank of the British 2nd Army, which was ordered to land between Ouistreham and Graye-sur-Mer on beaches codenamed Sword and Juno. Firstly, the airborne troops were to capture intact two bridges, over the Caen Canal and the River Orne, and hold these until the seaborne troops could advance and relieve them. Secondly, it had to destroy the heavily fortified gun battery at Merville, which could fire directly on Sword Beach. Thirdly, it had to blow up five bridges over the River Dives to the east, to prevent German reinforcements moving up from that direction.

The operation to secure the two bridges was carried out by six Horsa gliders flown by pilots of the Glider Pilot Regiment and towed by RAF Halifaxes. These took off at about 23.00 hours on 5 June and the tows were released when over the French coast. Five Horsas landed in precisely the correct places and the troops rushed out and captured the two bridges, overcoming German opposition. They were reinforced at 03.00 hours by paratroops who had been dropped slightly to the east, and these men held the bridges against attacks until relieved by a commando brigade which arrived at 13.30 hours.

The Merville battery was taken by paratroops, but at heavy cost. It was intended that they would make their assault immediately after ninety-nine

Lancasters and Halifaxes delivered a bombing attack, but the weather closed in and most of the bombs fell to the south of the battery, while those which scored hits did not penetrate the thick concrete roofs. Some of the paratroops missed the correct landing zones. Only 150 of the 600 troops ordered to make the assault were in position at the correct time, but they accomplished the task at the cost of 65 dead or wounded. On the other hand, the task of blowing up the five bridges to the east was achieved by sappers who were dropped with paratroops, against determined opposition from German defenders.

While the seaborne troops were afloat, Bomber Command carried out a series of operations, part of which concerned deception. False signals had already convinced the Germans that the Allies intended to land further east, between Boulogne and Dieppe. One of Bomber Command's tasks was to reinforce this deception on D-Day itself. Two squadrons of Lancasters flew from the area of Dover, one towards Fécamp and the other towards Boulogne, circling small ships flying balloons fitted with reflectors which the German radar could pick up. Most of the German radar stations had been knocked out by Allied air attacks, but a few in the Pas de Calais had been left deliberately untouched. The Lancasters also dropped strips of *Window*, specially cut into shapes that simulated approaching ships on radar screens. The whole procession moved towards the French coast at about seven knots, giving the impression of a huge convoy.

These obstacles along the beach between Le Tréport and Berck-Plage (south of Le Touquet) were anti-tank obstructions about 5 ft high to which mines or explosive charges were fitted. They were photographed about a month before D-Day by a Lightning F-5 of the US Ninth Air Force, flying at 50 ft. The Allies landed further west, on the Normandy beaches.

Author's collection

Over the true convoy to the west, RAF Halifaxes and USAAF Fortresses used *Mandrel* (Monitoring and Neutralizing Defensive Radar Electronics) equipment to jam any radar stations ahead that might have been repaired by the Germans. To the east Lancasters and Fortresses of the RAF used *ABC* (AirBorne Cigar) equipment and *Window* to jam the enemy's radar stations and night-fighter aircraft. Stirlings and Halifaxes dropped dummy paratroops, fireworks and rifle-fire simulators over the village of Yvetot, north of Rouen, to deceive the Germans into believing that an airborne operation was taking place in that area. The plan worked and a German battalion was sent to that area to investigate matters.

Bomber Command was out in force on the night of 5/6 June. Apart from the 99 aircraft which bombed the Merville battery, 913 more bombed other coastal batteries. Over 5,000 tons of bombs were dropped, the heaviest tonnage of the war so far. When the seaborne troops reached the beaches, swarms of RAF and USAAF fighters overwhelmed the Luftwaffe while fighter-bombers and medium bombers gave close support to the troops. The RAF squadrons alone numbered 171, controlled from three 'fighter direction' ships. Tactical photo-reconnaissance aircraft ranged further afield, monitoring every sign of German activity. At the same time Coastal Command stood guard over both flanks of the Channel, combing the area for U-boats and making low-level attacks on those warships which attempted to penetrate the screens formed by the Royal Navy.

By the end of D-Day the beachheads had been secured, inevitably at the cost of heavy casualties although mercifully these were far lower than the gloomiest forecasts. The troops began to move inland while Typhoons, Mustangs and Spitfires from England shot up enemy columns and destroyed hundreds of enemy vehicles. On 7 June the RAF's Servicing Commando and Construction Wings began to construct airstrips, often while under fire. These airstrips were in

The Airspeed Horsa, which carried two pilots and up to twenty-five armed men, became the standard troop-carrying glider in the Second World War from 1942 onwards. The structure was manufactured in sections by woodworking firms and assembled on RAF stations. This Horsa was photographed after returning from its initial air test.

Author's collection

operational use within three days, and eventually thirty-one were constructed in the British zone. In addition the USAAF constructed forty in the American zone.

For six weeks after D-Day, Bomber Command hammered enemy communications, ammunition and fuel dumps, airfields and troop concentrations, mostly at night but sometimes in daylight. Other targets were flying-bomb sites. British Intelligence had known for many months of the existence of the German *V-1* flying-bomb, but the first did not arrive over England until 12 June 1944. It was followed by 2,000 others during the remainder of the month, all aimed against London, and many more arrived during the next few months. Travelling at speeds of about 400 mph, only the fastest fighters could catch them, but others were shot down by anti-aircraft fire. About half reached the London area, where they caused considerable damage and about 6,000 fatalities. However, most of the launching ramps were either knocked out or overrun by 5 September, and thereafter the *V-1*s were launched by Heinkel He111s over the North Sea, although these bombers suffered heavy losses at the hands of Mosquito night-fighters. The other missile, the *V-2* rocket, first arrived on 8 September. It was launched vertically and flew at a height and speed which made it almost impossible to shoot down. However, it was not accurate and the launching sites could be located and bombed. These *V-2* rockets resulted in almost 3,000 fatalities before the last arrived on 27 March 1945.

'THUMBS UP OVER NORMANDY (I)'
by Charles J. Thompson
A North American Mitchell II of the RAF's
226 Squadron, based at Hartfordbridge in
Hampshire, accompanied by Mosquito PR16 of
the USAAF's 653rd Bomb Squadron, based at
Watton in Norfolk, on missions over Normandy
on D-Day, 6 June 1944.

The American, Canadian and British troops enlarged their beachheads until all were connected. German armoured divisions that tried to penetrate the defensive ring were shattered by hundreds of fighter-bombers which descended on them in great swarms. In early August the Allies began to break out and race through France, the Canadians to the north, the Americans to the south and the British between them, with the RAF and the USAAF blasting the way ahead, moving from airstrip to airstrip. The Luftwaffe lost control of the skies. Paris was liberated on 25 August. British troops entered Belgium on 2 September and the following day drove past ecstatic crowds lining the streets of Brussels. Meanwhile, on 14/15 August the Americans had landed in southern France and began their drive northwards. Pockets of Germans still held out in some Channel ports and western France, but these were bombed repeatedly and eventually forced to surrender.

The advances seemed irresistible but the next major operation ended in disaster. This was the famous airborne operation around Arnhem in Holland, which had the objective of seizing bridges over the Rhine, to enable the Allied armies to cross over and enter Germany. It began on 27 September 1944 when RAF Albemarles, Stirlings and Halifaxes towed gliders with men of the 1st Airborne Division, while USAAF Dakotas carried men of the 1st Parachute Brigade. The armada was preceded by 1,400 aircraft which plastered the German anti-aircraft defences. Then came the tugs and the gliders, numbering about 2,000 in all, protected by 1,500 fighters and fighter-bombers. There was another

'THUMBS UP OVER NORMANDY (2)'
by Charles J. Thompson
P-51C Mustang III of 306 (Polish) Squadron, based at Coolham in Sussex, with Spitfire VB of 85 Group, Air Spotting Pool of the 2nd Tactical Air Force (flown by a pilot of the USNAF's Cruiser Scouting Squadron 7), based at Lee-on-Solent in Hampshire, over Normandy on D-Day, 6 June 1944.

lift the following day, but then fog descended on English airfields and only supply drops were possible, some of which fell into the hands of the Germans. Unexpectedly, two crack Panzer divisions were resting in the locality and even the most gallant actions could not withstand their attacks. The divisions battling forward to relieve them were stalled by determined defences. By 24 September the position at Arnhem had become untenable and the survivors were ordered to pull out if they could. Almost 14,000 airborne soldiers were lost in the operation, either killed, wounded or missing, while 55 aircraft failed to return. There would be no advance into Germany for another four months.

While these dramatic events were taking place, Coastal Command was playing a full part in the war. The Strike Wings in Cornwall were reinforced with detachments from the east coast of England, and Beaufighters and Mosquitos rampaged down the west coast of France and sank armed merchant ships and warships. By the end of August they had destroyed every available target and moved up to Lincolnshire and Scotland, to attack the convoys which still moved along the coasts of Denmark, Germany and Norway. The advance of the Allied armies had rendered the coasts of Belgium and Holland useless to the Germans. The Strike Wings sank ship after ship until the Germans ceased daylight sailings. Even when the vessels sheltered in fjords, the Strike Wings sank or damaged them while at anchor. Those U-boats which survived the onslaught on the ports of western France streamed round Ireland to Norway. Some of the more modern

Airborne troops entering a Horsa glider for a training flight at a Heavy Glider Conversion Unit. Although they carried parachutes in training, the men did not take them on operational sorties. This photograph was taken in England shortly before the airborne operation that spearheaded the Allied invasion of Italy on 10 July 1943.

Author's collection

U-boats were fitted with schnorkel tubes and were thus more difficult to detect. Most of these were ordered to concentrate on British waters. Other larger and faster U-boats were coming into service, but the construction yards were being smashed by Bomber Command and the USAAF. From July 1944 until the end of the war, Coastal Command sank forty-nine more U-boats and was in complete ascendancy over its enemies.

From mid-August 1944 Bomber Command was able to resume much of its activity over the German heartland, combining with the US Eighth Air Force in 'round-the-clock' bombing. The strength of Bomber Command was increasing markedly, from 1,028 aircraft in April 1944 to 1,513 in December 1944. Moreover, the carrying capacity rose even more, since most of the new arrivals were Lancasters. It was estimated that 46 per cent of the tonnage dropped by Bomber Command fell in the last nine months of the year. In addition to its night operations, from 27 August Bomber Command was also able to resume some daylight operations over Germany, escorted by RAF fighters which had the range to reach the targets from advance airfields.

A new radar aid, known as *G-H*, was introduced in this period. This was similar to *Oboe* but in reverse. The aircraft carried a small radar device which enabled the navigator (instead of the ground station) to use the interrogation and display system. Thus many aircraft could use the system at the same time, enabling heavy bombers as well as the Pathfinder Force to operate more effectively. Moreover, ground stations were set up in France as the Allies advanced, extending the range of this very effective navigation aid.

Horsa gliders taking off from a Heavy Glider Conversion Unit. Army or RAF volunteer pilots took a four-week course at one of these units after training on General Aircraft Hotspur gliders and being given their wings. There were eight of these training units in England.

Author's collection

The American contribution to the combined bombing offensive was even greater than that of Bomber Command, in terms of aircraft although not bomb-carrying capacity. The US Eighth Air Force expanded from 1,049 bombers in April 1944 to 1,826 in December 1944. The US Fifteenth Air Force, which was based in Italy but capable of bombing Germany, was eventually equipped with almost 1,600 bombers.

By this time, it was believed by most Allied planners that the combined bomber offensive should be directed to synthetic oil production as a first priority and the transport system as the second. The attack against oil had begun in earnest on 12 May 1944 when 886 bombers of the US Eighth Air Force, escorted by 735 fighters, attacked targets in Germany and Czechoslavakia. On 25 September a directive was issued to both Bomber Command and the US Eighth Air Force, requiring them to implement this policy. However, Harris still favoured the destruction of the remaining cities and entered into a protracted wrangle with Portal over the issue. Meanwhile, his bombers were directed to oil installations on some occasions, but also continued to attack city centres.

On 16 December 1944 the Wehrmacht launched its last major effort against the Western Allies, with an all-out attack in the Ardennes. The objective was to drive a wedge between the American and British forces and reach Antwerp, then crush each in turn. The assault gained ground at first, under cover of low cloud which continued for a week. However, when the weather cleared the RAF and the USAAF were able to resume their attacks in daylight. The Panzers were halted and eventually driven back. The Luftwaffe also made its last great offensive, on 1 January 1945, with a determined attempt to destroy much of the 2nd Tactical Air Force on the ground. In fact, there were plenty of aircraft in Germany, for the dispersed factories were still turning them out in quantity. The major problems were the shortage of experienced pilots and an acute lack of fuel to train new entrants. Nevertheless, over 800 aircraft were mustered for this surprise attack on airfields, which destroyed 144 aircraft and damaged 84 more. But it was estimated that some 200 German aircraft were shot down, and these were flown by irreplaceable pilots.

The military situation in the Ardennes did not stabilize until the end of January 1945, and meanwhile the arguments between Harris and Portal continued. These culminated in Harris's offer of resignation in a letter of 18 January. Portal replied the following day, refusing this offer and effectively backing down. However

Horsa gliders were used for carrying equipment as well as troops, such as these motor cycles being made fast to the floor during a demonstration on 22–3 April 1944. This event was watched by the Deputy Supreme Commander of the Allied Expeditionary Force, Air Chief Marshal Sir Arthur Tedder.

Author's collection

history might judge Harris, he was a very popular figure with the British public at the time and was revered by his aircrews. A resignation would have been extremely damaging to general morale, and he was allowed to continue with his programme of selective attacks against oil and transportation coupled with heavy attacks against those German cities which had not yet felt the weight of Bomber Command's massive and increasing strength.

However, the much-publicized attack against Dresden on the night of 13/14 February 1945, followed by a heavy attack by the US Eighth Air Force the next day, was primarily one of the results of the Yalta Conference earlier that month, attended by Stalin, Roosevelt and Churchill. On 4 February the Russians had asked for heavy attacks to be made against Dresden, Chemnitz and Liepzig, to hinder the movement of German troops being brought up to resist their own advancing forces. The two Western leaders had agreed to this request and instructions were issued accordingly. The combined attacks against Dresden, which resulted in enormous destruction and a minimum of 35,000 fatalities, were not initiated by Harris although they accorded with his preferred bombing policy.

When the Allies finally crossed the Rhine, it was one of the best-executed operations of the war, stemming from excellent planning. It began on 24 March

'D-DAY DAWNING' by Charles J. Thompson
On D-Day, 6 June 1944, over seventy General
Aircraft Hamilcar gliders were towed by
Halifaxes and Stirlings to landing zones in
Normandy. They carried army vehicles which
were driven out of the hinged noses to support
airborne troops carried in Airspeed Horsa
gliders.

1945 in the Wesel sector, which was held relatively weakly by the Germans. It
was also within easy range of Allied fighters and even of artillery fire. The assault
was preceded by a night-bombing attack on Wesel by Bomber Command, which
finally obliterated this unfortunate town and left some of the surviving defenders
too dazed to put up an effective resistance. They were further pounded by the US
Eighth Air Force immediately preceding the airborne operation. About 1,750 heavy
bombers were despatched, escorted by almost 1,300 fighters, many of the targets
being the nearby airfields. The airborne assault consisted of 541 Dakotas carrying
paratroops and 1,050 aircraft towing 1,350 gliders, some in double tow. They were
protected by fighters of the 2nd Tactical Air Force and the US Ninth Air Force. Flak
was still intense and 53 aircraft were shot down and many more damaged, but all
objectives were achieved and the amphibious forces then crossed the Rhine.

This was the decisive battle of the European war on the Western Front. The
Allied armies broke through all along the German frontier and began fighting
throughout the country. The Americans linked up with the Russians at the Elbe
on 23 April and the British reached the Baltic on 2 May. Hitler committed suicide
in his Berlin bunker on 30 April and Germany surrendered unconditionally on
7 May. VE-Day was celebrated the next day, but it seemed to many in the armed
forces that a long and bitter war lay ahead before the Japanese could be defeated.

The Tetrarch light tank of 7.5 tons, armed with a two-pounder gun and a 7.92 mm machine-gun, was designed to fit into the Hamilcar glider. Sixteen of these tanks were on the strength of the 6th Airborne Reconnaissance Regiment, and six were carried to the battle front on D-Day. This Tetrarch was backing into a Hamilcar, even though the soldier seems to be motioning it forward.

Author's collection

A Halifax towing a General Aircraft Hamilcar glider over the airfield at Tarrant Rushton in Dorset during an exercise prior to D-Day. The Hamilcar, designed as a freight carrier, was the largest and heaviest glider employed by the Allies during the Second World War.

Author's collection

Officers of the 22nd Independent Parachute Company, 6th Airborne Division, synchronizing their watches at RAF Harwell in Berkshire for the D-Day operation. They took off shortly before midnight in Armstrong Whitworth Albemarles. Left to right: Lt R. de Latour; Lt D. Wells; Lt I. Vischner; Lt R. Midwood. Bobby de Latour took off in the first aircraft, at 23.03 hours on 5 June 1944. This was flown by Sqn Ldr C. Merrick, with Air Vice-Marshal Leslie H. Hollinghurst (commanding the Air Transport Groups) as a passenger.

Author's collection

Paratroops of the 22nd Independent Parachute Company, 6th Airborne Division, entering Albemarle serial V1740 of 295 Squadron at Harwell for the D-Day invasion, watched by the RAF crew of four and another officer. Three Albemarles of 295 Squadron and three of 570 Squadron carried sticks of ten paratroops apiece to dropping zones in France, where the men acted as pathfinders with 'Eureka' transmitters for the following assault troops. The twin-engined Albemarle was designed as a reconnaissance bomber but was employed by the RAF from July 1943 as a glider-tug or for dropping paratroops.

Author's collection

One of the main tasks of the airborne troops was to capture two bridges, over the Caen Canal and the Orne River, and to hold these until the arrival of seaborne troops. Six Horsa gliders containing men of the Ox & Bucks Light Infantry were towed by Halifaxes of 298 and 644 Squadrons from Tarrant Rushton. The first glider to land in France on D-Day was Horsa No. 91 flown by Sgt Jimmy Wallwork, shown here with its nose embedded in barbed wire by the Caen Canal bridge at Bénouville. A concrete blockhouse and the bridge-keeper's cottage are in the background.

Museum of Army Flying

All three Horsa gliders, Nos 91, 92 and 93, landed successfully by the Caen Canal bridge by 00.16 hours GMT on 6 June 1944. The troops overcame the German garrison after a stiff fight and captured the bridge intact.

Museum of Army Flying

Two of the other three Horsa gliders landed successfully by the bridge over the Orne River. One can be seen in this photograph. Both bridges were held by the airborne soldiers, reinforced by paratroops, until seaborne commandos of the 1st Special Service Brigade arrived in the afternoon of 6 June.

Museum of Army Flying

Empty landing craft at Asnelles, on Gold Beach to the west of the British landing positions, photographed at about 13.00 hours on 6 June 1944.

Author's collection

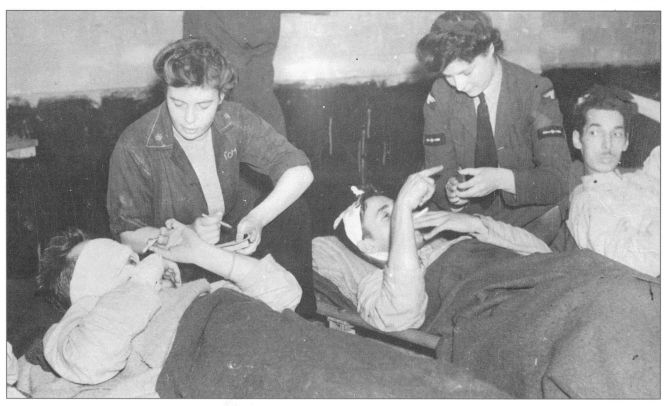

WAAF volunteers in the medical service photographed while looking after wounded men from France brought by air ambulance to a fighter airfield on the south coast of England. The girl on the left is writing a letter for a soldier wounded in the face.

Author's collection

Rockets fired by a Typhoon of the 2nd Tactical Air Force reaching their target on a railway line behind the front in Normandy in July 1944. The explosion of another rocket can be seen at the bottom of the photograph.

Author's collection

On 15 July 1944 the Langham Strike Wing despatched thirty-four Beaufighters to Cape Lindesnes on the coast of south-west Norway, where they attacked a German convoy. The Norwegian tanker *Irania* of 2,249 tons was badly damaged and several other vessels were set on fire by cannon fire and rockets. All the aircraft returned.

Author's collection

The German flak ships *Vp810* of 314 tons and *Vp812* of 386 tons were sunk on 22 July 1944 when attacked by Beaufighters of the North Coates Strike Wing off the island of Wangerooge in the East Frisian Islands. A group of survivors from one of these vessels can be seen clinging to a life-raft in the foreground.

Author's collection

On 27 July 1944 Bomber Command despatched seventy-two aircraft to attack flying-bomb sites, as shown in this photograph of Lancasters. There were no losses but the targets were cloud-covered and some of the aircraft bombed using *G-H* radar instead of visual bombsights.

Author's collection

Twenty-four Beaufighters of the Davidstow Moor Strike Wing were despatched on 8 August 1944 on a sweep down the west coast of France. They attacked four German minesweepers in the Bay of Bourgeneuf with cannon and rockets. One Beaufighter was shot down but the minesweepers *M366, M367, M428* and *M438*, all of 637 tons, were sunk.

Author's collection

On 15 August 1944 Bomber Command dispatched over a thousand aircraft in daylight to attack nine airfields in Belgium and Holland used by German night-fighters, preliminary to a renewed bombing offensive against Germany. This airfield at Melsbroek near Brussels was blanketed with bombs.

Author's collection

This photograph of a mêlée of aircraft was taken on 25 August 1944 when forty-four Beaufighters of the Strubby, North Coates and Langham Strike Wings made a combined attack on a German convoy off Schiermonnikoog in the West Frisian Islands. All the torpedoes missed but many vessels were damaged and the German minesweeper *M347* of 637 tons was sunk. All aircraft returned.

Author's collection

Bomber Command despatched 675 Lancasters, Halifaxes and Mosquitos in daylight on 3 September 1944 to attack six enemy airfields in southern Holland. Only one aircraft was lost. This airfield at Volkel, 12 miles north of Helmond, was pitted with craters after the attack, although it should be noted that the Germans were adept at faking these on runways, to fool photo-interpreters into assuming that airfields were out of action.

Author's collection

When Antwerp was captured by the Allies on 4 September 1944, supplies sent by ship to the port could not reach the front line until the Scheldt Estuary had been cleared of the enemy. On 3 October attacks by 259 aircraft of Bomber Command breached the wall near Westkapelle on the island of Walcheren, thus flooding some of the German defences.

Author's collection

The *V-2* rocket establishment at Peenemünde, photographed in September 1944, showing the damage caused by Bomber Command's heavy raid on the night of 17/18 August 1943, after which much of the work on the site was transferred to Blizna in Poland. The arrow marked 'A' indicated that light flak positions on the roof of the damaged building had been removed.

Author's collection

British Taylorcraft Austers, designed in the USA and built under licence in Britain, operated over many battle fronts during the Second World War as Air Observation Post aircraft. They entered squadron service from July 1941 onwards, and five marks were produced. This Auster I, serial LB375, was taken on charge by 653 Squadron in December 1942 and later served with 43 Operational Training Unit, 451 Squadron and 164 Squadron. It was sold to the Royal Flying Club in 1946.

Museum of Army Flying

Supply containers being dropped from Dakotas to troops on the ground at Arnhem.

Author's collection

Operation 'Market Garden', the airborne landings at Arnhem, began in the morning of 17 September 1944. This photograph of the gliders was taken on the same day by a photo-reconnaissance Spitfire.

Author's collection

Flak over a German fleet near Den Helder, photographed on 25 September 1944 during an attack by Beaufighters of the North Coates and Langham Strike Wings. The German M-Class minesweeper *M471* of 750 tons and the harbour defence vessel *Jannetje* of 107 tons were sunk but three Beaufighters were shot down and seventeen damaged.

Author's collection

On 12 October 1944 Bomber Command despatched 137 aircraft in daylight, with fighter escort, to attack the synthetic oil plant at Wanne-Eickel in the Ruhr. According to German reports the oil plant was not seriously damaged but the chemical factory was destroyed and a number of civilians killed. This photograph of a Halifax was taken over the oil plant, which was covered by smoke.

Author's collection

On 31 October 1944 twenty-five Mosquitos of the 2nd Tactical Air Force made a low-level attack against the headquarters of the Gestapo at Aarhus University in Denmark, escorted by eight Mustangs of 12 Group. The building was destroyed, together with the records of the Danish Resistance.

Author's collection

This merchant vessel, the German *Ferndale* of 5,684 tons, was attacked on 16 December 1944 by twenty-two Mosquitos of the Banff Strike Wing while in the narrow fjord of Krahellesund in Norway. She was badly hit and her destruction was completed by six more Mosquitos which arrived an hour later. A Mosquito from the first formation was forced to ditch and another from the second attack was also shot down.

Author's collection

'BLACK FRIDAY' by Mark Postlethwaite
On 9 February 1945 thirty-two Beaufighter TFXs of the Dallachy Strike Wing, escorted by ten Mustangs of 65 Squadron from Peterhead, attacked enemy warships in Fördefjord. These included a destroyer, minesweepers and several flak ships. The attackers came under very heavy flak and were also in combat with Focke Wulf FW190s. Nine Beaufighters and a Mustang were shot down while many more were damaged, for the loss of five FW190s. This painting shows serial NE831 of 144 Squadron, flown by Flt Sgt S.A. Butler with Flt Sgt C.B. Nicholl as navigator, being engaged by an FW190 of Jagdgeschwader 5. The Beaufighter was damaged but the men were not injured and managed to land safely at Dallachy.

A damaged Beaufighter after the attack by the Dallachy Strike Wing on shipping in Fördefjord on 9 February 1945.

Author's collection

This Mosquito XIII night-fighter of 604 Squadron was photographed in the winter of 1944/5 on the snow-covered airfield of Lille-Vendeville airfield, from where the squadron was engaged on intruder operations as part of the 2nd Tactical Air Force. Beneath the thimble-shaped nose containing airborne-interception radar, the navigator WO D. Gosling (left) was talking to Sqn Ldr G.H. Hayhurst.

Author's collection

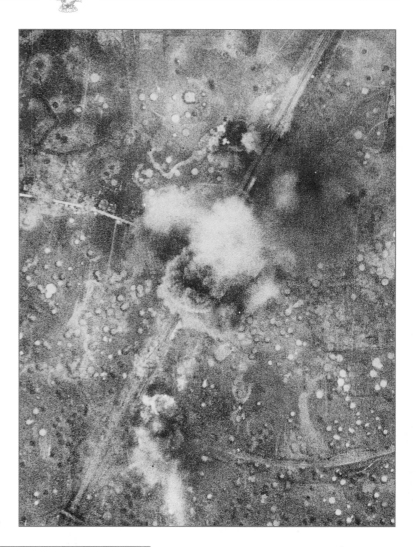

On 14 March 1945 the first 'Grand Slam' bomb of 22,000 lb,
developed by Barnes Wallis, was dropped from a Lancaster of
617 Squadron on the railway viaduct at Bielefeld in Germany.
In addition, 'Tallboy' bombs of 12,000 lb were dropped on this target.

Author's collection

The 'earthquake' effect of the huge bombs caused part of
the railway viaduct at Bielefeld to collapse.

Dr E.V. Hawkinson

The scale of the air effort made by RAF's Transport Command may be judged by these Dakotas lined up on an airfield in Belgium, with army trucks beside each. The photograph was taken in March 1945, when the Allied armies were pressing on into Germany, and the stream of Dakotas was bringing supplies and taking out the wounded. The Luftwaffe had been almost wiped out at this stage and there was little interference from the air.

Author's collection

On 9 April 1945 the Banff Strike Wing despatched thirty-five Mosquitos to the Skaggerak to hunt for U-boats on the surface. They sank the Type IXs *U-804* and *U-843* and the Type VII *U-1065*. A Mosquito of the RAF Film Unit which had accompanied the force was brought down in the explosions. Three other Mosquitos were damaged by enemy fire but headed for safety in Sweden.

Author's collection

The Danish freighter *Java* of 8,651 tons at anchor in the Danish harbour of Nakskov, under attack on 3 May 1945 by rocket-firing Beaufighters of the Dallachy Strike Wing. The vessel sank and the two freighters behind her were also damaged.

Author's collection

The remains of the synthetic oil plant at Gelsenkirchen in the Ruhr, which was a primary target for night attacks by Bomber Command and day attacks by the US Eighth Air Force. The photograph shows the remains of the compressor house in the foreground, the reaction cylinders (in which the coal paste was made) on the left, and the tanks for the lubricating oil plant in the background.

Dr E.V. Hawkinson

This trainload of *V-2* rockets was captured by the Allies at Bromskirchen, near Kassel in central Germany, in the closing weeks of the war. The rockets had not been assembled and were hidden under camouflage in the freight cars.

Author's collection

Hitler's fortified retreat at Berchtesgaden in the Alps of south-east Bavaria, named 'The Eagle's Nest'.

Dr E.V. Hawkinson

CHAPTER NINE

A DISTANT
WAR

The initial victories by the Japanese in the Far East were stunning blows against the British forces in the area. They also humiliated the British Empire and accelerated its decline. No one in authority seems to have anticipated the effectiveness of the Japanese war machine, or the fanaticism and ruthlessness of its servicemen. Indeed, there was a general and mistaken belief that the Japanese fighting men and their equipment were far inferior to those of a world power such as Great Britain. Japan was considered to have been drained by years of conflict with China, which it had invaded in July 1937, and to possess no more than a weak and dislocated industry.

The main defect appears to have been a failure in military intelligence. This was the responsibility of the Far East Combined Bureau in Singapore, which was controlled by the Royal Navy and largely devoted to its needs. Although the Japanese were already established in Indo-China and within striking range of Malaya, there was almost no knowledge of their air force or the performance of their aircraft. Moreover, after the fall of France the RAF had been forced to neglect the Far East in favour of Britain and the Middle East. Compounding the problem, when Russia was attacked by the Wehrmacht in June 1941, there was an urgent need to send RAF fighters to that country instead of to the Far East.

Thus the aircraft available to defend Singapore and Malaya were either obsolete or too few for the task they faced. There were two squadrons of Vildebeest torpedo-bombers, four of Blenheim light bombers, two of Hudsons, four of Brewster Buffalo fighters and one of Catalinas. These were seriously outclassed and outnumbered by Japanese aircraft, particularly the fighter squadrons. There were insufficient pilots and some of these had not been trained on operational machines. The only photo-reconnaissance aircraft were two modified Buffalos, plus a single Beaufort which had arrived from Australia. The radar system was patchy and did not cover the whole of the Malayan archipelago. There were too few airfields, and those which existed were ill-defended and provided with inadequate servicing facilities.

On 8 December 1941, the day after their crippling air attack on Pearl Harbor, the Japanese landed near RAF Khota Bharu on the east coast of Malaya. RAF Vildebeests and RAAF Hudsons attempted to hinder the landings but with only limited success. Indeed, the Vildebeests were almost wiped out in this and subsequent engagements. On the same day Japanese bombers made their first

The Brewster Buffalo, a single-seat fighter fitted with four .50 inch machine-guns, entered service with the RAF's 71 Squadron at Church Fenton in Yorkshire during July 1940, such as serial AS430 in this photograph. The performance was considered inferior to that of other fighters, however, and the machines were shipped to Singapore where the armament was changed to .303 inch machine-guns. Although outclassed by Japanese fighters, the squadrons gave good accounts of themselves before retiring to Burma and India, where they were re-equipped with Hurricanes.

Aeroplane Monthly

attack on Singapore itself, a city that was so unprepared that it had no air raid shelters or black-out arrangements.

The Japanese took Khota Bharu the following day and began their jungle version of the Blitzkrieg. This was a method of warfare they had developed from studying the events in Europe, with the help of German military advisers. Lightly equipped troops filtered rapidly through jungle tracks, surrounding British and Commonwealth positions, while their air forces, both Navy and Army, began to wrest control of the skies from the RAF and Commonwealth squadrons. It was a war of co-ordination and movement, and the defenders had no real answer, although pockets of men fought stubbornly. Twenty-two Glenn Martin bombers and nine Buffalos of the Royal Netherlands Air Force arrived on 9 December from the Netherlands East Indies, but the aircraft available to the defenders were steadily whittled away. Every RAF airfield was attacked in turn, and the surviving aircraft were forced to fly south.

On 10 December torpedo-bombers of the Japanese Navy Air Force sank the British battleships *Prince of Wales* and *Repulse*, which had been sent up the east coast of Malaya to oppose the landings, but without adequate air cover. Some of the survivors were picked up by the destroyer escorts. From this time the British lost control of the seas around Malaya, while in retreat over land and in the air. Further afield, Hong Kong and British Borneo were without air cover or adequate defences. Hong Kong fell into Japanese hands on 25 December and British Borneo on the following day.

In Malaya the defending troops were forced into a fighting retreat down the peninsula, destroying their equipment when possible. By the beginning of February 1942 all the survivors had crossed the causeway into Singapore and were preparing to resist from the island. Meanwhile, 51 Hurricanes, originally intended for the Middle East, had arrived in crates and 21 pilots had landed. These carried out their first operation on 20 January and shot down eight Japanese bombers over Singapore, giving the impression that the island might be able to defend itself. On the next attack, however, the bombers were escorted by fighters which shot down five Hurricanes.

'SUMATRA SCRAMBLE' by Charles J. Thompson
Five days before the fall of Singapore on
15 February 1942, the last Hurricanes and
Buffalos were withdrawn to hastily constructed
airstrips near Palembang in Sumatra, part of the
Dutch East Indies. They joined a party of
35 Hurricanes which had flown off the aircraft
carrier HMS *Indomitable* on 26 January. The
pilots made valiant attempts to protect the
Hudsons and Blenheims which attacked
Japanese transports invading the island, and they
also destroyed several Zero fighters which had
landed on Bangka Island on the east of Sumatra.
However, Japanese paratroops overcame
resistance on Sumatra and the remaining RAF
aircraft completed a retreat to Java on
18 February.

The island and its airfields came under both shellfire and bombing, and it was soon evident that continued defence was impossible. It was time to evacuate the personnel and their equipment, but there was no Dunkirk miracle awaiting the desperate forces. The Catalina squadron had already moved its base to Java and by the end of January the aircraft in Singapore had also left. The twin-engined aircraft, reduced to a fraction of their original number, had also flown off the island, with the intention of continuing the struggle from bases in Sumatra, across the Strait of Malacca. Only 6 Buffalos remained serviceable in Singapore, together with 21 of the 51 Hurricanes which had arrived shortly before.

The 6 Buffalos and 8 Hurricanes remained for a heroic last-ditch defence while the others were shipped out in the few vessels available, amid scenes of chaos. On 15 February, Singapore surrendered. The Malayan campaign had cost the Japanese about 3,500 dead and 6,150 wounded. About 9,000 of the defenders had lost their lives. Some 130,000 British and Imperial troops were taken prisoner and suffered appallingly inhuman cruelty leading to the deaths of tens of thousands. A huge arsenal fell into enemy hands. It was Britain's worst defeat of the war.

The Vultee Vengeance saw operational service with the RAF only in the Burma theatre, four squadrons being equipped with this two-seat dive-bomber from August 1942 onwards. It was armed with four machine-guns in the wings with two more in the rear cockpit and could carry 2,000 lb of bombs. Other Vengeances delivered to Britain were converted to target-tugs.

Author's collection

Many vessels which escaped from Singapore were sunk or crippled by the Japanese, but some reached Sumatra. The RAF had set up its headquarters at Palembang, to the south-east of the huge island. About 48 twin-engined bombers remained, some in poor condition. There were also a number of Hurricanes, some of which had been withdrawn from Singapore while 35 had been flown off a British aircraft carrier. Lastly, a handful of Buffalos had arrived from Singapore. This small force had no respite, for it was already under air attack. A Japanese invasion fleet had already sailed and was nearing the entrance of the Palembang River. This convoy was attacked repeatedly on 15 February by Blenheims and Hudsons, escorted by Hurricanes, with considerable success. Japanese fighters, flown off a carrier to an airfield on nearby Banka Island, were also strafed.

These successes could not be exploited, for there were insufficient aircraft or ground troops. Japanese paratroops descended on the area of Palembang and advanced on the weakly defended RAF airfields. Another retreat was necessary, this time across the Sunda Strait to Java. By 18 February all available aircraft had flown to the island, and about 10,000 men from various units had arrived in miscellaneous ships. This retreat was carried out in great confusion, compounded by masses of refugees in a state of panic. By this time only 18 Hurricanes remained serviceable, together with 12 Hudsons and 6 Blenheims. The bombers returned to Sumatra on two occasions, attacking Japanese shipping, but by 22 February almost all were destroyed on the ground by enemy air attacks.

Java was defended by the Dutch, supported by some Australian, British and American troops, but these were inadequately armed and air cover was extremely limited. A strong Japanese fleet was spotted approaching the island on 26 February, and a mixed force of British, American, Australian and Dutch warships sent out to intercept it was wiped out the following day. The aircraft available attacked the transports on 1 March, sinking some ships, but the great majority of the Japanese landed and began to overrun the Allied positions, including the airfields. The Allies and the remnants of the squadrons fought on until 8 March, when the Dutch surrendered. A handful of aircraft managed to take off for Australia, but most were destroyed. A few ground personnel escaped in ships but most became prisoners and were subjected to the usual Japanese methods of starvation and brutality.

These episodes were not the end of the string of disasters for the British in the Far East. The Japanese were intent on occupying Burma, partly to obtain its output of oil and partly to cut off the military supplies from the Western powers passing along the 'Burma Road' to China, which was still resisting the Japanese attempt at conquest. Their forces had already occupied Siam and on 14 December 1941 crossed the frontier of southern Burma. Air raids against Rangoon began nine days later, causing panic among the civilian population, many of whom streamed out of the city.

However, a squadron of the American Volunteer Group, equipped with Curtiss P-40 Tomahawks, flew down from the north to operate from Mingaladon, near Rangoon, joining an RAF fighter squadron with 16 Buffalos on its strength. These aircraft shot down many Japanese bombers and long-distance fighters, deferring the inevitable retreat which would follow an attack by superior forces. A squadron of Blenheims arrived on 7 January 1942, followed by about 30 Hurricanes to augment the Buffalos. The Blenheims made successful attacks on airfields in Siam and the Hurricanes acquitted themselves well. For a brief period, the Allies established air superiority over Rangoon, but on the ground the

British forces were retreating stubbornly in the face of some 70,000 Japanese troops. The Army began to withdraw to the north, blowing up installations as it went, and the military evacuation was completed on 7 March.

The RAF's fighters and the American P-40s also suffered losses. They flew northwards in stages, covering the Army's retreat to the best of their ability. By 12 March the survivors formed a small Wing at Magwe, a civil airfield to which the Blenheims had withdrawn on 21 February. Eight days later the Blenheims and Hurricanes made a very effective attack on Mingaladon, destroying many Japanese aircraft on the ground. The Japanese responded with a series of bombing attacks in overwhelming strength, which left the Wing with no more than 6 Blenheims, 11 Hurricanes, and 3 P-40s. The Americans flew north to join their comrades at Lashio and the RAF retired to the island of Akyab, where once again they were subjected to waves of attacks by Japanese bombers. These destroyed almost all the remaining RAF aircraft, the few survivors making for Lashio. This town also fell to the Japanese, on 29 April. Some of the RAF men were evacuated to India by Dakotas while others moved further north to China.

By May 1942 the Japanese were in control of the whole of Burma and had cut the road to China. They were poised to cross the hills, advance through the Indian plains to Calcutta and then continue to Delhi, but the heavy monsoon broke and brought operations to a halt for several months. Meanwhile, they occupied the Andaman and Nicobar Islands in the Bay of Bengal, which had hitherto provided bases for RAF reconnaissance aircraft.

Then Ceylon came under attack. This was protected by the British Far Eastern Fleet, while four RAF squadrons of Hurricanes had arrived in early March to help defend the island. On 5 April a strong Japanese force which included four carriers approached the island and their aircraft launched raids against shipping in Colombo harbour and the RAF airfield of Ratmalana. There was little damage at the airfield, but an armed merchant cruiser and a destroyer were sunk in the harbour. In the air battle, 15 Hurricanes and 5 FAA Fulmars were shot down but the defenders claimed 18 enemy aircraft destroyed, while the anti-aircraft batteries claimed another 5. Later that day, the cruisers HMS *Cornwall* and HMS *Dorsetshire* were sunk south of Ceylon by bombers from the same carrier force.

The Japanese returned to the attack on 9 April and sank the carrier HMS *Hermes*, together with a destroyer and a corvette, off Ceylon. They also bombed Trincomalee and the RAF airfield of China Bay, but many of the attackers were shot down for the loss of 8 Hurricanes and 3 Fulmars. The Japanese fleet then withdrew to refuel and replenish its losses, but never returned. It was urgently required in the Pacific, but three of the carriers were among the four sunk by American dive-bombers in the Battle of Midway of 4 June 1942. The tide of war began to turn against Japan.

American-backed Chinese troops were continuing to fight the Japanese along the northern frontier of Burma. To support these, a US military airlift began from Bengal to Kunming. The first experimental flight was made in April 1942 and during the summer US transport aircraft carried Chinese troops and supplies for 500 miles over the great wall of mountains that separates India from southern China. This astonishing achievement took place in spite of the monsoon, without fighter protection, and over terrain which was partly unmapped and where the Japanese Air Force had mastery. The service, which soon became known as the 'Hump Run', continued throughout the war, with RAF Dakotas joining from December 1943.

The respite afforded by the monsoon enabled the British, supported by the Americans, to build up their forces in India. Air Chief Marshal Sir Richard Peirse

'OUT IN THE MIDDAY SUN'
by Charles J. Thompson
Four RAF squadrons were equipped with Vultee Vengeance dive-bombers for service in Burma. This painting depicts one of these aircraft on an airstrip near Imphal in north-east India, where the Japanese launched an assault on 7 March 1944. After a hard-fought battle at Imphal and Kohima, the Japanese were forced to withdraw and began their long retreat down the length of Burma.

arrived in March 1942 to take over command of the RAF. There were only five RAF squadrons in the country at the time of the Japanese victory, but these were augmented by the light bomber squadrons brought out of Burma and made up to strength. From this time, the Command was increased rapidly to twenty-six squadrons by June 1942. Six fighter squadrons of the Indian Air Force were added to these. A photo-reconnaissance unit was also formed. It was unfortunate for the Japanese that the Allied victories in North Africa released military resources and more squadrons arrived in India. By the end of the year, the Command had increased to a total of 1,443 aircraft, although not all these were fully operational. There were three Groups, one of which was in Ceylon, and the squadrons were equipped with Hurricanes, Vengeances, Blenheims, Hudsons, Wellingtons, Beauforts, Lysanders, Dakotas, Catalinas and Liberators.

The RAF had few contacts with the enemy up to the end of November 1942 and it was not until the middle of the following month that the Japanese began bombing raids against Calcutta. These took place at night and were on a limited scale but they created panic among the volatile population. It was estimated that about 1,500,000 people fled the city after the first attack. However, a flight of Beaufighter night-fighters arrived in January 1943 and shot down five Japanese bombers in two nights. This seemed to discourage the Japanese, for they did not return and the refugees drifted back to the city.

At the beginning of December 1942 British and Indian troops under the overall command of General Sir Archibald Wavell began the first Arakan campaign, advancing down the Mayu Peninsula with the intention of recapturing the island of Akyab. RAF and US aircraft bombed Japanese positions and the troops progressed as far as the port of Indin by 27 December. Here the Japanese resistance stiffened and further progress was stalled. Fighting continued for several weeks, with the RAF giving close support, but by March the Japanese were able to launch a counter-offensive and threatened to surround the force.

The British and Indians retreated to their starting point by May, at the cost of some 2,500 casualties.

Another assault coincided with this event. Seven columns of men, known as Chindits and trained in commando methods to operate behind enemy lines, marched eastwards on 7 February 1943 from Imphal in the State of Manipur. They were led by an expert in guerrilla tactics, Brigadier Orde Wingate, and crossed the Chindwin River to penetrate Japanese lines and spread whatever confusion they could. A novel aspect of the operation was that they had no lines of communication to their rear but depended wholly on two squadrons of RAF Dakotas for supplies parachuted to them in containers. The troops endured gruelling hardships and suffered casualties but managed to blow up bridges and destroy sections of railway lines, while the angry Japanese pursued and tried to locate them, usually in vain. The operations came to an end in June 1943 with the onset of the summer monsoon, and the survivors marched out, mostly to the west but some to join the Chinese in the east.

Their achievements were limited, but some of them had marched for 1,000 miles and a great deal of knowledge and experience was gained. Above all, this legendary campaign demonstrated that a close co-operation between the Army and the RAF could bring success and indeed that whole divisions could be sustained from the air, even in extremely difficult terrain. If surrounded by the Japanese, as had happened so often to British and Imperial forces in the past eighteen months, they could stay and fight. It was also believed that with the aid of air power it would be possible to continue warfare in the monsoon period.

By June 1943 the RAF in India had already expanded to 53 squadrons and most of the older types of aircraft had been replaced with modern machines. Following the Chindit expedition there was an enormous expansion in squadrons, including those equipped with Dakotas. South East Asia Command was formed under Admiral Lord Louis Mountbatten in November 1943, and by early the following year its Air Command had expanded to 48 RAF and 17 USAAF squadrons. At the same time, a great programme of airfield building was taking place, with 275 already constructed and 15 more being completed. A radar network was also established and an intensive programme of air reconnaissance was under way.

General William Slim had been appointed by Mountbatten to command the 14th Army and oust the Japanese from Burma. A second Arakan campaign opened on New Year's Eve 1943, and once again the British and Indian troops began pushing down the Mayu Peninsula. Prior to this assault the RAF had established supremacy over the Japanese Air Force in Burma. When the attacking troops were surrounded in early February in what became known as the 'Admin Box', supplies poured in from the air and this time it was the Japanese who were forced to withdraw.

At this point, the Japanese decided to invade India through the State of Manipur, with 100,000 of their crack troops. The assault began on 7 March 1944 when patrols began to press against British forward positions, and ten days later three Japanese divisions approached the main defensive lines. Allied garrisons had been reinforced and ferocious battles began around Kohima and Imphal, but the defenders were supplied from the air by RAF Dakotas and USAAF Commandos, while RAF Hurricanes and Vengeances attacked enemy positions and the Allies used their mastery of the air to strafe enemy airfields. Even the most fanatical Japanese attacks could not prevail and in April the 14th Army launched a counter-attack. Of course, the Japanese resisted stubbornly but by the end of June many were trapped and they were gradually annihilated. The number of their dead cannot be calculated accurately, but the Japanese never regained their strength in Burma.

Meanwhile the Chindits had begun a major operation further north in Burma. On 5 March 1944 some 9,000 men and 1,000 pack animals were flown in Dakotas or towed in gliders over the mountain ranges to natural clearings far behind enemy lines, in order to cut their lines of communication. Other Chindits set off on foot. At the same time, Chinese and American troops under General J.W. Stilwell continued to push south, fighting the Japanese as they went. All these troops were supplied from the air and supported by fighter-bombers, the Chindits with the aid of RAF officers with R/T and W/T sets who accompanied them. Operations continued throughout the monsoon and everywhere the Japanese were in retreat.

By the beginning of July 1944 the Air Command in South East Asia possessed ninety RAF and USAAF squadrons, equipped with Liberators, Venturas, Catalinas, Wellingtons, Dakotas, Hudsons, Sunderlands, Mosquitos, Mitchells, Warwicks, Beaufighters, Beauforts, Thunderbolts, Spitfires, Hurricanes, Lightnings, Tomahawks and Vengeances. It was an overwhelming force, against which the Japanese could pit only about 125 aircraft. In the following November Air Chief Marshal Sir Trafford Leigh-Mallory was killed in an air crash while en route to take over command from Air Chief Marshal Sir Richard Peirse. His post was filled temporarily by Air Marshal Sir Guy Garrod until another appointee, Air Marshal Sir Keith Park, arrived at the end of February 1945.

RAF photo-reconnaissance aircraft completed the mapping of a huge part of Burma in preparation for the coming campaign. The Japanese evacuated Akyab in January 1945, enabling the 14th Army to mount an amphibian assault on the mainland. Allied troops broke through in the north and Lashio was occupied by Chinese troops on 6 March. Mandalay fell to the 14th Army a fortnight later, after fighter-bombers had destroyed its defences. The way was now clear to advance down the central plain, with over 350,000 troops being supplied from the air. Everywhere, bombers attacked enemy supply dumps and communications. The advance was remorseless, with the Japanese being destroyed or falling back. On 3 May the 14th Army entered Rangoon.

The Chinese and Americans were able to quit this theatre of war and leave the 14th Army to finish off the remaining Japanese, consisting of only about 17,500 in the district of Pegu. These tried to cross the Sittang River into Siam but were strafed by the RAF or cut down by guerrilla forces led by British undercover teams. Very few survived.

Meanwhile, Mountbatten had made plans to recapture Malaya, under a combined operation codenamed 'Zipper'. Most British servicemen expected a long and bloody fight ahead even after this conquest, when they would join the Americans in the Pacific, moving from island to island and nearing Japan itself. It was anticipated that the invasion of the Japanese homeland would result in at least a million Allied casualties, in addition to a far larger number of enemy deaths. But then, to the astonishment of most of the world, the atomic bombs were dropped on Hiroshima and Nagasaki, and Japan surrendered unconditionally on 14 August 1945. VJ-Day had at last arrived.

Seven columns of Chindits, led by Brigadier Orde C. Wingate, left Imphal in February 1943 to carry out operations 170 miles behind Japanese lines in northern Burma. They were supplied throughout by Dakotas of 31 and 194 Squadrons. In response to an SOS from one of the columns, two aircraft took off on 25 April to attempt a rescue. They were unable to land and pick up the sick and wounded but dropped supplies and ammunition.

Author's collection

Dakotas returned a few days later, dropping more supplies which were picked up by files of men. The Chindits had hacked a landing strip out of the jungle and arranged other parachutes into a notice reading PLANE LAND HERE NOW.

Author's collection

One of the Dakotas landed on the strip and picked up seventeen sick and wounded men. In this photograph, an RAF despatcher is handing a can of water to a Chindit suffering from dysentery and an infected hip, and holding on to the static line used for parachute hooks. The Chindit operations came to an end in June 1943 with the advent of the summer monsoon, after the columns had marched for over 1,000 miles and lost a third of their number.

Author's collection

The Japanese merchant ship *Asakasan Maru* of 8,709 tons being bombed from low level off Moulmein in Burma by B-24 Liberators of the USAAF on 27 February 1943. The crew can be seen taking to the lifeboats before the ship sank.

Author's collection

Stationary trucks on the railway line between Mandalay on the Irrawaddy River and Monya on the Chindwin River, under attack on 18 July 1943 with cannon and machine-gun fire by Beaufighter VIs of 27 Squadron based at Agartala in India.

Author's collection

An oil barge off Steamer Point on the Irrawaddy, south-west of Pakoku, under cannon and machine-gun fire from a Beaufighter.

Author's collection

An oil pumping station on the pipeline at Thegon, north-west of Moulmein, set on fire by Beaufighters.

Author's collection

In the second Arakan campaign, which began in early November 1943, the 81st West African Division advanced down the Kaladan valley while the 5th and 7th Indian Divisions fought their way down the Mayu Peninsula. The West Africans were supplied from the air, mainly by Dakotas of 62 Squadron, as shown in this photograph of containers descending by parachute near the Kaladan River.

Author's collection

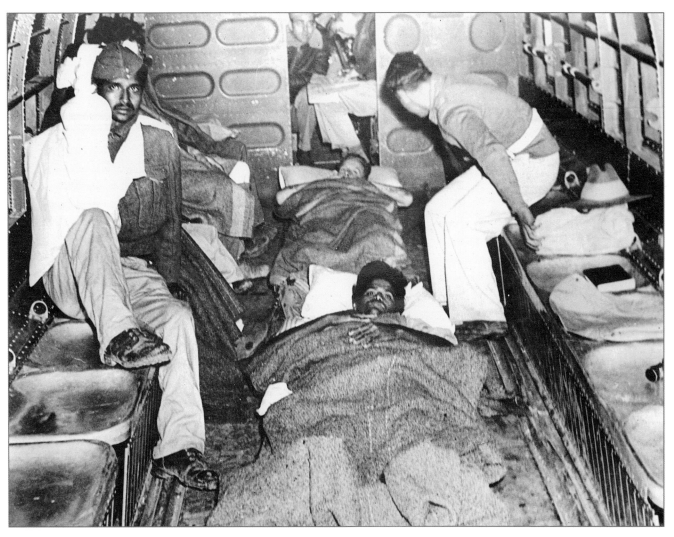

When the 7th Indian Division was surrounded by the Japanese at Sinzweya, in a position known as the 'Admin Box', supplies were brought in from 8 February 1944 by Commandos and Dakotas of the India/China Wing of the US Air Transport Command. The wounded were taken out by air, as shown in this photograph. The Japanese were subjected to dive-bombing and by the beginning of April had been defeated.

Author's collection

Hurricanes were used extensively in the Burma theatre of war as fighter-bombers. This photograph, taken in the late summer of 1944, shows two bombs falling from the wings of a Hurricane during an attack on a bridge over the Tiddim road, with smoke from other bombs rising from the target.

Author's collection

'MONSOON MOSQUITOS' by Charles J. Thompson
Mosquito PRXVIs of 684 Squadron, based at Alipore in north-east India, flying over the Hooghly River during the monsoon of 1944. The squadron was engaged on long-range photo-reconnaissance missions over Burma, Siam and Malaya.

Opposite:
'OVER THE HUMP' by Charles J. Thompson
This air route over the Himalayas from India to China was opened by the USAAF in the summer of 1942 and became an American operation known as the 'Hump Run', as shown in this painting of a Curtiss C-46 Commando. However, from December 1943 RAF Dakotas also operated a regular service from Dum-Dum in Bengal to Kunming in China. Much of the terrain was unmapped, with snow-capped mountain peaks rising to 20,000 ft and dense jungle in the valleys below. There were vicious down-currents and tremendous cross-winds, with no possible landing places.

The Republic P-47 Thunderbolt was employed by the RAF solely in the Burma theatre of war, where it began to replace the Hurricane fighter-bomber in May 1944. Armed with eight .50 inch machine-guns and carrying three 50 lb bombs, it was fitted with long-range tanks to attack Japanese troops and supply lines.

Author's collection

Beaufighters made bombing attacks in early 1944 on the oil pipeline running south from Yenangyaung to Rangoon and succeeded in setting ablaze a suspension bridge carrying the pipeline near Kanhla.

Author's collection

This road from the railhead at Ledo in India, which wound up the passes of the 5,000 ft Patkai range and then over the upper Chindwin River, was built over a period of two years by the Americans. By November 1944 it connected with the pre-war Burma Road to China. This photograph shows the first convoy to China, setting off on a journey of 1,040 miles to Kunming.

Author's collection

Bombs dropped in March 1945 by RAF Liberators of 231 Group destroyed a railway bridge at Kalawthut, 22 miles south of Moulmein in Burma, as shown in this photograph taken from 500 ft. The southern part of this railway from Bangkok to Rangoon was built by British prisoners-of-war under appalling conditions of forced labour and starvation.

Author's collection

On 19 March 1945 Liberator VIs of the RAF's 231 Group in the Strategic Air Force, South East Asia Command, made sorties of over seventeen hours from India to attack railway sidings at Na Nien, 8 miles west of Chumphuan in the Gulf of Siam. They went in at low level, setting trains and oil tanks on fire. PoWs were seen waving to them as they passed over the Kra Isthmus.

Author's collection

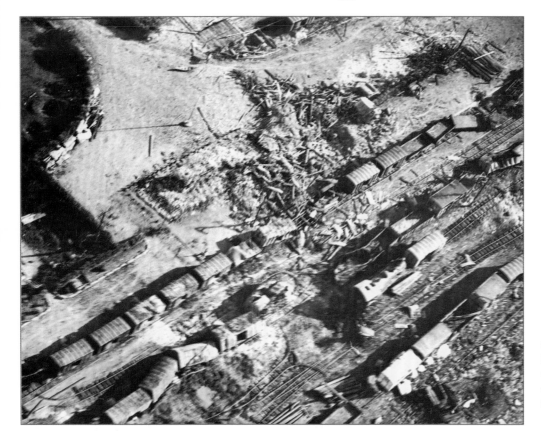

Some of the damage from the RAF's attack on Na Nien, showing wrecked coaches and trucks, with torn railway lines and gutted administration buildings.

Author's collection

On 18 April 1945 RAF Liberators of 231 Group attacked canals west of Bangkok which were being used by the Japanese after railway bridges in the area had been destroyed. Wrecked lock gates and sunken shipping can be seen in this photograph.

Author's collection

Men of the RAF Regiment on patrol in search of Japanese stragglers during the Allied advances in central Burma in May 1945.

Author's collection

A Japanese officer in front of a Tachikawa Ki-36 army co-operation aircraft at RAF Mingaladon, near Rangoon, photographed by the author after VJ-Day.

Author's collection

CHAPTER TEN

THE IRON CURTAIN

At the end of the war with Japan, the RAF was presented with the task of demobilizing most of its force of over a million personnel and cutting down its equipment, which consisted of about 9,200 aircraft in 460 squadrons, together with about 1,200 airfields. Within this organization, the 2nd Tactical Air Force, which had followed the Allied advances into Germany after the D-Day landings, remained in Europe and had been renamed the British Air Force of Occupation (BAFO) in July 1945. Germany was divided into four zones controlled by the USA, Britain, France and the Soviet Union, with the Oder–Neisse Line separating the Eastern Bloc from the three Western Powers. However, within the Soviet zone, Berlin was divided into four sectors controlled by the four Powers.

Much of the process of reducing the RAF was carried out rapidly and efficiently. The Empire Air Training Scheme, which had contributed so much in Canada, Southern Rhodesia and South Africa during the war, was wound down and dismantled. However, there were problems in the Far East and India, where some of the RAF men went 'on strike'. They felt that the men at home were being demobilized first and securing the best jobs, while the personnel in the Army and Navy overseas were being given priority in the scarce shipping and aircraft available for the return journeys. There was some justification in these grievances, for the RAF needed to maintain operational efficiency in distant parts of the world where trouble was brewing, but the strikes were classed strictly as mutinies. Disciplinary action was taken and each strike lasted only a few days.

Some of the photo-reconnaissance Mosquitos were employed on survey work in Britain, Europe and Commonwealth countries, assisting the Ordnance Survey in updating maps or providing information where little existed before. But in general this was an extremely difficult time for the RAF, since the country had been impoverished by the war and there were few resources available for defence. Air Chief Marshal Sir Arthur Tedder took over as Chief of Air Staff on 1 January 1946. By the end of 1947 the RAF had reduced its strength to fewer than 300,000 personnel, with about 1,350 aircraft in 141 squadrons. Only ten squadrons remained in BAFO, facing the might of the Soviet Union. These operated in collaboration with the squadrons of the United States Air Force (USAF), as the USAAF had been renamed when it became an independent body on 18 September 1947.

The RAF aircraft 'reduced to produce' went into industries where metal was urgently required for peacetime production. Unfortunately this procedure was short-sighted in one respect. Some well-known types of RAF aircraft and their equipment went into complete oblivion, so that examples which would be extremely valuable nowadays do not exist either in museums or in private hands.

External pressures began to force a change of policy towards the RAF. Winston Churchill, who had lost the General Election held in July 1945, declared in a speech delivered at Fulton in the USA on 5 March 1946: 'From Stettin on the Baltic to Trieste on the Adriatic an Iron Curtain has descended across the Continent.' Some regarded this as scare-mongering, but intelligence sources indicated that the Soviet Union would soon develop the atomic bomb. Meanwhile, the Russians were not reducing their armed forces but were maintaining them on a war footing. Britain had to decide whether to develop her own nuclear capability or rely on the Americans for defence.

In the course of 1947 the Government opted for the former policy. It was decided to fund atomic research and build up the RAF to about 1,500 modern machines. The emphasis had to be on quality of aircraft rather than quantity, for the RAF was still equipped mainly with piston-engined machines. Although Frank Whittle and other British scientists had been in the forefront of jet engine development in the 1930s and early 1940s, production of suitable aircraft was lagging well behind that of the USA and possibly the USSR. The RAF had introduced its first jet fighter, the Gloster Meteor, in July 1944, and followed this with the de Havilland Vampire in April 1946. However, further

Gp Capt. Frank Whittle, who worked on jet-propulsion before the war and developed it from 1938 with Power Jets Ltd of Derby, with Rolls-Royce taking an interest in the results. In June 1941 the Ministry of Aircraft Production ordered Rolls-Royce to begin manufacturing the engine, known as the WR1, in conjunction with Power Jets and the Rover Company. Frank Whittle was promoted to Air Commodore and knighted.

Author's collection

The Gloster experimental aircraft E.29/39 serial W4041/G, which first took off from Cranwell on 15 May 1941, was powered by the turbojet engine designed by Frank Whittle. This was the first flight made by any British jet aircraft and led to the development of the Meteor I fighter.

Author's collection

advances with fighters had to be made for the defence of West Germany and the UK, while jet bombers capable of carrying nuclear bombs had to be designed. There were no aircraft specifically designed as advanced jet trainers, although there were trainer variants of operational jet fighters. Coastal Command was not provided with jet aircraft at this stage. This branch of the RAF had to be content with modified versions of wartime machines for several years, although long-range Lockheed Neptunes were borrowed from the USA in 1952. Another development coming to the fore was the helicopter, required by Coastal Command for its important function of air-sea rescue.

In December 1947 a four-power conference on the future of Germany broke down without agreement. The Cold War, as it was known, dated from February 1948 when the Soviets engineered a Communist *coup* in Czechoslovakia. Then, on 24 June 1948, the Soviets imposed a surface blockade on Berlin, where the West Berliners were dependent on the Western Powers for sustenance. The response of the British and Americans was to begin a massive airlift to the city, through the three air corridors they were entitled to use. Within a week, the whole of RAF Transport Command's fleet of Dakotas and Yorks was moved to Wunstorf, near Hanover, and began flying supplies through the northern corridor to Gatow in the British sector of Berlin. At the same time, the USAF employed its larger fleet of Dakotas and Skymasters from Wiesbaden and Rhein/Main through the southern corridor to Tempelhof in the American sector of Berlin. The third corridor, in the centre, was reserved by both the RAF and the USAF for their returning transports.

The American Skymasters could carry about 10 tons, the Yorks about 8½ tons, and the Dakotas about 3½ tons. Fortunately, more Skymasters were available to replace the Dakotas in the American part of the airlift. Meanwhile, the RAF Dakotas moved to Lübeck, relieving congestion at Wunstorf. By September 1948 the combined fleets were able to transport over 4,500 tons a day. In terms of weight, the main cargo was coal, which needed to be stocked up before winter set in. Foodstuffs were also vital requirements, and these were dehydrated where possible to reduce space and weight.

The RAF brought in their new Hastings transports in December 1948, and even used Sunderlands which landed on Havel Lake near Berlin. RAF airfields were provided in the British sector of West Germany for the USAF, which was able to increase its carrying capacity. The airport of Tegel in the French sector of Berlin was opened in December 1948, helping to relieve congestion at the receiving end. The tonnage transported rose to over 5,500 tons a day in January 1949 and to over 8,000 tons a day four months later. By this time the Russians were made to look ineffective and somewhat ridiculous in the eyes of the world. They lifted their blockade on 12 May 1949, but the RAF and USAF continued their operations for four more months, as a safety precaution.

This close collaboration between the RAF and the USAF was one of the factors which led to the creation of the North Atlantic Treaty Organization (NATO) on 24 August 1949, of which the founder members were the USA, Canada, Britain and nine other European countries. These formed a military alliance against any potential extension of Communist hegemony in Europe or elsewhere. In the following month, the Federal Republic of Germany was formed, marking the end of the control by the USA, Britain and France over West Germany. This was also the year in which it became known that the Soviet Union had developed its own nuclear weapon.

The conversion of the RAF to a more modern force continued, although new

recruits were required to serve in Bomber, Fighter, Coastal, Training and Maintenance Commands, at a time when there was almost full employment in a country which was busy building up its peacetime economy. Some wartime servicemen rejoined the RAF, but there was a shortage of skilled personnel in some branches and trades. The wartime WAAF had also been run down to a fraction of its former number, but in 1948 a new Short Service Scheme was introduced for both women officers and airwomen. It was renamed the Women's Royal Air Force (WRAF) on 1 February 1949.

On 1 January 1950 Air Chief Marshal Sir John Slessor took over as Chief of Air Staff. Thereafter, this post has been filled by Air Chief Marshals on a fairly regular three-yearly basis. In 1950 there were sixteen RAF squadrons in forward bases in Germany facing the Iron Curtain, equipped with Vampires and Meteors, under the control of NATO. In September of the following year, BAFO resumed its previous name of 2nd Tactical Air Force and was in course of expansion, with Venoms replacing the Vampires and Sabres arriving from the USA. In 1952 there were two Tactical Air Forces in central Europe, with the RAF forming the major part of the 2nd Allied Tactical Air Force in the north while the USAF assumed the leading role in the 4th Allied Tactical Air Force in the south.

Meanwhile, Britain continued to develop her own atomic bomb and chose the uninhabited Hermite Island, part of the Monte Bello Islands off the coast

The Gloster Meteor was the first jet aircraft to enter RAF service, when 616 Squadron began to receive these single-seat fighters at Culmhead in Somerset during July 1944. They were armed with four 20 mm guns and saw action over Europe in the closing months of the war. Other Marks followed and fighter variants of the Gloster Meteor continued in service to April 1957. The Meteor IIIs in this photograph were on the strength of 74 Squadron in August 1945 when based at Horsham St Faith in Norfolk.

Philip Jarrett collection

The single-seat de Havilland Vampire was the second jet fighter to serve with the RAF, entering squadron service in April 1946. Vampires served at home and abroad with distinction. A fighter-bomber variant appeared in 1949, capable of carrying rockets or 2,000 lb of bombs in addition to the normal four 20 mm guns. A night-fighter variant entered service in July 1951. Another variant was the T11 two-seat advanced trainer, which was introduced in early 1956 and continued until 1969, long after the fighter and fighter-bomber versions had been withdrawn. This Vampire FB5 serial VV560 was on the strength of 16 Squadron in 1950, when based in Germany.

R.G. Gregory via A.S. Thomas

of Western Australia, for the first bomb, which was exploded in a Royal Navy frigate on 3 October 1952. It was followed by explosions on 14 and 16 October 1953 from towers erected on the Emu Field of South Australia. The next did not take place until 16 May 1956, once again on the Monte Bello Islands, and it was followed by another on 16 June. So far, all the bombs had been exploded from ground level or from towers. A series of tests followed in the area of Maralinga, north of the Nullarbor Plain in South Australia. Bombs were exploded on 27 September and 4 October 1956, but another on 11 October was dropped from the new Vickers Valiant B1 V-bomber, detached from Wittering in Northamptonshire. Four more A-bombs were exploded in this area, the last being on 9 October 1957, but these were not dropped by aircraft.

This arms race was becoming more deadly. The USA had exploded the first hydrogen bomb in October 1952 and the Russians in August 1953. The Warsaw Pact had been signed in May 1955, a military alliance of Communist countries in Europe under the leadership of the Soviet Union, in opposition to the forces of NATO. Britain duly developed her own H-bomb. The first was dropped by a Valiant over Malden Island, south-east of Christmas Island, on 15 May 1957. Three more were dropped in the course of the year, and five more were exploded off Christmas Island itself in 1958. The RAF's nuclear force had become one that could rival the Soviet Air Force.

The second of the V-bombers, the Avro Vulcan, entered service in 1956 but did not become operational until the following year. The third and last of the V-bombers, the Handley Page Victor, entered squadron service in 1958. Britain's nuclear capacity was increased with the acquisition of sixty Douglas Thor surface-to-surface missiles, which were deployed around RAF bases in East Anglia and Yorkshire.

The Americans began to reconnoitre the Soviet Union on 4 July 1956 with the Lockheed U-2A, a single-engined spy plane that could fly even higher than the Canberra and carried a panoramic strip camera which could photograph a wide swathe of territory with high definition. However, the launch of the Soviet 'Sputnik 1' satellite in October 1957 came as a considerable shock to the Western Powers, for reconnaissance of their own territories could be obtained from such a source. This Russian success preceded the American satellites which were launched shortly afterwards. However, the U-2 operations continued, but ceased on 1 May 1960 when one of the spy planes was shot down by a ground-to-air missile at 68,000 ft over Sverdlovsk in the Ural Mountains. The pilot, Francis Gary Powers, baled out and was captured, but he was exchanged later for a Russian spy.

Such Soviet ground-to-air missiles gave warning that the RAF's nuclear bombers faced the strong possibility of being shot down before they could reach their targets. In February 1963 the V-bombers were equipped with the Blue Steel air-to-surface missile, made by Hawker Siddeley Dynamics. This was fitted with a thermo-nuclear warhead and could be released up to 200 miles from the target. In this year the RAF's V-bombers came under the command of NATO for nuclear strikes. However, the policy began to change when the Polaris nuclear missile, launched from British submarines, was introduced. The RAF began to disband its nuclear force in 1964, although some of the bombers were retained as conventional bombers, converted to the tanker role or employed as strategic reconnaissance aircraft. At the same time, the anti-submarine role of the RAF became more vital. The Hawker Siddeley Nimrod, developed from the Comet jet airliner, was introduced into service during 1969 in this capacity. It was equipped with homing torpedoes and special radar equipment, and backed the long-serving Avro Shackletons with maritime reconnaissance.

Meanwhile, the cost of pilot training in the RAF in fast jets was increasing steadily. This pattern of training consisted of passing through Flying Training School, Advanced Flying School and Operational Conversion Unit, before posting to a squadron. One method of achieving economies was to close down the flying elements of the Royal Auxiliary Air Force and the Royal Air Force Volunteer Reserve. These measures occurred in 1957 following a Defence Review, although some specialist personnel in the RAFVR and the RAuxAF continued to provide the RAF with their services.

A major administrative change took place in April 1964, when the Admiralty, War Office and Air Ministry were absorbed into a reconstituted Ministry of Defence. From this time, the Chief of Defence Staff was appointed from each of the three services in turn on a three-yearly basis, whenever possible. The RAF continued to appoint its own Chief of Air Staff, also for a normal term of three years.

In April 1968 the administration of the RAF contracted further when Fighter Command merged with Bomber Command to form the new Strike Command. Coastal Command was absorbed into this new Command in November 1969. Transport Command, which had been renamed Air Support Command in August 1967, was absorbed by Strike Command in September 1972. However, a new Support Command was formed in September 1973. In June 1977 this was merged with Training Command to form RAF Support Command, the main functions being maintenance, communications, and both flying and ground training.

'RAIN AT DAWN' by Mark Postlethwaite
On 7 July 1948 the thousandth aircraft to land at RAF Gatow in Berlin was Dakota IV, serial KN439, of 30 Squadron, based at Oakington with a detachment at Wunstorf. It was flown by Flt Lt J.F. Manning, with Flt Lt Hood as navigator and Signaller I.L. Barlow as wireless operator.

The Avro York was a long-range transport, carrying a crew of five and twenty-four passengers, which entered RAF service in May 1943. Freighter and passenger-freighter versions were produced later in the year. Six RAF squadrons equipped with Yorks took part in the Berlin Airlift, carrying about 230,000 tons of supplies to the city.

Author's collection

The Handley Page Hastings was introduced into RAF Transport Command in September 1948. There were five in the crew and the machine was designed to carry up to fifty troops on long-range work, but freight could be carried as an alternative. It was a reliable aircraft and gave long years of service. Although withdrawn from squadrons in 1967, some machines continued with the Strike Command Bombing School until June 1977. These Hastings C1s of 47 Squadron, with serial TG524 in the foreground, were photographed on 30 November 1948 while en route to Schleswigland in Germany to take part in the Berlin Airlift.

The late F.M. Taylor via A.S. Thomas

The Boeing Washington was the name given to the Boeing B-29 Superfortress when it entered RAF squadron service as a stop-gap in March 1950, soon after the beginning of the Cold War. A long-range bomber with a crew of ten, it was armed with twelve .50 inch machine-guns and could carry up to 17,500 lb of bombs. Most were flown back to the USA by March 1954, when they were superseded by Canberras. This Washington B1, serial WF491, of 149 Squadron was photographed in early 1952 while on a Bomber Command exercise.

G. Brown via A.S. Thomas

One of the RAF's well-loved aircraft was the Avro Shackleton, which entered squadron service in April 1951 to replace Coastal Command's long-range maritime reconnaissance machines such as the Liberator and the Fortress. The earliest variant carried a crew of ten and was armed with twin 20 mm guns in the nose as well as two more in a dorsal turret. The bomb load, usually consisting of depth charges, could amount to 20,000 lb. This photograph is of a Shackleton MR2 of 42 Squadron, which received this Mark from January 1953. Shackleton MR2s continued in front-line service until April 1972, by which time some had been converted into the airborne early warning variant.

I.M. Coleman

The two-seat Armstrong Whitworth Meteor was the RAF's first jet night-fighter, entering squadron service in August 1951. It was armed with four 20 mm guns in the wings but these were omitted in a two-seat trainer version which also appeared. The Gloster Javelin began to replace the Meteor night-fighter in 1956 but some remained in squadron service up to August 1961, while others continued until 1968 as target tugs. This Meteor NF11, serial WM293, of 68 Squadron in Germany was flown by the commanding officer in 1957.

G. Swanborough via A.S. Thomas

The Lockheed Neptune, a maritime reconnaissance and anti-shipping bomber with a crew of seven, entered service with Coastal Command in 1952. It was armed with six machine-guns and could carry 8,000 lb of bombs, with provision for rocket projectiles. It was also fitted with Magnetic Anomaly Detector (MAD) equipment in the tail, as well as searchlights and radar. All Neptunes were returned to the USA when replaced with Avro Shackletons. This example, serial WX543, of 33 Squadron, based at Topcliffe in Yorkshire, was photographed over Bermuda in 1956.

A.S. Thomas collection

The single-seat de Havilland Venom fighter-bomber began to replace the Vampire in August 1952. It was fitted with four 20 mm guns in the wings and could carry rockets or 2,000 lb of bombs. A two-seat night-fighter version also appeared, in June 1955. Vampires continued in squadron service until November 1957, when they were replaced by Javelins. This Venom NF3 of 151 Squadron was photographed in 1955 when starting up at Leuchars in Fifeshire.

I.G. Stott via A.S. Thomas

'THE MEATBOX' by Charles J. Thompson
The Meteor IV had uprated engines and entered RAF squadron service in November 1947, after having achieved new world airspeed records in November 1945 and September 1946. This Meteor IV, serial VZ413, was on the strength of 56 Squadron at Waterbeach in Cambridgeshire during 1950. The RAF nickname for the variants of the long-serving Meteor was 'Meatbox'.

The RAF introduced the North American Sabre in May 1953 as a stop-gap pending the arrival of the Hawker Hunter. A single-seat jet fighter armed with six .5 inch machine-guns and a maximum speed of 670 mph, it filled a vital need, equipping eleven squadrons at home and in Germany at a critical time during the Cold War. All Sabres were withdrawn by May 1956. These Sabre F4s of 130 Squadron based at RAF Brüggen were photographed in September 1954.

R. Lindsay via A.S. Thomas

'CANBERRA B2' by Charles J. Thompson

One of the most successful aircraft in the RAF's postwar era was the English Electric Canberra, the country's first jet bomber. The first to enter RAF service was the Canberra B2, in May 1951. It was an unarmed light bomber with a crew of three, capable of carrying a bomb load of up to 6,000 lb. The maximum speed was 570 mph and the service ceiling 48,000 ft. The Canberra has appeared in various guises during its long career, including photo-reconnaissance variants. This Canberra B2 was on the strength of 109 Squadron in 1952 while based at Hemswell in Lincolnshire.

The Supermarine Swift, a single-seat jet fighter with swept wings and two 30 mm guns, first entered service in February 1954. There were four Marks, F1 to F4, with various improvements in the later versions. Only 56 Squadron was equipped with these Swifts, which established several records but suffered a high accident rate. They were followed by the fighter-reconnaissance Swift FR5, such as serial XD904 in this photograph, with which two RAF squadrons in Germany were equipped from February 1956. With a lengthened nose to accommodate three cameras, the Swift FR5 was employed on low-level tactical photography until March 1961.

Aeroplane Monthly

The Hawker Hunter began to replace the Sabre in July 1954 as the RAF's standard single-seat day fighter. With its swept wings, it was capable of Mach 0.95 at high level. It was fitted with four 30 mm guns in a removable pack and could carry rockets or up to 2,000 lb of bombs. Nine variants of this highly successful machine were built for RAF service, including a two-seat trainer. The last trainers continued in service until June 1976. These Hunter F6s of 14 Squadron were on patrol over Germany in 1959.

F. Davies via A.S. Thomas

The Vickers Valiant was the first of the RAF's nuclear 'V' bombers, entering squadron service in February 1955. Powered by four jet engines and unarmed, it could fly at 54,000 ft, carry a bomb load of up to 21,000 lb and had a maximum range of 4,500 miles. Valiants carried Britain's nuclear weapons, the atomic bomb which was first dropped over Australia on 11 October 1956, and the hydrogen bomb which was first dropped over Christmas Island on 15 May 1957. A reconnaissance version of the Valiant was also produced, the B(PR)1 which entered service in July 1955. All the machines were withdrawn from service in May 1965. This Valiant B(PR)1, serial WZ391, of 543 Squadron was photographed in 1960 when accompanied by a Canberra.

A.S. Thomas collection

The two-seat Gloster Javelin first entered squadron service in February 1956, providing the RAF with an all-weather fighter fitted with four 30 mm guns in the wings and the capacity of carrying rockets or four air-to-air missiles. There were nine variants of this successful machine, each improving on its predecessor, and the last was withdrawn in April 1968. There was also a trainer version, the Javelin T3. This Javelin FAW5, serial XA667, of 228 Operational Conversion Unit was photographed in March 1961 while taking off from RAF Leeming in Yorkshire.

R. Lindsay via A.S. Thomas

The last of the trio of 'V' bombers was the Handley Page Victor, which entered RAF service in November 1957. With a crew of five and no defensive armament, it had a service ceiling of 55,000 ft and was capable of carrying nuclear or conventional bombs up to 35,000 lb. The first Victor B1 was withdrawn in 1966 but meanwhile the more powerful B2 had been introduced. The B2 served from 1961 to 1974 in the bomber and strategic reconnaissance role, but K1 and K2 tanker versions of the Victor served from 1965 until 1993. In the Falklands War, some of these tankers reverted to the reconnaissance role. This Victor K2 from Marham in Norfolk was photographed in August 1977 while refuelling a Phantom.

British Crown Copyright/MOD/RAF Marham

The Beagle Basset was a light communications aircraft which entered RAF service in mid-1965. It was capable of carrying up to six passengers, the original purpose being to transport V-bomber crews. However, it suffered from performance and technical problems and was withdrawn in May 1974. This Basset CC1, serial XS771, of 26 Squadron, based at Wyton in Cambridgeshire, was photographed in 1972.

A.S. Thomas collection

The Avro Vulcan was the second of the RAF's 'V' Class bombers and the first RAF bomber with the delta-wing configuration. With a crew of five it was unarmed, but had a nuclear or conventional bomb-carrying capacity of up to 21,000 lb, and it first entered squadron service in July 1957. It was soon followed by several improvements such as electronic counter-measures and in-flight refuelling. The Vulcan B2, such as serial XM645 in this photograph, was introduced in October 1960. This was powered by four 17,000 lb thrust engines in replacement for the 11,000 lb thrust engines of the Vulcan B1. The last Vulcans flew as air-to-air refuelling tankers and were retired at the end of 1984.

G.R. Pitchfork collection

The Hawker Siddeley Nimrod MR1, evolved from the Comet airliner, entered RAF service in October 1969 as a marine reconnaissance and anti-submarine aircraft. Thereafter, the electronic equipment was updated to include 'Searchwater' radar and the aircraft became the MR2, as in this photograph of serial XV238 of 42 (Torpedo-Bomber) Squadron. The aircraft can carry nine homing torpedoes in its bomb bay. During the Falklands War some Nimrods were also fitted with Sidewinder missiles.

I.M. Coleman collection

The single-seat English Electric Lightning was the first fighter in the RAF to exceed the speed of sound in level flight. It entered squadron service in June 1960 and in fact the maximum speed of the Lightning F1A was Mach 2.1. It was armed with two 30 mm guns in the nose and could carry two air-to-air missiles. Six variants were built, as well as a two-seat trainer version, and the last of the type continued until April 1988. This Lightning F6, serial XR758, of 11 Squadron was photographed off Cyprus in June 1987.

A.S. Thomas collection

The Soviet 'space event' ship *Kosmonaut Yuri Gagarin* of 53,000 tons displacement, photographed by an RAF Nimrod in 1980. This vessel was completed in 1971 for controlling space vehicles and investigating conditions in the upper atmosphere.

British Crown Copyright/MOD/42 (Reserve) Squadron Archives

The Percival Proctor, such as serial P6062 in this photograph, was a four-seater adapted from the civil Vega Gull. It entered RAF service shortly after the outbreak of the Second World War and was used as a trainer for wireless operators or as a communications aircraft. A few continued in service after the war in the latter capacity.

Philip Jarrett collection

The Percival Prentice entered RAF service as a basic trainer in November 1947, replacing the Tiger Moth and the Miles Magister. Unlike its predecessors, it had an enclosed cabin and was fitted with flaps, a variable-pitch propeller and a radio, while the instructor and pupil sat side by side. The Prentice continued for about five years, until replaced by the Hunting Percival Provost. The example here is Prentice T1 serial VR230 of No. 3 Flying Training School at Feltwell in Norfolk.

Philip Jarrett collection

The Boulton Paul Balliol was a two-seat advanced trainer introduced in 1949 as a replacement for the Harvard. Only two schools were equipped with the Balliol and it continued as a trainer until 1956, by which time it was replaced by the Vampire T11 jet trainer which first came into service in 1952 with other Advanced Flying Schools. This Balliol T2, serial WN161, of the Transport Command Communications Flight was photographed on 25 May 1956 at Aston Down in Gloucestershire.

A.S. Thomas collection

The Vickers Varsity was introduced in October 1951 as an advanced crew trainer for pilots, navigators and bomb aimers. It enabled pilots to convert on to a heavier piston-engined aircraft while its long range, over 2,500 miles, gave excellent facilities for pupil navigators. It continued in service until May 1976. The Varsity T1 in this photograph is serial WF378, one of the earliest production batch.

Philip Jarrett collection

'CHIPMUNK' by Charles J. Thompson

From February 1950 the de Havilland Chipmunk began to enter service as the RAF's elementary trainer. It was designed in Canada, with seats in tandem for instructor and pupil. Although some were superseded by Provosts in November 1954, others were introduced and some continued until the mid-1990s. This Chipmunk, serial WP829, was flown by trainees of the University Air Squadron at Southampton in Hampshire during the 1950s.

The Hunting Percival Provost began to replace the Prentice in October 1953. Like its predecessor, it was a trainer with two seats side-by-side but in this machine the pupil pilot could move on from basic to more advanced training. This piston-engined Provost was replaced with the Jet Provost from August 1955. The Provost T1 serial WV614 in this photograph was fitted with two .303 inch machine-guns and carried two 250 lb bombs beneath the wings.

Philip Jarrett collection

'TARGET TUG' by Charles J. Thompson
The final development of the Bristol Beaufighter was the TTX target-towing variant. A number of torpedo-carrying Beaufighter TFXs were converted to this role after they had been withdrawn from operational duties. This Beaufighter TTX, serial RD802, was on the strength of 34 (Anti-Aircraft Co-operation) Squadron, based at Horsham St Faith in 1950.

The Handley Page Marathon was converted from a civil airliner to a navigation trainer, carrying a crew of three and two pupil navigators. It entered service in December 1953 and continued until June 1968. Twenty-eight of these four-engined machines, such as Marathon T11 serial XA274 in this photograph, were supplied to Air Navigation Schools.

Philip Jarrett collection

The Hawker Siddeley Gnat was developed for advanced training in jet aircraft. It first entered RAF service in February 1962 and became the standard advanced trainer until replaced by the British Aerospace Hawk in November 1978. There were two seats in tandem for pupil and instructor, and the aircraft was supersonic in a dive. This Gnat T1 of No. 4 Flying Training School was based at RAF Valley in Anglesey.

J.D.R. Rawlings via A.S. Thomas

The British Aircraft Corporation Jet Provost T3 first entered service in June 1959. It was a two-seat basic trainer similar to its predecessor, the Hunting Percival Jet Provost T1, but the engine was more powerful and there were other improve-ments such as wingtip tanks and ejector seats. The Provost T3 was followed by the T4 and then the T5, each incorporating various improvements. RAF aerobatic teams were also equipped with these machines. They continued to give good service until the Shorts Tucano began to replace them in January 1987. This Jet Provost T5, serial XW352, was photographed in August 1983 while on the strength of No. 6 Flying Training School at Finningley in Yorkshire.

British Crown Copyright/MOD/
RAF Finningley

The Scottish Aviation Jetstream, designed as an airliner, was developed by the RAF as a multi-engined trainer for pilots from June 1973. It is powered by two turbo-prop engines. Although all aircraft soon went into storage during a period of defence cuts, some reappeared in 1977 and are still in service for advanced pilot training. This Jetstream serial XX498 of No. 6 Flying Training School, based at Finningley in Yorkshire, was photographed in August 1983.

British Crown Copyright/MOD/
RAF Finningley

CHAPTER ELEVEN

WITHDRAWAL FROM EMPIRE

The RAF was presented with a stream of commitments outside Europe in the years following the Second World War. That enormous global conflict had left a legacy of unsettled conditions in which nationalists of countries within the British Empire felt that they could demand complete autonomy. While there is no doubt that the majority of British people were prepared to see these countries form their own governments, the main concern was whether the handovers would conform with the democratic will of the inhabitants and not be subject to Communist dictatorship. In some cases the withdrawals took place fairly peacefully but in others the nationalist causes were marred by terrorism or vicious civil war. The RAF was involved with them for over a quarter of a century, together with the Royal Navy and the British Army.

Of course, the RAF squadrons abroad suffered from the same drastic cutbacks as those in Britain and Germany at the end of the war. In the Mediterranean area, the withdrawal of the USAAF necessitated a change of command. The Mediterranean Allied Air Forces, with headquarters at Caserta in Italy, was disbanded in August 1945 and replaced by RAF Mediterranean and Middle East, with headquarters in Cairo.

One of the most unpleasant duties concerned Palestine, which had been mandated to Britain by the League of Nations at the end of the First World War. The cold-blooded murder of millions of Jews during the Nazi holocaust had created a desire among the survivors to form a new state in their ancient homeland, which their distant ancestors had left in the Diaspora of Roman times. World sympathy and international Jewry were on their side, but Britain was faced with the problem of dealing with the Arabs who formed the majority of the population. Ships containing Jewish illegal immigrants began streaming towards Palestine and the RAF was called upon to locate them with Lancasters and Warwicks converted to the maritime reconnaissance role, mostly based at Ein Shemer. Seventeen such ships were located by the RAF and turned back by the Royal Navy in the course of 1946, but Jewish terrorists began attacks on RAF bases in Palestine. Eventually, the United Nations decreed that Palestine should be partitioned between the Jews and the Arabs, and the new state of Israel was created on 30 June 1948. British servicemen were not unhappy when they left the country.

Indian nationalists had been clamouring for independence for many years, and this was finally proclaimed on 14 August 1947, but parts of that vast sub-

The first Avro Lincolns arrived for trials at East Kirkby in Lincolnshire in August 1945 but were too late for service in the Second World War. A heavy bomber armed with up to seven .50 inch machine-guns and capable of carrying 14,000 lb of bombs, the Lincoln had more powerful engines and a longer range than its famous predecessor, the Lancaster, although both carried a crew of seven. Lincolns served in Kenya and Malaya during the anti-terrorist campaigns, and then continued in the RAF until May 1963. Serial RE295 in this photograph was on the strength of 214 Squadron, which supplied a detachment at Eastleigh near Nairobi from June to December 1954, during the Mau-Mau uprisings.

P.J. Thompson collection

continent were formed into the new state of Pakistan. Both countries became republics within the British Commonwealth. Fortunately, the RAF was not involved in the bloodshed that followed the partition, although two Dakota squadrons remained in Pakistan until the following December. Relations between the RAF and the air forces of these two great countries have been on a cordial basis since they achieved independence. Burma became an independent country outside the Commonwealth on 4 January 1948, after the RAF had left the country. The independence of Ceylon within the Commonwealth was proclaimed exactly a month later, but the RAF maintained a headquarters in the country and was allowed to use the airfields as staging posts to the Far East.

Further afield, the RAF presence in Siam was whittled down in January 1946 to a few personnel in the airfield of Don Muang, near Bangkok, which was used temporarily as a staging post. Similarly, the RAF in French Indo-China pulled out in the course of early 1946, handing over to the French Air Force. However, several RAF squadrons supported a British division in Java, which was fighting with the Dutch against extremists. These operations continued until November 1946. The most serious conflict in the Far East during the years immediately following VJ-Day was known as the Malayan Emergency. During the war, the Allies had supplied arms to the Malayan Communist Party, which was conducting a guerrilla war from the jungles against the occupying Japanese. These guerrillas, who numbered about 40,000 at the end of the war, refused to hand back their weapons and in June 1948 began an attempt to wrest control of the country from the British and set up a Communist republic. Their methods were to terrorize civilians, both British and Malayan, and to attack the rubber plantations and tin mines which formed the backbone of the economy.

The British responded with combined operations. By this time, the Far East Air Command had been formed, with its main headquarters at Changi in Singapore and subordinate headquarters in Ceylon and Hong Kong. RAF manpower had been reduced from about 125,000 at the end of the war to under 9,000. Fortunately Singapore possessed excellent airfields and there were others in the Malayan peninsula which could be re-activated. As always, intelligence was vital, and this was partly supplied by Spitfires and Mosquitos which carried out air reconnaissance of the encampments and clearings in the thick jungles from which the terrorists operated. Sunderlands combined with the Royal Navy in patrolling the seas and identifying small craft which might be smuggling arms to the insurgents.

'BEVERLEYS OVER KILIMANJARO'
by Mark Postlethwaite
Two Blackburn Beverleys of 30 Squadron from
Eastleigh in Kenya flying over the snow-capped
summit of Mount Kilimanjaro in 1962. The
squadron was engaged on famine relief drops at
this time. The Beverley, capable of a payload of
almost 22 tons, was first introduced into
squadron service in March 1956. It was the
largest RAF aircraft of its day and some
continued in service until December 1968.

Attacks on terrorist positions were made by Beaufighters, Spitfires, Meteors and
Vampires, while troops were transported to airstrips by Dakotas. The terrorists
withdrew into deeper jungle and continued their activities, including attacks on
road convoys. The RAF squadrons were reinforced with Lincoln heavy bombers,
Brigand light bombers and Hornet long-range fighters. The first time the RAF used
helicopters operationally was with the formation of a Casualty Evacuation Flight in
April 1950. Dragonfly, Sycamore and Whirlwind helicopters were employed in this
campaign. Scottish Aviation Pioneers also proved their worth on liaison duties. The
RAF Regiment also played a prominent part in the actions, on defence duties and
directing air attacks from the ground.

On 25 June the Communist state of North Korea invaded South Korea across
the 38th Parallel which had been established at the end of the Second World War
as a dividing line between the areas controlled respectively by the Russians and
the Americans. Although British and Commonwealth troops, together with the
Royal Navy, were able to join the forces of South Korea and the Americans
against this aggression, the RAF was heavily engaged in Malaya as well as the
Middle East. The only contributions that could be made were detachments of
Sunderlands which were moved from Singapore to Iwakuni in Japan, from where
they were engaged on anti-submarine patrols and air reconnaissance. This war
continued until an uneasy truce was declared on 27 July 1953.

Perhaps the most effective measure adopted during the Malayan Emergency was
the movement of Chinese and Malayan villagers into encampments where they
could be protected. This was carried out by the police with the help of British and

Gurkha troops. The civilians were afforded kindness and sustenance which contrasted sharply with the brutality and extortions of the Communists, who were then denied foodstuff and means of intelligence. However, the campaign continued until the thwarted terrorists began to surrender in 1956. On 11 August 1957 the Federation of Malaya came into being as an independent country within the Commonwealth, and any sympathy for the remaining Communists disappeared. Nevertheless, some acts of violence continued until the emergency was officially proclaimed at an end on 31 July 1960, by which time the RAF had handed over its responsibilities to the emergent Royal Malayan Air Force. The counter-insurgency campaign in Malaya is often regarded as a model for this type of warfare.

The de Havilland Hornet was designed as a long-range fighter for use in the Far East but was too late to see action in the Second World War. A single-seater armed with four 20 mm guns in the nose and provision for rockets or up to 2,000 lb of bombs beneath the wings, the first examples were supplied to an RAF squadron in May 1946. Hornets became best known for their operations against Communist terrorists in Malaya from March 1951, using rockets against bands in the jungle. They continued in service until June 1955. This Hornet F3, serial PX302, was on the strength of 41 Squadron at Church Fenton in Yorkshire during 1949.

H.H. Moon via A.S. Thomas

Meanwhile, events in Africa and in the Mediterranean were engaging the attention of the RAF as well as other branches of the British armed forces. One of these took place in Kenya from 1952 when a particularly brutal section of the Kikuyu people began committing atrocities against both whites and blacks in order to gain control of lands which they believed had been unjustly taken away from them years before. A State of Emergency was declared in October 1952 and the Police Air Wing, together with a flight of armed Harvards from Southern Rhodesia, supported the King's African Rifles in an attempt to root out the terrorist gangs. They were hidden in the dense forests and defiles of the Aberdare Mountains, but from March 1954 some of their positions were located by RAF Meteors sent from Egypt and Lincolns detached from Britain. Bombing attacks by Lincolns and Vampires followed, and these proved extremely accurate. The morale of the gangs broke and they began to emerge and surrender, although some mopping-up of the remainder continued throughout 1955.

While these events were taking place, trouble also arose in the Trucial States, on the Arabian side of the Persian Gulf, where Britain continued to maintain a military presence. The Buraimi Oasis, on the border of Abu Dhabi with Muscat and Oman, was occupied by forces of Saudi Arabia in August 1952, with the intention of annexing this part of the territory. To avoid open hostility, the supply lines of the invaders were blocked by troops of the Trucial Oman Levies, while RAF Vampires and then Lancasters operated from Sharjah in identifying the camel trains. These measures did not succeed and in the following October the

The Bristol Brigand light bomber entered service in February 1949, armed with four 20 mm guns in the nose and provision for rockets under the wings or up to 2,000 lb of bombs. It carried a crew of three and served in only three squadrons, all overseas. Brigand BIs of 45 Squadron, such as these photographed over the Johore Strait, went into action against terrorists in Malaya in early 1950. They continued in this role for over two years.

C.G. Jefford via A.S. Thomas

intruders were removed by force. Saudi Arabia was furious and diplomatic relations were broken off for some time.

The remaining RAF squadrons were withdrawn from Iraq in April 1956, under fairly amicable conditions and leaving some staging posts in the country. A military alliance known as the Baghdad Pact had been signed on 4 April of the previous year, the participants being Britain, Iraq, Turkey and Pakistan. This was closely associated with the USA and formed an extension of NATO's eastern boundary with the Soviet Union.

Cyprus then assumed greater importance as an RAF base, but hostility had been growing from April 1955 with the formation of EOKA (Ethniks Organosis Kypriou Agonistou), bands of terrorists who began a campaign of bomb explosions and murder of British personnel. These groups were the military wing which supported the policy of Archbishop Makarios, whose objective was union with Greece. Makarios was arrested in March 1956 and exiled to the Seychelles.

Following the deposing of the monarchy in June 1953, Egypt had declared itself a republic outside the British Commonwealth. However, British troops remained in the Canal Zone for defensive purposes until April 1956. In the interim, Sudan also became an independent republic on 1 January 1956. By this time Egypt was ruled under conditions approaching dictatorship by Colonel Gamel Abdel Nasser, whose sympathies lay with the Soviet Union rather than the Western Powers. He was also violently opposed to Israel. When the USA refused to sell arms to his country, Nasser turned to the Russians for supplies and America promptly withdrew financial support for the construction of the Aswan High Dam on

The Vickers Valetta C1, such as serial VL280 in this photograph, was a version of the Viking airliner supplied to the RAF from May 1949 as a medium-range transport carrying a crew of three and up to thirty-four troops. It replaced the Dakota in overseas commands and proved a reliable aircraft which continued until April 1966. The Valetta T3 was also produced for training navigators and some T3s were converted into the more advanced T4.

Philip Jarrett collection

the River Nile. This measure was followed by Britain and the International Bank. On 26 July 1956 Nasser seized the assets of the Universal Suez Canal Company, which were owned by Britain and France for the benefit of all users.

Diplomatic efforts having failed, Britain and France determined to regain control of the Suez Canal by military force. To achieve this end, covert arrangements were made with Israel. On 29 October 1956 the Israelis struck at Egypt with a parachute drop over Mitla Pass in the Sinai Peninsula while other troops advanced overland. The Egyptian Air Force strafed the invaders and air battles took place with the Israeli Air Force, with losses on both sides.

This conflict gave Britain and France an opportunity to assert that their own actions were intended to bring this conflict to a halt. Meanwhile, the squadrons and airborne troops of both countries had been built up in Cyprus, while additional longer-range RAF bombers had flown to Malta. The combined air force eventually amounted to a total of 548 aircraft. Partly owing to insufficient transport aircraft, the formation of this invasion force had taken about three months.

Reconnaissance of Egyptian airfields by RAF Canberras and French RF-84 Thunderstreaks took place on 31 October 1956, and night-bombing raids by RAF Canberras and Valiants followed a few hours later. Meanwhile, the Anglo-French invasion fleet of about 130 warships and support vessels was nearing Egyptian waters, and on 1 November carrier-borne aircraft were able to join in these attacks. It was estimated that 158 of the 216 modern aircraft in the Egyptian Air Force were destroyed, while most of the remainder fled the country. Only one RAF aircraft was lost in these operations, a Venom which hit the ground accidentally.

French F-84F Thunderstreaks also operated from Israel. By 5 November almost the whole of the Sinai Peninsula was in Israeli hands. Anglo-French transport aircraft dropped paratroops on airfields near the Egyptian coast. Seaborne landings began the following morning, supported by naval bombardment and air-to-ground attacks. Two Sea Hawks, two Wyverns and two Whirlwinds of the FAA were lost in these engagements. Stiff fighting followed, but the invaders broke through and made rapid progress to the Suez Canal. However, these actions were severely criticized by the United Nations, which ordered a cease-fire for midnight on 6 November. The British, French and Israelis complied, although the last troop withdrawals did not take place until 22 December, after handing over to a United Nations Emergency Force.

This operation, codenamed 'Musketeer', signalled the end of Great Britain as a first-class military power. There were two main results for the RAF. The first was a strengthening of the British Government's desire for a nuclear bombing force independent of the USA, which had opposed the Anglo-French action over Suez. The other was the need for a rapid reaction force which could fulfil the country's remaining commitments around the world independent of Egypt and the Suez Canal, and for this longer-range transport aircraft were required. A military version of the Comet airliner had already entered RAF service, but this was followed by the Andover and the Britannia, also converted from civil use.

The Sultan of Muscat had called for assistance from the British military in 1955, to counter insurgents backed by Saudi Arabia who were attempting to take over the vast territory of Oman which was ruled from his Sultanate. In June 1956 this rebel force was reinforced by an 'Oman Liberation Army' which landed on the coast and penetrated the interior. RAF Shackletons, Meteors and Venoms were flown from Malta to Kormaksar in Aden to assist forces of the Sultan and elements of the British Army who were engaged in dislodging the invaders from the high and rocky ground they were holding. Operations were protracted in the difficult terrain but were successfully wound up by February 1959.

Meanwhile, the anti-terrorist campaign in Cyprus intensified, primarily with the use of RAF Sycamore and Whirlwind helicopters to locate hide-outs in the Troodos Mountains and land small bodies of troops. In March 1957 the EOKA terrorists offered a truce provided Makarios was released. This was agreed but the archbishop was not allowed to return to Cyprus and the violence resumed. It continued until February 1959 when an agreement was reached between Britain, Greece and Turkey, whereby Cyprus was granted sovereign status but the RAF was allowed to retain its base at Akrotiri and the British Army kept its base at Dhekelia. Cyprus became a republic within the British Commonwealth on 21 September 1960.

The RAF had been allowed to maintain forces in two air bases in Jordan, for a friendship between Britain and this kingdom had existed since 1921. However, hostility to the British presence intensified during 1956. The RAF withdrew its squadrons and other units in May 1957, helping to fly out the British elements of the Arab Legion at the same time. Incongruously, Jordan called for military assistance the following year, when violence threatened from neighbouring Lebanon, and British troops and the RAF returned for a brief period.

A coup took place in Iraq during July 1958 and the country withdrew from the Baghdad Pact. The remaining participants formed the Central Treaty Organization (CENTO) on 20 August 1959, which operated from Turkey. Iraq then cast covetous eyes on the small but independent state of Kuwait, which was developing huge oil reserves and looked to Britain for protection. The RAF sent squadrons and flew troops to Bahrein in the Persian Gulf, another country which enjoyed friendly relations with Britain, and the threat from Iraq receded.

The Westland Dragonfly was based on the American Sikorsky S-51 but manufactured in Britain. Known as the Dragonfly HC2, it entered RAF service in 1950 with the Casualty Evacuation Flight (later 194 Squadron) in Malaya. Later versions of the Dragonfly continued with the RAF until June 1956. The helicopter in this photograph is serial XD649.

The Westland Group

The next major conflict in which the RAF was involved occurred when it was proposed in 1962 to form a new Federation of Malaysia from the territories of Malaya, Singapore and British North Borneo. The latter consisted of the Crown Colonies of Sarawak, Sabah and Brunei. The Indonesian Government, which was strongly influenced by Communist ideology, fostered terrorist acts in North Borneo. In December 1962 the RAF flew British and Gurkha troops from Singapore to help the local security forces. RAF Gan in the Maldives had been opened in August 1957 as a staging post for aircraft crossing the Indian Ocean to the Far East. The local rebellions in Brunei and Sarawak were suppressed, but armed incursions from the neighbouring Indonesian territory, named Kalimantan, began in September 1963.

The RAF provided reconnaissance with Canberras, while Whirlwind, Wessex and Belvedere helicopters transported troops and supplies to flashpoints in the dense jungles and also evacuated casualties. Ground-attack Hunters were employed, and V-bombers flew to Singapore to act as a deterrent. In August 1964 a party of regular Indonesian troops landed on the Malayan Peninsula while others parachuted in. A total of 451 men arrived, in the mistaken belief that they could whip up insurrection and cause serious sabotage, but every man was either killed or captured. Singapore decided to leave the Malaysian Federation in August 1965 but continued to support the operations in North Borneo. These dragged on, the defenders gaining the upper hand with their experience and knowledge of jungle fighting, until a peace treaty was signed with Indonesia in August 1966. Britain then began the process of withdrawing from the region, the last units leaving Singapore on October 1971. Gan was closed down about five years later. Only Hong Kong remained as an RAF station in the Far East.

Aden and its Protectorates, renamed the Federation of South Arabia in February 1959, had remained fairly quiescent during the turbulent times in the Middle East, but in the early 1960s the area was affected by developments in

The first RAF helicopter designed and built in Britain was the Bristol Sycamore HR12, which entered service in February 1952. It was followed by the improved versions HR13 and HR14. With a crew of two and provision for three passengers or two stretchers, it was employed mainly on communication, air-sea rescue and casualty evacuation duties at home and overseas. This Sycamore HR14, serial XG502, was on the strength of the Joint Experimental Helicopter Unit from March 1955, then took part in the Suez crisis of 1956 and afterwards was reissued to 225 Squadron, which continued with these helicopters until March 1962. Sycamores were withdrawn from front-line service in October 1964 but some continued on communication duties until August 1972.

Museum of Army Flying

other possessions of the British Empire. British and Italian Somaliland combined to form a separate state outside the Commonwealth in July 1960. Independence within the Commonwealth was achieved by Tanganyika in December 1961, Uganda in October 1962, Kenya in December 1963 and Zanzibar in the same month. Insurrections broke out in Aden in the course of these, and during 1964 armed parties crossed the border from the neighbouring state of Yemen, encouraged by Egypt. RAF Hunters, Shackletons, Twin Pioneers, Beverleys, Argosies, Valettas and Sycamores were all employed in supporting the ground forces, but in any event the British Government was determined to divest itself of this responsibility. At the end of November 1967 the territory of Aden left the Commonwealth and became part of the People's Republic of South Yemen. The RAF units were withdrawn, some moving to friendly states in the Persian Gulf, where a few remained until December 1971, when the oil-rich states had built up their own air forces.

While these events were taking place, two independent states were formed within the Commonwealth, on 6 July 1964. These were Zambia and Malawi, part of the former Federation of Rhodesia. However, the British Government refused to grant independence to Rhodesia, the third country within the Federation. Rhodesia announced a Unilateral Declaration of Independence on 11 November 1965, but Britain declared this to be illegal and invoked economic sanctions through the United Nations.

RAF Javelins were sent to Zambia as a protection force while RAF Britannias and RCAF Hercules ferried oil to that land-locked country for about nine months. To prevent Rhodesia obtaining clandestine supplies via Beira in Portuguese East Africa, RAF Shackletons were sent to Majunga in Madagascar, from where they carried out anti-shipping patrols over the Mozambique Channel in collaboration with the Royal Navy. These continued until early 1972, by which time guerrilla activities were preventing the passage of supplies across Mozambique. The war between the Rhodesian regime and guerrilla forces of the country continued until a settlement was reached at the end of 1979.

Apart from Cyprus and Gibraltar, the only bases the RAF could use in Britain's former possessions in the Mediterranean were those in Malta. An anti-Western society had been developing in that small group of islands, and it was decided that the RAF should pull out. The last squadron left in October 1979, severing formal links with a country which had played such a prominent part in the history of the RAF.

The Hunting Percival Pembroke was a useful communication aircraft, with a crew of two and accommodation for eight passengers, which entered service in 1953. Some were converted to photo-reconnaissance aircraft and employed over Malaya from 1958, such as Pembroke C(PR)1 serial XF796 of 81 Squadron, shown here on 19 July 1960 at Seletar in Singapore when leaving the squadron. Others were fitted with dual controls as trainers. A few of these reliable aircraft continued in squadron service until 1988.

A.S. Thomas collection

The Scottish Aviation Pioneer was introduced in February 1954 as a light liaison aircraft capable of landing in confined areas such as jungle clearings. It could carry five casualties and was operational in Malaya during the anti-terrorist war. The Pioneers in this photograph, serials XL702, XL703 and XL686, were on the strength of 215 Squadron, which was equipped with these aircraft from April 1956 to September 1958 while based at Dishforth in Yorkshire.

Aeroplane Monthly

The Westland Whirlwind, with a crew of three and a carrying capacity of eight passengers, entered RAF service in September 1954 to replace the smaller Dragonfly. It was employed for tactical transport or search and rescue, at home and in Germany, the Near East and the Far East, the last continuing in squadron service until March 1982. This Whirlwind HAR10, serial XP347, was photographed with a Wessex helicopter of the Royal Navy.

P. Batten

A military version of the de Havilland Comet was modified from the world's first jet airliner and entered RAF squadron service in June 1956. The first eight aircraft were designated Comet C2s and carried a crew of five with forty-four passengers. In February 1962 five Comet C4s were delivered to 216 Squadron at Lyneham in Wiltshire, including serial XR396 shown here. These were capable of carrying ninety-four passengers. By June 1975 all Comets had been withdrawn from the transport role.

The late O.G. Thetford via
A.S. Thomas

This Royal Navy fleet auxiliary lay off the island of Gan, where it was used as a refuelling depot guarded only by a couple of watchmen. A party of RAF men approached quietly one night and painted UNDER RAF PROTECTION on her side, to the annoyance of the Royal Navy.

P.J. Thompson collection

RAF living quarters in the lonely island of Gan in the Maldives Islands, which was used primarily as a staging post in the Indian Ocean from August 1957 until the spring of 1976.

P.J. Thompson collection

The Scottish Aviation Twin Pioneer followed the single-engined version in 1958 and was capable of carrying up to eleven men as well as a crew of three. It saw service as a troop-carrier and casualty evacuator in Aden, Kuwait, Kenya and Indonesia before being withdrawn at the end of 1968. This Twin Pioneer CC1, serial XM958, was on the strength of 21 Squadron, which served with these machines in Kenya, Aden and at home.

Aeroplane Monthly

The Bristol Britannia, converted from a civil airliner, provided the RAF with its first turbo-prop transport when it entered squadron service in March 1959. Intended for long-range work, it carried a crew of five and up to 113 troops or 37,400 lb of freight. Twenty-three Britannias served in the RAF and all were given the names of stars or constellations, such as serial XL636 of 99 Squadron in this photograph, which was named *Argo*. They gave long service and were finally retired in January 1976.

J.D. Oughton via A.S. Thomas

The Hawker Siddeley Argosy was a medium-range tactical transport which entered squadron service in February 1962. With a crew of five, it could carry up to sixty-nine troops or 29,000 lb of freight. Its short landing and take-off facility, twin booms and large rear door gave it the ability to deploy troops and their vehicles with rapidity. Argosies proved their worth in operations in both the Middle East and the Far East, including the confrontation with Indonesia. The last were retired in January 1978. This Argosy C1, serial XN820 of 70 Squadron, named *Hermes*, was photographed in 1970 at Akrotiri in Cyprus. It bore Red Cross markings while on relief flights to Jordan.

R.J. Wozencroft via A.S. Thomas

Whirlwind HAR10, serial XP398, of the RAF, based at Kuching, landing at an Army outpost in May 1964 during the Indonesian confrontation.

P. Batten

The Westland Belvedere, with twin engines and rotors, entered RAF service in September 1961 as a short-range tactical helicopter, carrying a crew of two and up to eighteen troops with their equipment. They continued in service until March 1969. This Belvedere, serial XG456 of 66 Squadron, was photographed in June 1964 at Nanga Gaat in North Borneo while transporting a downed Wessex of the Royal Navy's 845 Squadron.

P. Batten

The Short Belfast was the first aircraft in the RAF designed specifically as a long-range transport. It carried a crew of six and had a capacity for 150 troops or freight up to 80,000 lb. Only ten were built and all were supplied to 53 Squadron from January 1966. They were given individual names, serial XR362 in this photograph being *Samson*. Belfasts were finally retired in September 1976.

A.S. Thomas collection

The Hawker Siddeley Andover C1 was developed from the Avro 748 civil aircraft and entered service with the RAF from December 1966 as a tactical transport. It carried a crew of four and had a capacity of forty-four troops or up to 14,000 lb of freight. It gave excellent service both at home and overseas, continuing until August 1975. Other versions were the Andover CC2, which was equipped solely for passengers, and the Andover E3, which was employed on special Signals Command duties; these continued until the mid-1990s. This Andover C1, serial XS608 of 52 Squadron in the Far East Air Force, was photographed over the Johore Strait in 1968.

D. Bennett via A.S. Thomas

CHAPTER TWELVE

BACK ON
OPERATIONS

The Hawker Siddeley Dominie was a jet-powered aircraft employed as an advanced navigation trainer, with a crew of two pilots, a staff navigator, an extra crew member and two pupils. It first entered service in December 1965. This Dominie T1, serial XS710, was on the strength of No. 6 Flying Training School at Finningley in Yorkshire.

G.R. Pitchfork collection

As the commitments of the RAF in the former British Empire diminished, the responsibilities towards NATO and home defence increased. Since the formation of NATO in 1949, the squadrons in Germany had come under the operational control of the Supreme

Allied Commander, Europe (SACEUR). From 1963 the number of these squadrons was settled at about twelve, varying in equipment but increasing in performance and firepower. By early 1972 there were four squadrons of Phantoms, three of Harriers, two of Lightnings, two of Buccaneers and one of Wessex helicopters. Then Jaguars arrived to replace the Phantoms, which were able to return to home defence. More Harriers arrived to replace the ageing Lightnings, and the performance of these remarkable new aircraft was steadily improved with new variants. From 1970 Bloodhound Mark 2 ground-to-air missiles were also deployed with the RAF in Germany, followed by Rapier ground-to-air missiles two years later. These were air-transportable in small aircraft or helicopters and manned by men of the RAF Regiment. Another development in defence was the introduction of hardened concrete shelters for aircraft and operation rooms, with improved camouflage.

At home, the RAF fighter aircraft were increasingly involved in intercepting Soviet aircraft attempting to intrude air space around the United Kingdom. By 1975 these fighters numbered about seventy-five, mostly Phantoms and Jaguars. There was also a squadron of airborne early warning Shackletons, with which they operated. Radar stations had faced the east for many years but more were built in the north-west and west of Britain, to cover this increased activity.

The home-based maritime squadrons formed part of the NATO alliance forces in the eastern Atlantic and operated in close co-operation with the Royal Navy in this region. In early 1971 there were four squadrons of Nimrods, each with six aircraft, plus a single squadron of Buccaneers in the maritime strike role, with two more Buccaneer squadrons to follow. By 1975 two search and rescue squadrons were equipped with Whirlwind helicopters, one of which converted on to the Wessex the following year and the other to the Sea King in 1978.

Sea King HAR3, serial XZ597, of the Sea King Training Unit at Culdrose in Cornwall, in Falklands livery.

Westland Group

The need for long-distance transport aircraft diminished with the reduction of overseas commitments in the late 1970s. Belfasts were phased out but the VC10, first introduced in July 1966, continued to perform this function. The backbone of the RAF's medium-range facility was the Lyneham Transport Wing, formed in mid-1968 and equipped entirely with Hercules C1s or Hercules tanker variants. Shorter-range transport duties were carried out by helicopters such as the Puma, introduced in 1971, supplemented by the heavier Chinook, which first appeared in RAF service in December 1980. The main duties of the RAF's Support Command consisted of lifting troops and equipment to Gibraltar, Cyprus and Northern Ireland, as well as strategic and tactical exercises in combination with other NATO forces.

When the next conflict came, it was in a part of the world unknown to some of the British public. Argentine forces invaded the Falkland Islands on 2 April 1982 and its dependency of South Georgia the following day. The defences were quickly overwhelmed. British rule over the Crown Colony of the Falklands had lasted for over two hundred years and its inhabitants naturally depended on their mother country for protection, even though they were some 8,000 miles distant from the United Kingdom and only 400 miles from the Argentine mainland.

The ejection of the invaders seemed an impossible task, but Britain surprised the world with the speed of her response. A South Atlantic Task Force was formed immediately and the first vessels left Portsmouth on 5 April. All branches of Britain's front-line armed services were carried in this convoy. By this time the RAF's overseas presence was only a shadow of its former self, apart from the squadrons based in Germany. Nevertheless, the service was able to play a crucial part in the operation. Seaborne helicopters were mainly drawn from the Fleet Air Arm, the Royal Marines and the Army, but the RAF provided four Chinooks. In addition, RAF Harrier GR3s joined the seaborne forces while more RAF pilots were made available to fly Sea Harriers of the Fleet Air Arm.

The operation would not have been possible without the facilities provided by Ascension Island, a British dependency in the South Atlantic 3,750 miles from the

The British Aircraft Corporation VC10 was the heaviest aircraft to serve in the RAF when it was delivered to 10 Squadron at Fairford in Gloucestershire from July 1966. Fourteen of these long-range transports, adapted from the civil airliner, were supplied to the squadron, which moved to Brize Norton the following year. The VC10 C1 has a crew of five plus stewards, and a capacity of 150 passengers. From June 1982 more were supplied in the tanker role as K2s, K3s and K4s. All VC10 C1s were named after RAF holders of the Victoria Cross. This example, serial XR808, was named after Fg Off Kenneth Campbell of 22 Squadron, who was awarded a posthumous VC in 1941 after torpedoing the German battleship *Gneisenau*. It was photographed on 11 January 1983 at Ascension Island while transporting the Prime Minister, Margaret Thatcher, to the Falkland Islands.

A.S. Thomas collection

Falklands. The American staging airfield of Wideawake had been built on Ascension and supplies were flown there by Hercules of the RAF's Transport Wing at Lyneham, refuelled in flight by Victor tankers. Vulcan B2 bombers from three RAF squadrons also arrived at Wideawake. Nimrods from St Mawgan in Cornwall and Kinloss in Morayshire flew there with the aid of Victor tankers. These Nimrods carried out reconnaissance patrols, armed with Harpoon anti-ship missiles and fitted with pylons which enabled them to carry Sidewinder air-to-air missiles. Sea King helicopters also arrived to carry out search and rescue duties from Ascension.

The first element of the South Atlantic Task Force set sail from Ascension for the Falklands on 16 April, led by the aircraft carriers HMS *Hermes* and *Invincible*. The vessels carried twenty Sea Harriers as well as Sea King, Wessex, Lynx, Wasp, Scout and Gazelle helicopters of the Fleet Air Arm, the Army Air Corps and the Royal Marine Commandos. Three RAF regiments also accompanied the Task Force, one of which was equipped with Rapier ground-to-air missiles for airfield defence. Meanwhile, some of the Victors were converted back to the role of long-range reconnaissance and from 20 April carried out flights over South Georgia. This dependency was retaken on 25 April by a small task force which had sailed from Gibraltar in early April, under the command of the Royal Navy.

Hostilities on the Falklands opened at an early hour on 1 May when one of the Vulcan B2s from Wideawake, refuelled by a succession of Victor tankers, dropped a stick of twenty-one 1,000 lb bombs across the runway at Stanley airport, to prevent its use by the Mirage VIIIs and Super-Etendards with which the Argentine Air Force on the mainland was equipped. This was followed at dawn by low-level strikes by the Sea Harriers from the Task Force against this airport and an airfield at Goose Green. Bombardment from the sea followed. Over the next days, the Task Force was attacked from the mainland with great determination by the Argentine Air Force and on 4 May the destroyer HMS *Sheffield* was hit by an Exocet missile and later sank. The battle was hard fought for the next six weeks, with an uncertain outcome for some of this time.

In early May, nine Harrier GR3s flew from Wittering in Northamptonshire to Wideawake, refuelled en route by Victor tankers. Six of these Harriers and four Chinooks were carried in the container ship MV *Atlantic Conveyor*, which set sail for the Falklands on 8 May. The Harriers flew off the container ship on 18 and 19 May, together with four Sea Harriers, and landed on the carrier HMS *Hermes*. The RAF aircraft were able to take over the duties of ground attack and release some of the Sea Harriers for defence of the Task Force.

On 21 May, 3 Commando Brigade was able to establish a beachhead at San Carlos and also destroy many Argentine aircraft. However, the frigate HMS *Antelope* was badly hit on 23 May and sank the following day, although the attacking aircraft were suffering heavy losses. Also on 23 May, the container ship *Atlantic Conveyor* was badly damaged, sinking three days later. Three of the RAF's Chinooks were destroyed. The remaining helicopter carried out a herculean task until the end of the conflict.

At the end of May five more Harrier GR3s flew out to Ascension Island, joining those which had remained for defensive duties. Phantom FGR2s arrived to relieve them and two Harriers flew out to HMS *Hermes* on 1 June, followed by two more a week later. Four left on another container ship, but did not arrive until the war was over. Meanwhile, paratroops and commandos made gradual progress on the Falklands, and 5 Brigade landed at San Carlos Bay on 1 June. The Royal Fleet Auxiliary *Sir Galahad* was sunk on 8 June and *Sir Tristram* was badly damaged. The RAF Harriers were able to operate from an aluminium strip at St Carlos from 9 June, while the land battle moved across the island.

The Lockheed Hercules became the RAF's medium-range tactical transport after its introduction in December 1966. With a crew of five, the first of these highly reliable machines could carry up to ninety-two troops for about 2,400 miles. In 1978 many were 'stretched' by lengthening the fuselage by 15 ft, the type being designated the Hercules C3. The squadrons form the Lyneham Transport Wing, where this photograph of Hercules C3, serial XV301 of 47 Squadron, was taken in 1991. It was fitted with a refuelling probe.

Author's collection

The campaign ended on 14 June when the remaining Argentines surrendered and 11,400 were taken prisoner. Their aircraft losses are estimated as 117 destroyed, of which about half were helicopters. Many other aircraft were captured. The Task Force lost 23 helicopters from its deployment of about 100, but 19 of these were sunk in vessels or destroyed in accidents. The FAA and RAF lost ten Harriers, of which five were in accidents. Civilian and Task Force casualties amounted to 255 lives and 777 injuries, but 700 of the latter were soon able to return to full duties.

One defect in the RAF's equipment shown up during the Falklands War was the lack of a suitable airborne early warning aircraft to replace the ageing Shackleton AEWs which had been adapted for this purpose. A lengthy but unsuccessful attempt to develop the Nimrod AEW3 was finally abandoned and the Boeing E-3 was ordered in its place and given the RAF name 'Sentry'. This new aircraft, combined with the Tornado GR1 and later the Tornado F3, gave the RAF an increased ability to defend Britain's air space and contribute to the defence of Germany. Humanitarian operations occupied much of the attention of the Lyneham Transport Wing from October 1984, when Ethiopia suffered an appalling famine. Hercules aircraft and crews were sent to Addis Ababa, from where they transported supplies such as grain, high-protein biscuits and blankets to airstrips near relief camps in the north of the country. Some supplies were dropped from low level to the more inaccessible parts of the stricken areas.

However, the main duty of the RAF at home and in Germany in the years immediately following the Falklands War was to combine with NATO in guarding the skies against any potential threat from the Soviet Air Force. NATO had always declared that it would never conduct a war of aggression and that its

The remarkable British Aerospace Harrier entered squadron service in July 1969. It was developed from the experimental Hawker Siddeley Kestrel, which was the world's first strike aircraft capable of vertical take-off and landing. A single-seater, it is armed with twin 30 mm guns and can carry weapons of up to 5,000 lb for ground attack. The maximum speed is Mach 0.95. Several variants have been produced, the example in this photograph being a GR3 of 1 Squadron at Wittering in Cambridgeshire, which participated in the Falklands campaign.

British Crown Copyright/MOD/RAF Wittering

function was purely one of defence. But in 1985 the Soviet empire began to collapse, partly from the failure of the communist economies and partly from unrest within its satellite states and even within some of its older republics. Western countries looked upon the social and political upheavals with astonishment mixed with caution, but a gradual easing of tension between their governments and that of the Soviet Union occurred. One by one the satellite countries of Eastern Europe obtained their freedom from Soviet rule and on 3 October 1990 the re-unification of Germany took place. It was becoming increasingly obvious that the need for NATO defences had diminished. By this time the RAF had been reduced to fifty-two squadrons and seven flights, with a total of 83,200 personnel.

Nevertheless, a massive commitment for Western countries cropped up in another part of the world, when Iraq invaded Kuwait on 2 August 1990. Saudi Arabia asked foreign governments for protection against such aggression, and a military alliance of Western and Middle East countries was rapidly formed, while the Security Council of the United Nations imposed sanctions on trade with Iraq. The major contribution of the Coalition Forces, as they were known, came from the USA, but the part played by Britain was not inconsiderable. Strong contingents of the USAF began flying to Saudi Arabia on 7 August and two days later the British Government announced that it would participate in the attempt to liberate Kuwait.

The McDonnell Douglas Phantom first entered an RAF operational squadron in September 1969. This was the FG1, a two-seat ground-attack fighter capable of Mach 2.1 and armed with air-to-air missiles, rockets and cannon, carrying up to 7,000 lb of bombs. The role of the FGR2, such as serial XT909 of 228 Operational Conversion Unit at Leuchars in this photograph, was that of an air defence interceptor. Phantoms defended the Falklands after the end of the war in 1982.

British Crown Copyright/MOD/RAF Leuchars

The final version of the Avro Shackleton was the Airborne Early Warning adaptation, twelve of which were converted from Shackleton MR2s from 1971 onwards. The bulky radome under the nose carried the special equipment. All twelve were supplied to 8 Squadron, at first based at Kinloss in Morayshire but moving to Lossiemouth in August 1973. Shackleton AEW2s remained in service until 1991. They were named after characters in the children's TV programme *Magic Roundabout*, serial WR963 in this photograph being Ermintrude.

British Crown Copyright/MOD/RAF Lossiemouth

A load of supplies being parachuted from the loading bay of a Hercules, photographed on 27 February 1981.

British Crown Copyright/MOD/47 Squadron Archives

Twenty-five Hercules of the Lyneham Transport Wing were ordered to begin lifting equipment to King Khalid International Airport near Riyadh in Saudi Arabia, using Akrotiri in Cyprus as a staging post. They also flew to Dhahran in Saudi Arabia and Thumran in Oman, operations continuing round the clock. In early October they began lifting British troops to the region, mainly from Germany and routed through Lyneham. Some of these, together with their equipment, were then flown to forward areas prepared by the Royal Engineers. Other RAF aircraft flew out, refuelled en route. This part of the operation was known as 'Desert Shield'.

By 16 January 1991 the RAF had contributed to the Coalition Forces 18 Tornado F3s, 40 Tornado GR1, 6 new Tornado GR1As, 12 Jaguar GR1As, 17 Victor K2 or VC10 tankers, 12 Chinook HC1 helicopters, 19 Puma helicopters, 7 Hercules transports and a BAe 125 communications aircraft. About 7,000 RAF personnel were detached to the region, including squadrons of the RAF Regiment. These were not the only RAF aircraft or units to serve in the Gulf War, for more arrived after operations began. In addition to the combined air forces of the countries in the Coalition Forces, about 600,000 troops with 4,000 tanks were based in Saudi Arabia, the Gulf States and Turkey. There were also 150 warships in nearby waters. These Coalition Forces formed the greatest accumulation of firepower ever assembled on earth.

The Hawker Siddeley Buccaneer first entered service in October 1970 as a maritime strike aircraft but it was also employed on low-level tactical work over land. Buccaneers also served in Germany and later in the Gulf War, where one of their tasks was to act as target designators for Tornados, carrying Paveway laser-guided bombs. This photograph shows Buccaneer serial XN981 of 12 Squadron from Lossiemouth in Morayshire. It was armed with Martel anti-shipping missiles, TV-guided with the blunt nose and anti-radar with the pointed nose. Behind it was serial XZ432 of 237 Operational Conversion Unit from the same station.

British Crown Copyright/MOD/RAF Lossiemouth

When the air assault began, under operation 'Desert Storm', it was with unparalleled effectiveness in the history of warfare. The RAF Tornado GR1s were in the van of the attack, on the night of 16/17 January 1991. Their targets were Iraqi airfields and they carried JP233 dispensers which contained runway-cratering bombs and anti-personnel mines. These attacks continued for three nights and were followed by others with free-fall bombs against bridges and various targets. Twelve RAF Buccaneers then arrived, fitted with Pavespike designator pods, and from 2 February worked in combination with the Tornados, which dropped Paveway laser-guided bombs 'marked' by the Pavespikes. On 6 February five more Tornado GR1s arrived, fitted with TIALD (Thermal Imaging and Airborne Laser Designator) pods, which enabled the Paveway bombs to be dropped without the assistance of the Buccaneers. About forty GR1s flew in the conflict, and they suffered the highest ratio of losses in all the Coalition Air Forces, six in combat and one in an accident. No Buccaneers were lost on the operations.

The Jaguar GR1s began operations in daylight on 17 January, the first day of 'Desert Storm', their initial targets being missile sites on the coast of Kuwait and Iraqi naval vessels. When the ground war, known as 'Desert Sabre', began on 24 February, they used free-fall and cluster-bombs to attack Iraqi artillery, troop concentrations, barracks and storage areas. Although they flew over 600 sorties, the Jaguars suffered no losses. The three Nimrod MR1s carried out

The Westland Wessex, a short-range helicopter with a crew of three and provision for up to sixteen passengers, entered RAF service in January 1964 for tactical transport and ground assault. This Wessex HC2, serial XT601 of A Flight, 22 Squadron, from Chivenor in North Devon, was photographed by the author when taking off from Lundy Island during a practice exercise on 15 December 1986.

Author's collection

The last flight of a Phantom FGR2 of
74 Squadron took place on 31 October 1992.
Serial XV460 was photographed over
RAF Wattisham in Suffolk.

British Crown Copyright/MOD/Sgt Rick Brewell

The Scottish Aviation Bulldog entered RAF
service in April 1973 as a primary trainer, fitted
with side-by-side seats for instructor and
trainee pilot. The example in this photograph,
Bulldog T1 serial XX692, was on the strength of
the RAF's Yorkshire University Air Squadron at
Finningley.

G.R. Pitchfork collection

The Westland/Aérospatiale Puma, carrying a crew of two and up to sixteen armed men, entered RAF service in June 1971. It was employed as a gunship equipped with two machine-guns, as a troop-carrier or for casualty evacuation.

Westland Group

reconnaissance missions with their Searchwater radar, supplementing the information supplied by Boeing E-3s of the USAF to the US aircraft carriers. These enabled naval and air attacks to be made on Iraqi warships and auxiliary vessels, twenty-five of which were sunk.

About thirty Tornado F3s flew air patrols and there were no losses. The six Tornado GR1As, which were fitted with TIRRS (Tornado Infra-Red Reconnaissance System), flew on many missions and provided vital information, also without loss. The RAF's Support Helicopter Force also went into action when the ground war began. Nineteen Puma HC1s flew in close support of the British Army, carrying troops and supplies to forward areas as they advanced, and operating from improvised airstrips. Fifteen Chinook HC1s transported troops and supplies, sometimes operating at night. No helicopters were lost.

The Iraqis began to pull out of Kuwait two days after the ground war began but were cut off by American and British armoured forces. The road to Basra was soon strewn with wrecked vehicles. It was estimated that 3,000 of their 4,300 tanks were destroyed, as well as 1,850 of their 2,900 armoured personnel carriers and 2,140 of their 3,100 artillery pieces. The survivors began to surrender in droves. At the end of February, the Iraqi Governemnt under its dictator, Saddam Hussein, admitted defeat and agreed to obey all the resolutions of the Security Council. These included 'no-fly zones' for the Iraqi Air Force in the north and south of the country as well as acceptance of inspectors from the United Nations Special Commission to Oversee the Destruction of Weapons of Mass Destruction (UNSCOM) which were believed to exist in Iraq. These weapons were chemical and biological, such as those known to have been employed in the war with Iran from 1980 to 1998 and against the Kurdish people in the north of Iraq. It was also believed that nuclear weapons were being developed. The Coalition Forces were ordered to cease fire at 08.00 hours on 1st March. It was estimated that the Iraqi armed forces had lost 100,000 men, with the same number captured, compared with less than 500 killed among the Coalition Forces.

The Gulf War demonstrated that the RAF was capable of considerable striking forc, but its squadrons were given little respite. A vicious civil war began in Yugoslavia and its various republics broke away from each other after bitter fighting and genocide. On 16 October 1992, a United Nations resolution declared that all flights over Bosnia-Herzegovina, in the western and central part of the country, were to be monitored so as to prevent further attacks by Serbian aircraft. The RAF's Boeing E-3D Sentries were quickly on the scene and were given permission to use the airfield at Aviano in northern Italy as well as fly over Hungarian air space on their missions. As the situation in the former Yugoslavia deteriorated, more active policing was required by the United Nations from March 1993. Britain, together with the USA, France, Netherlands and Turkey, deployed fighters in the area. The RAF moved detachments of Tornado F3s to the Italian Air Force base of Gioia Del Colle in southern Italy. RAF Harriers and Nimrods were also sent to Italy, to join in operations. However, actions in the mountainous terrain were difficult to monitor and the area was a potential powder keg which could explode again.

In April 1994, the command structure of the RAF underwent further changes. Strike Command remained unchanged but two others were formed, Personnel and Training Command and Logistics Command. Afterwards, there were many improvements in equipment and firepower. The service was awaiting the new Eurofighter Typhoon and the EH Industries multi-role Merlin Helicopter.

There were no major international incidents requiring operational activities for the next few years but the RAF remained vigilant, as did the other services in the UK. In October 1994, Iraq once again massed forces on the border with the Kuwait, resulting in deployment of ground forces by the US and Britain. In September 1996, military operations by Iraq in the northern Kurdish regions of the country were followed by the launching of twenty-seven US cruise missiles as a warning to Saddam Hussein. In the following year, weapons inspectors from the United Nations were denied access to several sites, although they were allowed back following threats of military action.

The RAF of 1998 consisted of forty-three squadrons, of which six were based in Germany and one in the Falklands. There were also three flights, two in the Falklands and one in Croatia. There were ten squadrons of the RAF Regiment, three of which were in Germany. In addition, some units of the RAF were stationed in Northern Ireland, Ascension Island, Bosnia, Cyprus and Turkey. The last RAF unit in Hong Kong had left when the colony was handed back to China in June 1997. At home, the various training units included those of the University Air Squadrons. The RAF was also backed by units of the Royal Auxillary Air Force Regiment, the Royal Auxillary Air Force and the Royal Air Force Volunteer Reserve.

The long-serving Sepecat Jaguar was first
introduced into squadron service in 1974 and is
still a potent force in the modern RAF.
A supersonic and single-seat tactical aircraft, it
began to replace the Phantom FG1 in the
ground attack role. It is armed with two 30 mm
Aden guns and carries up to 10,500 lb of
ordnance, including air-to-air missiles. The Jaguar
GR1 of 41 Squadron in this photograph is
painted in special colours for the squadron's
75th anniversary in 1991 and carries a
reconnaissance pod.

British Crown Copyright/MOD/RAF Coltishall

Westland Sea King HAR3 helicopter, serial
XZ597 of 202 Squadron, which has its
headquarters at Boulmer in Northumberland,
together with A Flight. D Flight is at Lossiemouth
in Morayshire while E Flight is at Leconfield in
Yorkshire. Other areas of the coasts are covered
by 22 Squadron, also equipped with Sea Kings.
All are engaged on air-sea rescue.

British Crown Copyright/MOD

On 1 May 1982 a Vulcan B2 of 44 Squadron, with a crew from 101 Squadron, made a long-distance bombing sortie from Ascension Island to Stanley airport, refuelled en route on numerous occasions by Victor tankers. The two Vulcan B2s in the background were photographed at Goose Bay in Labrador during an exercise, with Victor B2 serial XL161 in the foreground.

G.R. Pitchfork collection

The British Aerospace Hawk T1 is justly famous for the remarkable performances of the *Red Arrows* aerobatic team, but it is also the RAF's standard advanced trainer for pilots moving on to fast jets. First appearing at No. 4 Flying Training School at Valley in November 1976, it has two seats in tandem with the rear raised to give the instructor a clear field of vision. This Hawk T1A of the *Red Arrows* is unusual since it is armed with Sidewinder air-to-air missiles for air defence duties.

A.S. Thomas collection

The Westland/Aérospatiale Gazelle was employed by the RAF as a trainer and short-range communications helicopter from October 1976. It had seats for a crew of two or instructor and pupil, and could carry up to three passengers in cramped conditions. This example, serial XW902 of No. 2 Flying Training School at Ternhill in Shropshire, was still in RAF service in 1995.

Philip Jarrett collection

The Boeing Vertol Chinook was imported to provide the RAF with a medium-lift helicopter. The first were supplied to No. 240 Operational Conversion Unit at Odiham in Hampshire in December 1980, as shown in this stream of Chinooks landing in misty weather the following year. The twin-rotor helicopter has a crew of four and can carry up to thirty troops or an equivalent amount of freight. It can be armed with a machine-gun on the port side. The performance of the single Chinook of 18 Squadron, which survived the hit by an Exocet missile on the container ship *Atlantic Conveyor* during the Falklands War, has entered the annals of RAF history.

R.A. Forsythe via A.S. Thomas

This photograph of Stanley airport in the Falklands, which had been named Aeroporto Malvinas for a few weeks by the Argentines, was taken on 16 June 1982, two days after the capitulation. Fake bomb craters made from dirt had been placed on the runway, close to the genuine bomb craters, in an attempt to fool the British into believing that Vulcan bombers from Ascension Island had put the airport out of action.

British Crown Copyright/MOD/

47 Squadron Archives

The Tornado GR1A is a variant of the supersonic tactical strike aircraft which first entered service in 1981. It carries infra-red scanners and can operate at very low level, sweeping large areas and recording the results on a TV-type screen in the navigator's compartment. These machines carried out valuable work in the Gulf War.

British Aerospace

The container ship MV *Atlantic Conveyor* carried six Harrier GR3s, four Sea Harriers and four Chinook HC1 helicopters, cocooned against the elements and lashed to her deck. She left Ascension Island on 8 May 1982 for the Falkland Islands but was hit by an Exocet missile on 25 May, after the Harriers had taken off. Only one Chinook was saved. The vessel sank three days later.

British Crown Copyright/MOD

The 'Air Defence Variant' of the Panavia Tornado is the F3, which first entered an RAF squadron in April 1987. It is a two-seat supersonic interceptor, fitted with a more powerful engine than the GR1 and carrying more fuel for its longer range. The armament is one 27 mm cannon with four Sky Flash and four Sidewinder air-to-air missiles. This photograph of a Tornado F3 of 25 Squadron and another of 11 Squadron, both from Leeming in Yorkshire, was taken on 24 March 1997.

British Crown Copyright/MOD/Sgt Rick Brewell

The Shorts Tucano, based on a Brazilian design, began to enter RAF service in January 1987 as a replacement for the Jet Provost. A turbo-prop basic trainer with two seats in tandem, it has also proved successful in many other countries. These Tucano T1s were photographed at the RAF's Central Flying School at Scampton in Lincolnshire.

Short Bros PLC

Nine Lockheed Tristar Civil airliners were purchased from 1982 to provide the RAF with a long-range transport which could also be used in the tanker role. The first entered service with 216 Squadron at Brize Norton in November 1984. The TriStar has a crew of four plus stewards and accommodation for up to 204 passengers. This Tristar, serial ZD051 of 216 Squadron, was photographed in early 1995 while refuelling Jaguars of 54 Squadron.

R.A. Marshall via A.S. Thomas

The British Aerospace BAe 146 is a VIP transport which was first delivered to RAF Brize Norton in 1983 for evaluation. It has a crew of six and can carry nineteen passengers. This aircraft, serial ZD696, was photographed on 23 June 1983 while unloading at RAF Wildenrath in Germany. Three BAe 146 Mark 2s, serials ZE700, ZE701 and ZE702, now serve as part of 32 (The Royal) Squadron at RAF Northolt. The Queen first flew in one of these on 2 August 1986 and since then they have been in frequent use. On 1 September 1997 the body of Princess Diana was flown home from Paris in one of these transports.

British Crown Copyright/MOD/RAF Wildenrath

Tornado F3, serial ZE760 of 5 Squadron at Coningsby in Lincolnshire, flying 'very close escort' to a Tupolev Tu-142 'Bear F', followed by a Phantom. The Russian aircraft was employed on long-range reconnaissance and anti-submarine work, but the equilibrium of the crew may have been upset by the attention of the RAF.

British Crown Copyright/MOD/RAF Coningsby

The Canberra PR9 first entered service in January 1958 as the RAF's high-altitude photo-reconnaissance aircraft, capable of flying above any potential enemy fighters at that time. This photograph shows serial XH168 of 39 (No 1 PRU) Squadron, which finally disbanded on 31 July 2006.

British Crown Copyright/MOD/39 (No. 1 PRU) Squadron

A Hercules camouflaged in desert pink, crewed by members of 47 Squadron, returning to Riyadh in Saudi Arabia during the Gulf War.

Dave Fry

A Harrier GR5 of 1 Squadron, flanked by two Harrier GR3s of 233 Operational Conversion Unit, photographed near Dunsfold in Surrey. The GR5 was developed to give the Harrier a higher performance and increased weapon load. It entered squadron service in 1989.

British Crown Copyright/MOD/RAF Wittering

Jaguar GR1A, serial XZ367 of 54 Squadron, armed with Sidewinder air-to-air missiles, taking off from Muharraq in Bahrain. Twelve of these aircraft from the Coltishall Wing flew out to Thumrait in Oman on 11 August 1990 and moved to Muharraq in October. They were replaced later in that month by twelve which had been fitted up with more sophisticated equipment and pylons for air-to-air missiles. These completed over 600 missions during the Gulf War, without loss.

British Crown Copyright/MOD

This Buccaneer, painted in desert pink, was photographed at RAF Lyneham in Wiltshire shortly after the end of the Gulf War. The 'Hello Sailor' nose art was particularly suitable for the role of maritime strike, but the main role of the aircraft in the war was laser designation for bombs dropped by Tornados.

Author's collection

A lengthy project to develop the British Aerospace Nimrod AEW3 as a replacement for the RAF's ageing airborne early warning Shackletons was finally cancelled in December 1986, since the electronic equipment did not meet the requirements of the Air Staff. The Boeing AEW1 was ordered in its place. This prototype of the Nimrod AEW3 was serial XZ286.

British Crown Copyright/MOD

The Boeing Sentry AEW1, based on the Boeing 707 civil airliner, entered service with 8 Squadron at Waddington in Lincolnshire during 1991 and was named the A-3 Sentry. The rotodome radar antenna provides the crews with airborne early warning of the presence of potential enemies or it can be used for peaceful purposes. The RAF has seven of these machines, shared between 8 and 23 Squadrons. Serial ZH101 in this photograph is accompanied by Tornado F3s serials ZE254 and ZG730 of 5 Squadron.

British Aerospace via A.S. Thomas

The EH101 is a multi-role helicopter developed by EH Industries, a company formed by Westland Helicopters and Agusta. A military-utility variant is on order for the RAF, while the variant for the Royal Navy shown in this photograph is known as the Merlin and carries the latest detection equipment and four homing torpedoes.

Westland Group

Eurofighter 2000, serial ZH288 of the Ministry of Defence's Procurement Executive, photographed by Sgt Rick Brewell over British Aerospace's establishment near Warton in Lancashire on 15 January 1998, while being refuelled from VC10 K3 tanker, serial ZA149, of 101 Squadron from Brize Norton in Oxfordshire.

British Crown Copyright/MOD

When it comes into RAF squadron service, the single-seat Eurofighter Typhoon will perform four roles. These are replacement of Jaguar and Tornado interdictors, air defence of the United Kingdom, superiority within NATO over enemy fighters, and the possibility of operations outside NATO in the cause of world peace. With twin engines and a delta-canard design, it possesses maximum aerodynamic agility in a small airframe. It has twelve weapon points and the expected service life is twenty-five years. This Eurofighter, serial ZH288 of the Ministry of Defence's Procurement Executive, was photographed over British Aerospace's establishment near Warton in Lancashire on 15 January 1998.

British Crown Copyright/MOD/Sgt Rick Brewell

CHAPTER THIRTEEN

IN DEFENCE OF DEMOCRACY

The situation in Iraq took an ominous turn in 1998. American and British intelligence officials became convinced that Saddam Hussein was frustrating the efforts of weapons inspectors from UNSCOM, by clearing sites of evidence before allowing any examination for 'weapons of mass destruction'. It was believed by the Allies that the country possessed in secret as much as seventeen tons of material from which chemical and biological weapons could be produced. During January, America began gathering support for a military strike against Iraq, although such measures were strongly opposed by Russia and France. Possible targets for air strikes, mainly in the central region of the country had been identified. A 'three-day blitz' against these was planned, unless Sadam Hussein could be persuaded to collaborate.

The capacity of American and British aircraft to hit these sites precisely had been enhanced by improvements to the methods employed in the previous Gulf War and known as 'smart bombing'. These utilised Advanced Mission Planning Aids (AMPA), a computer-generated system providing a route to the target based on intelligence and reconnaissance photographs. AMPA took into account the terrain, avoided known danger points, and was loaded into a disk before take-off. The crew then had the advantage of their Inertial Navigational System (INS), a gyroscopic-based method which tracked their position from the take-off point. This was coupled with the Global Positioning System (GPS) which confirmed the INS position. When approaching the target, the crew used the Thermal Imaging and Laser Designator (TIALD), linked to the AMPA system. This provided the final direction, using GPS co-ordinates. By selecting either television or infra-red, the crew could identfy the target on a screen, magnified six times, by either day or night. When the bomb was released, a laser 'cone' of energy was created by the TIALD, which directed it on to the target. The TIALD could also be used to direct the bomb or bombs in an accompanying aircraft. Although the system worked less well through heavy cloud or smoke, it was estimated that on average it achieved an accuracy of at least 85 per cent.

In February, America warned Saddam Hussein of the outcome if he employed chemical or biological weapons against his neighbours. At the same time, the RAF was instructed to move eight Tornado GRIs to Kuwait to improve Britain's firepower in the Gulf region, which at the time included the aircraft carrier HMS *Invincible* with her Sea Harrier FA2 fighters. Saddam Hussein gave his assurance but then continued to frustrate attempts by the weapons inspectors to enter suspected sites, on the basis that they were spying on his government. There the matter rested until, on 7 August 1988, terrorists struck at US embassies in Kenya and Tanzania, killing over 200 people. American intelligence identified the shadowy terrorist group al-Qaeda as responsible, operating from the Sudan but based in Afghanistan. It was believed that this group was supported covertly by Saddam Hussein.

The crisis worsened when, on 31 October, Saddam Hussein again withdrew co-operation with the UNSCOM inspectors. He backed down when military strikes were ordered but then refused access to a suspect site near Baghdad on 9 December. By this time it was clear that reprisals were inevitable and on 16 December 1988 the United Nations ordered the inspectors in Baghdad to leave the country. Hours later on the same day, the air strikes began.

Only the United States and Britain carried out the attacks, named operation 'Desert Fox'. The aircraft carrier USS *Enterprise* with seventy-five aircraft was already in the Gulf. Accompanying her were the cruiser USS *Gettysburg* together with six destroyers, a frigate and a submarine, all equipped with Tomahawk Block III cruise missiles. Over 200 of these missiles were the first to be launched, each carrying its warhead of 1,000 lb and guided by a computer software and satellite global positioning system, aimed primarily at air defences and control facilities. They were soon followed by McDonnell Douglas F-18A Super Hornets of the US Navy, carrying missiles intended to destroy anti-aircraft batteries. Other participants were Boeing B-52 Stratofortress bombers of the US Strategic Air Command, operating from the island base of Diego Garcia in the Indian Ocean, leased from the British by the US military. Each carried sixteen cruise missiles.

The contribution of the RAF to the strike force consisted of twelve Tornado GR1 ground attack aircraft of 12 Squadron, comprising only about a twentieth of the total effort made by US aircraft. These were based at the Ali Al-Salem airfield in Kuwait and they joined in the second wave of attacks, operating in pairs. The leader of each pair carried a TIALD pod and a Paveway III bomb of 2,000 lb. The accompanying aircraft carried either two Paveway III bombs or three Paveway II bombs of 1,000 lb each, these being guided on to the target by the leader's TIALD pod. Their main targets were radar installations, radio antennae and a hangar where a prototype unmanned drone capable of carrying 'weapons of mass destruction' was believed to be stored. Despite heavy anti-aircraft fire, all aircraft returned safely, bringing evidence of their success. It was known that the Iraqis also possessed surface-to-air missiles (SAMs), but these were suppressed by US aircraft carrying anti-radiation missiles to deal with the batteries.

As originally planned, these air attacks lasted for three days, intended to provide a salutary lesson to Saddam Hussein. They were called off only a few hours before 20 December, the day when the holy month of Ramadan began, to avoid offending Islamic sensibilities throughout the world. Some RAF Tornados were in the air en route to targets when their missions were aborted, to the dismay of the crews. Their attitude is understandable to anyone with experience of operational flying. It is often extremely dangerous, but most of the tension builds up during briefing and pre-flight preparation. Once in the air, crews are usually too busy and intent on their task to worry about their survival. Any recall signal comes as an anti-climax, so that they have to burn off fuel before they can land back at base with the ignominy of still carrying their weapons.

It was reported that, by this time, a total of 650 sorties had been flown and about 250 targets had been hit. No RAF aircraft were lost but two US Hornets collided over Kuwait and the pilot of one was killed. It was never established whether any 'weapons of mass destruction' had been destroyed or, indeed, whether they still existed at that stage. The UNSCOM inspectors did not return for the next four years. Saddam Hussein remained defiant and a few days later his defences fired at American and British jets patrolling the 'no-fly' zone in the south of the country. The whole episode was soon forgotten by the world media.

The next operation in which the RAF was involved lasted far longer than the 'three-day blitz' in Iraq. This took place in the troubled country of Yugoslavia, where insurrection and reprisals were continuing. It was estimated that some 200,000 people had been killed and many more made homeless in the three and a half years of internecine war which had ended in December 1995. In that month the President of the Federal Republic of Yugoslavia, Slobodam Milosevic, had returned from Paris after signing an agreement which seemed to offer peace to the constituent parts of the country.

However, the region of Kosovo in the south-east, enclosed by Serbia, Montenegro, Albania and Macedonia, continued to seek autonomy. The people were mainly Albanian in ethnic origin but there was a substantial Serb minority. The Kosovo Liberation Army was formed and began to acquire weapons. Some clashes which took place in 1998 were followed by extreme suppression of the Kosovans by Serb forces. Peace talks in Paris were brokered by Russia and the North Atlantic Treaty Organisation (NATO) during February 1999. These offered limited autonomy to Kosovo but President Milosevic refused to sign the agreement.

Following warnings, NATO began air strikes against targets in Yugoslavia on 24 March 1999, in an action named operation 'Allied Force'. Thirteen of the nineteen countries forming part of NATO provided combat aircraft for the campaign. These were the United States, Britain, France, Germany, Italy, Spain, Portugal, Canada, Belgium, the Netherlands, Denmark, Norway and Turkey. The Americans flew the majority of the missions but smaller numbers of bombing aircraft were provided by Britain, France and Canada. The air forces of the other countries were not equipped with laser-guided bomb technology but contributed fighters and support aircraft.

Some 360 NATO aircraft were available initially, of which about 80 were capable of delivering bombing attacks. On that day, 24 March 1999, the German Luftwaffe flew in combat for the first time since the Second World War. During the first two days, American and Dutch pilots reported shooting down five Mikoyan MiG-29 fighters of the Yugoslav Air Force, which became far less in evidence for the remainder of the air operations.

The campaign was carried out in three phases. It was hoped that the first, Phase I, would be very short but sufficient to convince Milosevic that he should back down and agree to the terms of the peace proposals. The bombing targets were strategic, mainly consisting of the country's air defence network, aircraft and military communication centres. Scores of Tomahawk cruise missiles were launched from warships and submarines in the Adriatic, including the submarine HMS *Splendid*. They were followed by aircraft. Among these were Harrier GR7 ground attack fighters of the RAF's 1 Squadron, normally based at Wittering in Northamptonshire but operating from Gioia del Colle airfield in southern Italy. B-52 bombers of the USAF carrying cruise missiles operated from RAF Fairford in Gloucestershire.

Phase I lasted for only four days and did nothing to weaken the resolve of Milosevic. The Serbs had had the benefit of advance warning coupled with knowledge of the preliminary bombing of Iraq. They had been able to move aircraft and military equipment from the danger areas and to hide them elsewhere. Their rugged and mountainous country was quite different from the Iraqi desert, thus being far more capable of concealment. It was frequently covered with fog and low cloud, diminishing the ability to identify targets. A Lockheed F-117 Nighthawk 'stealth bomber' of the USAF was lost but the pilot was rescued by helicopter. The initial bombing had little effect and was used by Milosevic to accelerate the policy of 'thnic cleansing' by military operations against Kosovan civilians. Hundreds of thousands of refugees began streaming out of Kosovo and across the borders into Albania and Macedonia. Milosevic was encouraged by his friendship with Russia, the Serbs having an ethnic affinity with the Slavs.

NATO began Phase II on 29 March, extending the range of bombing attacks to the Serb forces attacking Kosovo. The new targets included military barracks, oil terminals and supply facilities. Some of the operations were increasingly dangerous since low-flying brought the aircraft within the range of surface-to-air missiles. The RAF despatched four more Harriers to Gioia del Colle. Supplies were brought into this air base by Lockheed C-130 Hercules transports from Lyneham in Wiltshire, while air-to-air refuelling was carried out by Lockheed Tristar tankers of the RAF's 216 Squadron based at Brize Norton in Oxfordshire. On 5 April, the RAF employed its Tornado GR1s in the conflict for the first time, on bombing sorties after taking off from their base at Bruggen in Germany. An offer by Milosevic to resume talks was rejected, but the NATO countries were extremely reluctant to employ ground troops since it was calculated that these would need to number about 100,000 and that there would be heavy casualties in a terrain suitable for guerilla war. This phase lasted for about two weeks but did not have the desired effect.

Phase III began when it became clear that Milosevic was stepping up his oppression of the Kosovans. The participating countries of NATO, principally the USA, increased their air power in Italy. A tragic incident took place on 14 April when the US pilots of Lockheed F-16s flying at 15,000 feet over Djakovica spotted what seemed to be a military convoy and attacked. It proved to be a refugee column of tractors en route to Albania, and more than seventy Kosovans were killed. The British contribution to the conflict was strengthened when the aircraft carrier HMS *Invincible* arrived on station in the Arctic on 15 April, equipped with eight Sea Harrier FA2 fighters of 800 Squadron from Yeovilton in Somerset, together with ten Sea King helicopters from 814 and 849 Squadrons. These Sea Harriers could give air cover to the RAF Harriers against Mikoyan MiGs of the Yugolsav Air Force, while the Sea Kings could be employed on humanitarian work.

It was known that the weak point in the Serbian defence was oil. On 18 April, NATO aircraft bombed a petrochemical complex at the north of Belgrade. Albania had granted air space to NATO and on 20 April the capacity of the Allies was increased with the arrival of the McDonnel Douglas AH-64 Apache gunships in that country. Known as 'the tank-busters', these had been used with deadly effect in operation 'Desert Fox'. However, the capacity of these helicopters to operate over the Yugoslav mountains of about 10,000 feet remained in doubt.

A further blow against the oil supplies to Serbia was struck on 27 April when

NATO aircraft destroyed the last remaining bridge over the Danube, at Novi Sad, severely restricting the flow from the direction of Hungary. Serbian forces immediately entered Montengro and took control of the Adriatic port of Bar, from where seaborne supplies could be carried overland. Meanwhile the resolution of Milosevic showed no signs of weakening.

Citizens of the major cities of Serbia, including Belgrade, experienced sudden and lengthy electricity power cuts in the late evening of 2 May. These were the result of NATO's 'soft bombs', dropped from above 14,000 feet by 'stealth aircraft' and guided to electricity stations by radar. These 500 lb soft bombs were fitted with proximity fuses and exploded over a target, showering it with fine carbon granules. The small electrical charges in these were attracted to electrical equipment and clustered round it. They caused a short circuit, followed by a long blackout, and even when the equipment was cleaned could return on the wind and cause more breakdowns. Such bombs were dropped over Serbia on frequent occasions for the remainder of the conflict.

The Allied air forces suffered their first casualties on 5 May when an Apache helicopter crashed during a training exercise in Albania, killing both crew members. On the following day US fighters shot down another MiG-29, bringing the estimated total destroyed to eight, half the number in the Yugoslav Air Force. In addition, some of the older MiG-21 'Fishbeds' had been destroyed. However, there was an accident of war on 7 May when a stray bomb hit the Chinese Embassy in Belgrade, killing three people and creating a serious international incident. But the bombing continued without prospect of complete success. There were renewed demands for an invasion by ground troops, but these were strongly resisted by some of the participating countries, particularly the United States and Germany.

On the night of 14 May, major cities in Serbia were blacked out once again by 'soft bombs', although Yugoslav engineers were showing ingenuity in repairing power stations quickly. There was no end to the conflict in sight and some Allied commentators were beginning to despair. Serbian forces showed no sign of withdrawing from Kosovo and indeed were increasing their policy of ethnic cleansing. More and more refugees were crossing into Albania. On 27 May, the United Nations estimated that almost 966,000 had fled since the beginning of the crisis. The International War Crimes Tribunal indicted Milosevic and four other Serb leaders for crimes against humanity.

The breakthrough came on 2 June, after Russian leaders had decided to play an important part in a new peace process. Together with the European Union, their negotiators proposed the withdrawal of all Serb military and police forces from Kosovo, which could then be occupied by an international force. Milosevic and the Serb Parliament had little option but to agree, but NATO insisted that the bombing would not stop until all the Serb forces began to leave the area. The peace deal did not become effective until 10 June, when the air operations ceased.

The 'Kosovo War' lasted for 78 days. It was hailed by some commentators as a most unusual victory for air power alone, but it is apparent that Milosevic's hand was finally forced by withdrawal of support from Russia. A postward evaluation established that the air attacks on the Serb ground forces were far less effective then estimated. On 3 June, the British Chief of the Defence Staff had announced that NATO had flown 30,000 sorties, of which 9,000 had been bombing missions. These were estimated to have destroyed over 100 main battle tanks and 500 armoured personnel carriers. However, a later evaluation stated that they had destroyed merely fourteen tanks and nineteen armoured personnel carriers.

The Serbs had been most adept at concealing their equipment in bunkers and even garages, while exposing models made of wood and plastic to deceive the Allies. The evaluation stressed the need for better air reconnaissance, which could have been provided by Unmanned Aerial Vehicles (UAVs) such as the 'Global Hawk' which was beginning to enter service.

The NATO troops duly arrived and supervised the return of many Kosovan refugees. Later, the Kosovans of Serbian origin became refugees in their turn, and it is estimated that about 200,000 were forced to leave the country. Milosevic remained president of the Federal Republic of Yugoslavia for over a year before being deposed by his own people. He was then arrested and taken to The Hague to face a tribunal for war crimes in Yugoslavia.

The more peaceful period in the world which followed was shattered when, on 11 September 2001, four airliners were hijacked by Islamic suicide bombers of the al-Qaeda terrorist organisation. Two of these airliners were flown into the twin towers of the New York Trade Center and another into the Pentagon building in Washington. The fourth crashed in Pennsylvania, apparently after action by passengers against the terrorists.

These disasters, which resulted in the loss of over 5,000 lives, shocked the world and resulted in a profound change of attitude within the American public. The enemies of their country who had committed these outrages had to be crushed and if possible completely wiped out. The perpetrators, al-Qaeda and its adherents in the Taliban (literally 'armed students'), were dominant in the government of Afghanistan and known to possess many terrorist camps in that country. Their leader was Osama bin Laden, a Saudi national and a civil engineer by profession.

Action against these terrorists was quickly mounted under political and military leadership. The USA established bases for military operations in the neighbouring countries of Pakistan, Uzbekistan and Tajikistan. An essential part of the American plan was to support the Northern Alliance of Afghanistan, consisting of the four main resistance groups which had fought successfully against Soviet occupation in 1992 but in turn had been ousted by the Taliban between 1994 and 1998.

During the night of 7 October, slightly less than a month after the attacks on the twin towers, three cruisers of the US Navy and two nuclear-powered submarines of the Royal Navy (HMS *Triumph* and HMS *Trafalgar*) in the Arabian Sea, fired about fifty cruise missiles against targets in Afghanistan. These were followed with sorties by twenty-five McDonald Douglas F-18 Super Hornet fighter/attack aircraft from the carriers USS *Enterprise* and USS Carl *Vinson*. Fifteen heavy bombers of the USAF also took part. These were Boeing B-52 Stratofortresses operating from Diego Garcia in the Indian Ocean, and Rockwell B-1B Lancers which flew on a round trip from Whiteman Air Force base in Missouri. With the aid of air-to-air refuelling, the latter 'bat-winged' stealth bombers were capable of flying to anywhere in the globe with a load of sixteen 2000 lb bombs or missiles and returning to base. In addition, two McDonnell Douglas C-17 Globemaster military cargo aircraft flew from the USAF base of Ramstein in Germany to drop 37,000 Humanitarian Daily Rations (HDRs) over some areas of Afghanistan where refugees were known to be in dire need. An operation named 'Enduring Freedom' by the Americans and 'Veritas' by the British had begun.

Over a hundred British and American men from special forces were already involved on the ground in Afghanistan, collaborating with the Northern Alliance

Four McDonnell Douglas C-17A Globemaster IIIs entered service in 2001 with 99 Squadron at RAF Brize Norton in Oxfordshire, as part of No 2 Group's Air Combat Support. With their huge carrying capacity, they have operated at twice their planned rate, extremely successfully. Millions of pounds of equipment and hundreds of passengers have been carried on numerous sorties throughout the world, including theatres of conflict.

A. S. Thomas Collection

and providing first-hand intelligence. A third aircraft carrier, the USS *Kitty Hawk* had been stripped of its aircraft to accommodate these special ground forces. It was announced that thirty-one targets had been struck from the air, consisting of Taliban positions around Kabul in the centre of the country and Kandahar in the south, as well as al-Qaeda training camps near Jalalabad in the east. Other objectives were the Taliban's military aircraft, believed to consist of about twenty old Mikoyan MiG-21 'Fishbed' and Sukhoi Su-22 'Fitter' interceptors, although these and the air defence network were considered totally inadequate by modern standards.

The RAF did not participate in these bombing operations, but twelve Tornado GR4s already in Oman for an exercise with other units of the armed forces were put on standby for possible attacks. B.A.C. VC10s and two Lockheed Tristars flew to the area from Brize Norton in Oxfordshire. The refuelling systems on these tanker aircraft were compatible with those of the F-18 Hornets of the US Navy, adding to the effectiveness of the Allied air operations. In addition, the four Canberra PR9s of 39 Squadron, based at RAF Marham in Norfolk, were despatched to the Gulf. Although these machines were about fifty years old, they were capable of high-resolution photography from 48,000 feet and thus invaluable for interpretation and intelligence. Other contributions from the RAF were three Nimrod R1s of 51 Squadron, which flew out to the Gulf from their base at Waddington in Lincolnshire.. These 'eavesdropping' aircraft were packed with highly advanced electronic equipment which was capable of picking up enemy communications and providing intelligence of positions as well as the content of messages, even of mobile phone conversations. They joined a fleet of USAF aircraft with similar equipment. The lessons of Yugoslavia had been learnt, and defects in the gathering of intelligence would not be repeated in Afghanistan.

On 10 October, NATO offered support to the Americans, but this was politely refused on the grounds that it was not required. However, offers by Britain and Australia to add to the special ground forces were accepted. The air strikes continued, with the Northern Alliance forces gradually gaining ascendancy over al-Qaeda. The USAF despatched Sikorski MH-60G Pave Hawk helicopters from Uzbekistan, from where special troops could be ferried into Afghanistan. On 16 October it used Lockheed AC-130 gunships, converted versions of the Hercules transport, to rake and bomb the Taliban positions at Kandahar, with devastating effect. One of these positions was then attacked by Rangers of the US Special Operations Command, flown in by helicopters. Pakistan had also agreed to allow American troops to use two of its air bases.

Progress on the ground was slow in this difficult terrain and it was feared that a considerable force from Western Allies might have to be flown in, with 4,200 troops pledged from Britain alone. However, the Northern Alliance began to make gains, with paths through the Taliban defences being blasted by sticks of heavy bombs dropped by the B-52s. A UAV 'Predator', manufactured by General Atomics Aeronautical Systems, achieved fame by firing a Hellfire missile which assisted in the destruction of an al-Qaeda compound near Kabul. However, the Predator was at its most effective at altitudes of 10,000 feet and thus vulnerable to anti-aircraft fire.

On 9 November the strategically important town of Mazar-i-Sharif, to the north-west of Kabul, fell to attacks from the Northern Alliance. The pace then quickened, Kabul being occupied on 13 November. Jalalabad, the headquarters of the Taliban, fell on the following day. This period is also notable for the use of the UAV 'Global Hawk', manufactured by Northrop Grumman and capable of operating as high as 65,000 feet while surveying areas with pinpoint accuracy.

It became known that, shortly before these territorial gains, Osama bin Laden had fled from the area. He had threatened the Western nations with a nuclear attack and was understood to have obtained radioactive material illegally from Pakistan. Although he did not have the facilities to make a nuclear bomb, the material could be used to contaminate a large area and cause much destruction. It was thought that he might have taken refuge in the complex network of caves of the White Mountains, south-west of Jalalabad. These had been reinforced by man-made tunnels and were capable of concealing a considerable number of guerilla fighters. Despite intense bombing with 'bunker-buster' bombs in this region, as well as other mountainous areas further south, no evidence of his death was ever found. However, he made no pronouncements to the world at large.

On 19 December, 200 Royal Marines of 40 Commando, part of 3 Commando Brigade, were flown to Afghanistan by helicopters from the carrier HMS *Illustrious*, to spearhead the new International Security Assistance Force (ISAF) with the role of helping to establish peace in the country. Three days later, a new government headed by the Northern Alliance was sworn in.

With the Taliban crushed, the USA could turn to the next threat to peace in the

Middle East, which was conceived to be Saddam Hussein's regime in Iraq. On 25 November 2002, the inspectors from the United Nations returned to Iraq and began to resume their work, their organisations being renamed UNMOVIC (UN Monitoring Verification and Inspection Commission). Some of this work seemed to confirm suspicions of Iraq's worst intentions, such as the discovery of warheads designed to carry chemical weapons, as well as documents found in the homes of Iraqi nuclear physicists which indicated progress on nuclear weapons. The inspectors reported in January 2003 that Saddam Hussein had failed to disarm.

Early in this month, the USA and the UK began to build up their forces in the Gulf, with the British contingent headed by the aircraft carrier HMS *Ark Royal*. Kuwait had agreed to provide a base for a new invasion of Iraq. On 7 March 2003, Saddam Hussein was given ten days to begin disarming or face war. On 16 March 2003, the Allies gave him a last warning: he had to leave Iraq and go into exile or his country would be invaded.

All the usual means of gathering intelligence were employed before the military campaign began. Iraqi newspapers, television and radio broadcasts were analysed, while valuable information was obtained from undercover agents. Satellites fitted with very long focal lenses were employed by the US military on a polar orbit, overflying the country for about fifteen minutes every two of three days and bringing back useful high-resolution imagery.

In the absence of any reply to the ultimatum, an operational named 'Iraqi Freedom' by the Americans. or 'Telic' by the British, began on 20 March 2003 with an immense air bombardment of Baghdad and Basra. The Iraqi air defences were immediately destroyed, enabling the UAVs as well as the high-altitude and low-flying reconnaissance aircraft from both the USAF and the RAF to bring back the imagery required for battlefield situations. The Americans made the first major use of their adapted Boeing 707–300 commercial airliners for this purpose; as part of the Joint Surveillance and Target Radar System (J-Stars), these could operate at altitudes of over 40,000 feet for 11 hours without refuelling of 20 hours with in-flight refuelling.

Although the Allied forces were smaller numerically than in the Gulf War of 1991, they were far stronger in terms of weaponry, while the Iraqi forces were considerably weaker. About two-thirds of the attacking force was supplied by the United States. Britain was the other main contributor but three warships, some air force units and special forces of her army had arrived from the steadfast Commonwealth member of Australia. Poland had supplied about 200 special troops.

In addition to HMS *Ark Royal*, the Royal Navy despatched the helicopter carrier HMS *Ocean*, three destroyers, three frigates, four minehunters, two submarines and eight Royal Fleet Auxiliaries. In addition to the two main warships, some of the vessels carried a few helicopters of the Naval Air Squadrons. The total in all vessels consisted of fifty-nine helicopters. They were Westland Sea Kings of 820, 845 and 849 Squadrons, Westland Lynxes of 815 and 847 Squadron, Eurocopter Gazelles of 847 Squadron and EH Industries Merlins of 814 Squadron. HMS *Ark Royal* also carried five Boeing Vertol Chinooks of the RAF's 18 Squadron. On board the various vessels was the amphibious force of No 3 Commando Brigade, including of course the Royal Marines.

Based in Kuwait, the British Army consisted of the 1st (UK) Armoured Division, with its 7th Armoured Brigade, 16 Air Assault Brigade and 102 Logistics Brigade. The Royal Air Force had committed detachments from strike and support squadrons which were normally home-based but had flown out to the Gulf states. These were Tornado GR4s from 9, 12, 13, 14, 31 and 617 Squadrons, Tornado F3s from 11, 25, 43 and 111 Squadrons, Jaguar GR3s from 6, 41, and 54 Squadrons, Harrier GR7s from 1, 2 and 4 Squadrons, C-130 Hercules from 24, 30, 47 and 70 Squadrons, VC10s from 10 and 101 Squadrons, Tristars from 216 Squadron, C-17 Globemasters from 99 Squadron, Canberra PR9s of 39 Squadron, Chinook HC2s from 7, 18 and 27 Squadrons, and Puma HC1s from 33 Squadron. In addition, there was a strong contingent from the RAF Regiment.

The contribution from Britain, although powerful and at a high state of efficiency, was dwarfed by the American forces. The US Navy consisted of six Carrier Battle Groups, two Amphibious Task Forces, three Amphibious Ready Groups and a Mine Countermeasures Division, amounting to eighty-five warships in all. Associated with its Navy, the US Marine Corps provided the 1st and 2nd Marine Divisions, as well as the 13th, 24th and 26th Marine Expeditionary Units. The US Army contributed the 3rd Infantry Division, the 82nd Airborne Division, the 101st Airborne (Air Assault) Division and the 173rd Airborne Brigade. The US Air Force was also enormously powerful, consisting of five Groups, twenty Wings and twenty-seven Squadrons. These were based at various airfields in Kuwait, Oman, Qatar, the United Arab Republic, Saudi Arabia, Diego Garcia and England.

Opposing this well-equipped and modern Coalition Force, the Iraqi army was able to muster six divisions of the Republican Guard, intensely loyal to Saddam Hussein; three of these were infantry and three armoured or mechanized, but all with out-of-date equipment. Then there was the regular army, consisting of seventeen divisions; eleven of these were infantry and six mechanized or armoured, but all were undermanned with conscripts of dubious loyalty, while their equipment was poor. Other than these, there were irregular units composed of *fedayeen*, or martyrs, some of whom could fight with extreme fanaticism and would prove the most dangerous opponents. The Iraqi Air Force had been almost obliterated in the previous campaigns.

It was decided not to continue with an independent air bombardment in advance of the land campaign, but to achieve a quick victory by coordination of all military arms. This was facilitated by the increased use of the so-called 'smart weapons' with which aircraft were equipped, directed precisely against military targets by laser or Global Positioning Satellite (GPS). The ground assault was spearheaded by US Marines and Royal Marines, transported to the south of Iraq amphibiously and by helicopter. Their paths had been preceded by special forces which had infiltrated the areas, the US Navy 'SEALS' (Sea-Air-Land Commandos) and elements from the British 3 Commando Brigade. The landings were supported by an intense artillery bombardment from land and gungire from Allied warships. They were everywhere successful, the day being marred by the accidental crash of a Boeing Vertol Sea Knight helicopter of the US Marines in Kuwait, killing four Americans and twelve Royal Marines.

On the second day, it was reported that the Coalition Forces (as they were known) had launched a thousand cruise missiles, as well as dropped a thousand bombs from aircraft, against military targets throughout Iraq. The bombers included B-52 Stratofortresses operating from RAF Fairford and almost every RAF Tornado GR4 based in the Gulf. By great misfortune, a Tornado was destroyed by a US Patriot missile on the third day, the first fatal accident of the war by 'friendly fire'. Under cover of a tremendous air bombardment, the

Coalition ground forces fought their way up the rivers Tigris and Euphrates towards Baghdad, experiencing only light casualties.

The British forces were ordered to invest Iraq's second city of Basra while the Americans continued north-west and approached the city of Nasiriyah en route to Baghdad. The Americans encountered some fanatical resistance at this city which was not fully overcome until the end of March. Then they continued towards Baghdad, which was defended by divisions of the Republican Guard. The marines in the spearhead were refuelled en route by C-130 transport aircraft which landed on highways and supplied 5,000 gallon bladders of diesel.

Meanwhile, the British surrounded Basra and began to probe the defences. On 27 March, fourteen Challenger 2 tanks of the Royal Scots Dragoon Guards engaged a column of fourteen Iraqi T-55 tanks which came out into the desert. The Challengers out-ranged and out-gunned the T-55s, destroying all of them without sustaining any damage in return. Three days later, A Global Hawk UAV located a column of twenty-one Iraqi armoured vehicles to the north of Shatt al-Arab waterway; all these were knocked out by British artillery fire.

By 2 April, thousands of American troops reached the outskirts of Baghdad, having destroyed an entire division of the Republican Guard with the aid of tanks and an intense air assault. On the following day, some of their armoured divisions occupied part of Saddam International Airport. In the same period, British troops entered the outskirts of Basra. Close support was given to the British by both the RAF and the USAF, with Tornados dropping laser-guided Paveway bombs of 2,000 lb as well as CBUs (Cluster Bomb Units). The Americans provided helicopter transport as well as fire from their deadly Apache helicopter gunships. It was not until the evening of 6 April when the British reached the centre of Basra. They were welcomed by cheering crowds who were relieved to be free of dictatorship, but there was still resistance from diehard *fedayeen* irregulars, some of whom were not Iraqi nationals. On the same day, the first RAF Hercules transport aircraft landed at Saddam International Airport, by then completely under the control of the Americans.

The Americans wiped out opposition from the Republican Guard on the outskirts of Baghdad, Iraqi T-72 and T55 tanks being destroyed by US Abrams tanks and strike aircraft. Among the latter were Fairchild A-10 'Warthogs', firing rockets. Waves of *fedayeen* were mown down in their suicidal attacks with rifles and RPG-7 grenade launchers. Thereafter, the Americans fought their way into the centre of Baghdad and finally occupied the whole city on 9 April, when the immense statue of Saddam Hussein in Firdos (Paradise) Square was toppled by a cable hauled by an armoured vehicle of the marines.

This became the official day of the ending of the war. It had lasted for twenty-one days and claimed the lives of 122 Americans and 33 British, many of whom were lost in accidents or from 'friendly fire'. The Iraqi losses were not counted but must have amounted to several thousand. However, casualties in the aftermath have been appalling. The disbandment of the Iraqi army and police force was followed by an orgy of looting and destruction which the Coalition Force had difficulty in suppressing. Thereafter suicide bombings, booby-traps and fire from moving vehicles have resulted in waves of casualties among Iraqis and Coalition Forces. Although Saddam Hussein was captured by the Americans on 13 December 2003, hiding in an underground hole near Tikrit in northern Iraq, the activities of the insurgents have continued unabated. By the end of 2004 they had caused the deaths of over 1,000 Americans and almost 100 British, in addition to numerous Iraqis. For the RAF, perhaps the worst incident took place

on 30 January 2005 when a Hercules of 47 Squadron crashed 25 miles north-west of Baghdad, as a result of a surface-to-air missile. All on board lost their lives, nine RAF men and one soldier.

A new National Assembly in Iraq was elected democratically in January 2005 but sectarian violence between the Sunni and Shia branches of the community intensified, resulting in the deaths or injuries of many thousands of civilians as well as numerous deaths among the Iraqi security forces. About 7,200 British troops remained in Iraq by the end of 2006, mostly stationed in the southern region.

Meanwhile, a resurgence of attacks by the Taliban in Afghanistan took place, despite the creation of a new government which followed a nationwide election in October 2004 and a United Nations peacekeeping force, the International Security Force (ISAF) from 26 nations, which was established in the country. The ISAF was built up to about 32,500 troops by 2006, of which 11,500 were provided by the USA and about 7,200 by Britain. The Americans had lost over 350 troops by July 2006. The majority of the British troops were then moved to Helmand province in the south-west, where most of the fighting against the Taliban was taking place at close quarters. Air support could usually be provided by 8 Apache helipcopters and 7 Harriers of the RAF.

The British troops had lost only 2 men in combat up to this time but 22 others were lost by the following December. In addition, 18 had died in accidents since the deployment began. the RAF suffered a major disaster on 2 September 2006 when a Nimrod MR2 of 120 Squadron engaged on a reconnaissance mission over the country suffered a technical fault at high level and crashed, killing all 14 on board.

In terms of aircraft and personnel, the RAF of today is only a fraction of its huge size at the end of the Second World War. With regard to operational aircraft, in February 2004 there were 243 aircraft in 1 Air Combat Group (Harriers, Tornados, Jaguars and Hawks), 88 aircraft in 2 Group Air Combat Support (VC10s, C-130 Hercules, C-17 Globemasters, Tristars and BAe 125s, 30 aircraft in 3 Group Air Battle Management (Sentry AEWs, Canberras and Nimrods), 87 in Support Helicopters (Chinooks, Merlins and Pumas), and 22 helicopters in Search and Rescue (Sea Kings and Griffins). The total personnel in the RAF numbered only about 53,000, of whom about 6,500 were aircrew.

The history of the Royal Air Force is short relative to the Royal Navy and the British Army. However, it is studded with numerous acts of heroism as well as remarkable achievements in technology and organisation. The RAF has never been defeated in any war and is much admired by the nation it serves as well as by its friends in other countries, especially within the USA, while it evokes dismay among its enemies. New crises will doubtless occur, so long as there are rogue states which attempt to impose their will on their neighbours and perhaps the world. The RAF stands ready to play its part in the defence of the United Kingdom and in the maintenance of world peace.

Opposite top: The Bell Griffin helicopter entered service in 1995 at the newly-created Defence Helicopter School at RAF Shawberry in Shropshire, replacing Gazelle and Wessex helicopters as an advanced flying trainer. Unarmed and with two seats, its has a wide cabin. Griffins are also employed with the Search and Rescue Training Unit at Raf Valley in Anglesey and with 84 Squadron at Akrotiri in Cyprus.

A.S. Thomas Collection

Opposite bottom: Agusta A109E helicopters entered service in 2006 with 32 (The Royal) Squadron at RAF Northolt in Greater London, engaged on light transport work. Three of these reliable helicopters are now on the strength of the Squadron.

A.S. Thomas Collection

ACKNOWLEDGEMENTS

In researching the material for this book, invaluable help with research was given by Air Cdre Jeaffreson H. Greswell, Paul Grundy, Ted Hooton, Wg Cdr J.F. Manning, Clive Richards of the Ministry of Defence's Air Historical Branch, Georges Van Acker and Gerrit J. Zwanenburg.

I am also extremely grateful to Sqn Ldr Dudley Cowderoy, Peter J.V. Elliott of the Royal Air Force Museum and Roger Hayward for their work in checking the narrative and the captions of photographs. Three aviation artists have contributed their splendid paintings to the book. They are J. Sidney Bailie, Mark Postlethwaite and Charles J. Thompson.

The book could not have been compiled without the help of those who provided photographs and guidance for the captions. They are *Aeroplane Monthly*, The Aviation Bookshop, British Aerospace, the Museum of Army Flying, Sgt Rick Brewell of Royal Air Force Public Relations, Short Brothers, The Westland Group, RAF Coltishall, RAF Coningsby, RAF Finningley, RAF Leuchars, RAF Lossiemouth, RAF Marham, RAF Wildenrath, RAF Wittering, 39 (No. 1 PRU) Squadron, 42 (Reserve) Squadron, 47 Squadron, the late Flt Lt Tom Armstrong, Peter Batten, Wg Cdr Dennis O. Butler, Rick Chapman, Sqn Ldr Ian M. Coleman, Dave Fry, Dr Eric V. Hawkinson, Flt Lt Stan J. Kernaghan, G. Stuart Leslie, Phillip Jarrett, Air Cdre Graham R. Pitchfork, Flt Lt Andrew S. Thomas, Sqn Ldr Peter J. Thomson and Flt Lt George G. Tuffin.

Finally, I shall always be grateful to three prominent members of the Association of Royal Air Force Photography Officers who presented me with numerous photographs which now form the basis of my own collection. They are the late Sqn Ldr Jack Archbald, the late Sqn Ldr Paul Lamboit and the late Flt Lt George Parry.

The publisher wishes to thank Air Chief Marshal Sir Richard Johns for kindly agreeing to write the foreword; Air Commodore Gordon McRobbie, Director of Public Relations (RAF); Dr Michael Fopp and Peter Elliott of the RAF Museum, Hendon; and the MOD Crown Copyright Unit, whose photographs are reproduced with the permission of the Controller of Her Britannic Majesty's Stationery Office.

BIBLIOGRAPHY

Ashworth, Chris. *RAF Coastal Command 1936–1969*. Patrick Stephens, 1992.

Bateman, Dennis C. *Home Commands of the Royal Air Force since 1918*. Ministry of Defence, Air Historical Branch (RAF), 1978.

Braybrook, Roy. *Battle for the Falklands: Air Forces*. Osprey, 1984.

Brown, David. *Warship Losses of World War Two*. Arms & Armour, 1990.

The Falklands Campaign: The Lessons. HMSO, 1982.

Fellows, P.F.M. *Britain's Wonderful Air Force*. Odhams, 1941.

Franks, Norman. *Search, Find and Kill*. Grub Street, 1995.

Goulter, Christina J.M. *A Forgotten Offensive*. Frank Cass, 1995.

Halley, James J. *The Squadrons of the Royal Air Force & Commonwealth 1918–1988*. Air Britain, 1988.

Harris, Sir Arthur T. *Despatch on War Operations*. Frank Cass, 1995.

Hinsley, F.H. *et al. British Intelligence in the Second World War*. Six volumes. HMSO, 1979–1990.

Jackson, Paul. *RAF Strike Command*. Ian Allen, 1984.

James, John. *The Paladins*. Macdonald, 1990.

Jane's Fighting Aircraft of World War II. Studio Editions, 1992.

Jones, H.A. and Raleigh, Sir Walter. *The War in the Air*. Seven volumes. Oxford University Press, 1928.

Jones, R.V. *Most Secret War*. Hodder & Stoughton, 1978.

Kampfner, John. *Blair's Wars*. The Free Press, 2004.

Keegan, John. *The Iraq War*. Pimlico, 2005.

Lee, Sir David. *Eastward*. HMSO, 1984.

———. *Flight from the Middle East*. HMSO, 1980.

———. *Wings in the Sun*. HMSO, 1989.

Lewis, Peter. *British Aircraft 1809–1914*. Putnam, 1962.

Middlebrook, Martin and Everitt, Chris. *The Bomber Command War Diaries*. Penguin, 1990.

Morse, Stan. *Gulf War Debrief*. Aerospace, 1991.

Postgate, Malcolm. *Operation Firedog*. HMSO, 1992.

Price, Alfred. *Instruments of Darkness*. Macdonald and Janes, 1977.

———. *Aircraft versus Submarine*. William Kimber, 1973.

Rawlings, John *et al. The History of the Royal Air Force*. Temple Press, 1984.

Richards, Denis and Saunders, Hilary St G. *Royal Air Force 1939–45*. Three volumes. HMSO, 1953–1954.

Robertson, Bruce. *British Military Serials 1911–1971*. Ian Allan, 1971.

———. *Aircraft Camouflage and Markings*. Harleyford, 1966.

Ross, Tony. *75 Eventful Years*. Wingham Aviation Books, 1993.

Sweetman, John. *Operation Chastise*. Jane's, 1982.

Taylor, John W.R. *Combat Aircraft of the World*. Ebery Press and Michael Joseph, 1969.

Thetford, Owen. *Aircraft of the 1914–1918 War*. Harborough, 1954.

———. *Aircraft of the Royal Air Force since 1918*. Putnam, 1989.

Willis, Steve and Hollis, Barry. *Military Airfields in the British Isles 1939–1945*. Enthusiasts Publications, 1989.

AIRCRAFT INDEX